Post-Christian Religion
in Popular Culture

Theology, Religion, and Pop Culture
Series Editor
Matthew Brake

The *Theology, Religion, and Pop Culture* series examines the intersection of theology, religion, and popular culture, including, but not limited to television, movies, sequential art, and genre fiction. In a world plagued by rampant polarization of every kind and the decline of religious literacy in the public square, *Theology, Religion, and Pop Culture* is uniquely poised to educate and entertain a diverse audience utilizing one of the few things society at large still holds in common: love for popular culture.

Select titles in the series
Post-Christian Religion in Popular Culture: Theology through Exegesis, by Andrew D. Thrasher

Nazi Occultism, Jewish Mysticism, and Christian Theology in the Video Game Series Wolfenstein, by Frank G. Bosman

The Last of Us and Theology: Violence, Ethics, Redemption? edited by Peter Admirand

Fantasy, Theology, and the Imagination, edited by Andrew D. Thrasher and Austin M. Freeman, with Fotini Toso

Theology and Wes Craven, edited by David K. Goodin

Theology and the DC Universe, edited by Gabriel Mckee and Roshan Abraham

Theology and Star Trek, edited by Shaun C. Brown and Amanda MacInnis Hackney

The Spirit and the Screen: Pneumatological Reflections on Contemporary Cinema, edited by Chris E.W. Green and Steven Félix-Jäger

Theology and the Avett Brothers, edited by Alex Sosler

Bob Dylan and the Spheres of Existence, by Christopher B. Barnett

Theology and Protest Music, edited by Jonathan H. Harwell and Heidi M. Altman

Post-Christian Religion in Popular Culture

Theology through Exegesis

Andrew D. Thrasher

LEXINGTON BOOKS/FORTRESS ACADEMIC
Lanham • Boulder • New York • London

Published by Lexington Books/Fortress Academic
Lexington Books is an imprint of The Rowman & Littlefield Publishing Group, Inc.
4501 Forbes Boulevard, Suite 200, Lanham, Maryland 20706
www.rowman.com

86-90 Paul Street, London EC2A 4NE, United Kingdom

Copyright © 2024 by The Rowman & Littlefield Publishing Group, Inc.

All rights reserved. No part of this book may be reproduced in any form or by any electronic or mechanical means, including information storage and retrieval systems, without written permission from the publisher, except by a reviewer who may quote passages in a review.

British Library Cataloguing in Publication Information Available

Library of Congress Cataloging-in-Publication Data

Names: Thrasher, Andrew D. author.
Title: Post-Christian religion in popular culture : theology through
 exegesis / Andrew D. Thrasher.
Description: Lanham : Lexington Books/Fortress Academic, [2024] |
 Series: Theology, religion, and pop culture | Includes bibliographical references and index. | Summary: "Post-Christian Religion in Popular Culture offers exegetical analyses of the post-Christian theological and religious messages found within twenty-first century popular culture. The author argues how the consumption of popular culture in the twenty-first century has the potential to reshape the possibilities of believing in late modernity."—Provided by publisher.
Identifiers: LCCN 2024024048 (print) | LCCN 2024024049 (ebook) |
 ISBN 9781978715875 (cloth) | ISBN 9781978715882 (epub)
Subjects: LCSH: Secularization (Theology) | Civilization, Modern. | Christian life.
Classification: LCC BT903 .T54 2024 (print) | LCC BT903 (ebook) |
 DDC 306.6—dc23/eng/20240613
LC record available at https://lccn.loc.gov/2024024048
LC ebook record available at https://lccn.loc.gov/2024024049

∞™ The paper used in this publication meets the minimum requirements of American National Standard for Information Sciences—Permanence of Paper for Printed Library Materials, ANSI/NISO Z39.48-1992.

*This book is dedicated to my Many Mothers.
To Susan, Tish, Lolly, and Jasmin for creating a safe haven
for a troubled youth. Your homes helped me survive. I
do not think I would be alive without you. Selah.
To Dr. Reese and Mrs. Goodman for advocating for me
when I had no hope. My life would have been very different
if you had not done so. I owe you much. Thank you.
To Donna, Irene, and Elizabeth, my spiritual mothers, who
loved me into the Kingdom and nurture me in it as I dwell
in anticipation for the Parousia. Such is Grace.
And finally, to Anita, my arduous love, for our relationship has ever been
marked by a struggle to love, and yet that love is Good. Love you, Mom.*

Contents

Foreword *Matthew William Brake*	ix
Preface	xi
Acknowledgments	xv
Introduction	1
PART I: THEORETICAL FRAMEWORKS	**19**
1 Consuming a Post-Christian Canon?	21
2 The Consumptive Poetics of Belief	43
PART II: METHODOLOGY THROUGH PRACTICE	**65**
3 Marveling Re-enchantment?	67
4 Deconstructing Inter-Religious Resourcement in *The Lion King*	91
5 Rescripting Theology in *Lucifer*	105
PART III: PROBLEMS AND PROPHECIES OF MODERNITY	**119**
6 The Tragedy and Trajectory of Modernity in *Cloud Atlas*	121
7 Grieving in the Wake of Wakanda	137
PART IV: RESCRIPTING SIN AS BROKENNESS	**155**
8 Doxologies of Brokenness	157
9 The Poverty of Sin in *Shameless*	175

PART V: CONSTRUCTIVE CONCLUSIONS **191**
  10 Messages of Post-Christian Theology   193

Bibliography   215

Index   227

About the Author   231

Foreword

Matthew William Brake

I didn't set out to become a scholar of popular culture. In fact, I kind of backed into it. I began college to train to be a Christian minister and work in the local church. I went to Bible college and then seminary. After I graduated with my MDiv, I joined a church plant. After six months, my time at that church ended in spectacular personal and professional defeat, a nervous breakdown, and the belief that I would never be cut out for ministry in a local parish setting.

Two years passed, and I found myself working in academia. During the day, I was mild-mannered Matthew Brake, academic advisor, but at night, I donned my dual identity as "Matthew Brake, Adjunct Professor." A year into teaching in the evenings, I realized that this might be a better alternative to becoming clergy. I could still mentor students, challenge their ideas, and discuss questions of ultimate meaning, but without the pressure of being in a pastoral role.

In 2013, I packed my bags and moved to Fairfax, Virginia, to attend George Mason University to pursue a second (and third) master's degree and to pursue the life of a full-time academic. My first year at Mason was defined by a constant stream of encyclopedic publications about Søren Kierkegaard (whom I thought would become my academic bread and butter), while my second and third years were defined by constant jet-setting to different academic conferences (which put me in quite a bit of debt). I was looking for my academic niche, which I thought would be Kierkegaard studies, but I found myself constantly branching out into different fields. Finally, I began to submit articles for Blackwell's Pop Culture and Philosophy series, and then I began to wonder, "Why isn't there a theology version of this?" So an idea was born, and the series of which this book is part was birthed.

Don't get me wrong. I had moments that reinforced to me pop culture's importance for theology and religious studies. Pop culture can illustrate any number of important theological ideas, but a person would be mistaken to simply treat pop culture as a source for useful analogies. Pop culture's power can be found in its ability to enchant the world by helping us to reimagine how the world works and what is possible. When I read Grant Morrison's *Animal Man* and the way he uses that story to blur the barriers between fiction and reality, it makes me aware of my own status as a fictional creation relative to a higher Creator. When I watch *Star Trek*, I remember the possibilities of human potential, for humanism finds its roots in the Renaissance Christian humanists. When I watch *Breaking Bad*, I'm reminded of just how corrupt humans are beneath the veneer of sanitized suburbia. Pop culture and the stories it tells can shape our imaginations and help us to see the enchantment of the everyday.

Of course, plenty has also been written about how pop culture can itself BE religion. Pop culture and its fandoms have their myths, their communities, and their rituals that, functionally, make them religions for people in a secular and pluralistic society.

The author of the book you're holding recognizes all of these realities. Andrew Thrasher and I have known each other for over a decade, and our paths intertwine in surprising ways. I met Andy at George Mason. He and I shared many of the same teachers. And then, Andy went to the seminary I attended, Regent University, where he shared many of my previous professors there as well. He and I also briefly lived together before I married my wife Rachel. I have not yet followed Andy to Birmingham for my PhD (but anything's possible!).

But Andy understands the importance of pop culture for the society that we live in and its ability to re-enchant what would otherwise be a dead, lifeless, materialistic existence. My hope is that the readers of this book will find its message helpful for navigating the theological landscapes of the twenty-first century. We live in interesting times that require interesting solutions.

The book you're holding is a useful guide for mapping the terrain.

Preface

This book seeks to answer a simple question: *What theological and religious messages are being presented in contemporary popular culture?* My answer is that these messages are *post*-Christian, or rather, that they reflect religious and theological messages that maintain a Christian *latency* while also moving *beyond* it. The cover art was commissioned with the following question in mind: *What would it look like to leave Christianity behind?* It should cause us to ponder the significance of it, as well as cause *grief* at what is left behind. This project should be seen as a project that wrestles with the realities of what post-Christian theological beliefs and religious messages look like throughout contemporary twenty-first-century popular culture. But it should also be seen as a constructive attempt to develop a post-Christian theology of culture that grapples with what it means to leave Christianity behind.

This book ought not to be the last of its kind in its attempt to take seriously how popular culture represents an enchanting resource by which to understand the spiritual, religious, and theological dimensions of post-Christian religion in popular culture. While this book can be seen as a post-Christian theology of culture, I am already planning another book that addresses the theological optionality, sociological narratives, and ecclesial demands of post-Christian belief. That book is to address the church from a post-Christian perspective around what the church would need to do and be for it to be a better witness to a post-Christian world. In the meantime, this book should be engaged as a post-Christian theological reflection upon popular culture.

In the study at the intersection of popular culture and theology or religion, Bruce David Forbes outlines four standard methodological approaches. The first approach is to analyze religion in popular culture. It should be very obvious that this book predominantly and primarily adopts this approach. It seeks to understand the theological messages found within contemporary popular culture. The second approach is to analyze popular culture in religion. This can mean seeing how real-world religions are utilizing popular culture to present their messages. In a sense, this book does this, insofar as my former Evangelical Christian background utilizes popular culture to make a subtle case for the Christian faith. The third approach is to view popular culture *as* religion. While I did not write this book to go that far, it still claims to analyze popular culture as post-Christian *scripture*. The fourth approach is to view popular culture and religion in dialogue. This is especially evidenced in part II, where I engage the Marvel Cinematic Universe, *The Lion King*, and *Lucifer* to generate a dialogue between them and how they problematize themes ranging between secularization, issues in sociology of religion, religious pluralism, Christian theology of religion, and rescriptions of traditional theology.

The central reflection of this book is how what we consume in popular culture can shape what is possible to believe. The working theory (found especially in chapters 1 and 2) emphasizes how what we consume in popular culture has the potential to shape what is believable because what we consume shapes what we can *imagine* as *desirable* and *credible*. That is, the possibilities of belief in the late modern world are intimately guided by whether we find belief desirable or credible, and the imagination and the messages of what we consume in popular culture implicitly shape these conditions for belief—they shape our wants and give us new ways of thinking about what we think is true, good, and beautiful. In light of this, I wrote this book with this theory in mind, and what it can generate goes beyond this book.

And yet, this book is also shaped by the latencies of my Evangelical formation as an adult convert to Christ. While by the time of the publication of this book, I am a practicing Anglican, this book was written throughout a period of my life in which I was a practicing non-denominational Evangelical. While not directly intentional, this book can be viewed as an attempt to be a post-Christian to the post-Christian, whether that saves some or not. I do, however, see this book as a subversion of typical Evangelical tendencies to merely preach Christ crucified to a culture where Christian messages lack relevance and where its people fail to make an effort to embody and contextualize their beliefs in credible and desirable ways. As such, this book may be viewed as another way to present Christ to a post-Christian world, and one that does not speak Christ into this world by condemning the world, but rather by showing how post-Christian popular cultural texts cry out for God.

Thus, this is a weighty book, even with all of its delight and lightness. As I sit at the end of the writing and final re-read of this book, I cannot but reflect on both how much I enjoyed writing it and how much it makes me cry out for God. It evokes pangs of longing in me, grief at the post-Christian human condition, and makes me weep and squirm as I critique modernity. This book sometimes makes me angry at the injustices written and reflected on throughout this book. And yet, I also have an inkling of the importance of this book. It engages with weighty things, even amid laughter, cringe, and shock. There are numerous places where shots are fired, and there are also places where I grieve with indignation and anger. I am not sold that I am the right person to speak some of the things found in this book. At times, I speak as if the terrible things reflected on are endorsed. The reader should note that I do not endorse these things. I often followed the logics of the research and voices engaged with, but in ways that make me angry and fill me with grief and repentance on the contextual conditions of modernity and what it means to believe in a post-Christian context.

Furthermore, this book often engages things that go against traditional morals, as well as the social and religious norms and convictions of some Christians. It calls religious folks to come to terms with the realities of our late modern world—the brokenness of the human condition as well as the afterlives of slavery and modern dehumanization. It engages with texts in popular culture that glorify sex and cringe, subverts traditional theological understandings of evil, and engages the reality of the Black experience in ways that prophetically call us to pay attention to the problems of modernity. It calls us who live in late modernity to come to terms with the trajectory toward which power and domination may lead, as well as with the brokenness of a world that cries out to an absent God. This book is in some sense prophetic, and in another sense, it should be approached seriously with both "pondering and repentance" as the cover art is titled.

This book may make you uncomfortable. I have taught some of this material to students in some of my courses. My religious students, especially the conservative Christian ones, have found chapters 5 and 9 uncomfortable—but did not condemn them. They were challenged because they go against the grain of their tradition, while yet recognizing the voices and arguments as valid and worth wrestling with. My non-religious students have viewed many of these same chapters with great delight, partly because they love the "scriptures" analyzed within those chapters. However, these non-religious students also have mixed feelings about the religious dimensions of some of the texts. They struggle with the Christian latencies used throughout this book, while also recognizing that the religious and theological dimensions of this book are still relevant. In light of this, please be aware this book is not for everyone. It will burst both religious bubbles and draw non-religious folks into dialogue with Christianity in ways that you may not want to go. But I hope that it will also cause us to reflect and ponder over the reality of what it means to leave Christianity behind—both to wrestle with this and to grieve it. Get ready to laugh and to delight, *but also to weep.*

One final note: *Spoilers—on nearly everything.* You've been warned.

Acknowledgments

This book was birthed out of my deep friendship with Matthew William Brake. Matt was the first to encourage me to contribute to his blog and then to the series in which this book appears. This book would not have been possible without his support. This book was also sustained by various friendships with those whom I call dearly beloved friends, brothers, and sisters. This includes, first, the "Grumpies" and those families who have grafted me into their own (the Gottliebs, Marshburns, Joneses, Williams/Wheelers, and Swartz's) who have brought me life, joy, delight, and shared love. Thank you, Grumpies, for giving me a life of deep friendship amid our pains with the American church. Thank you to my grafted family for allowing me to be an uncle to your kids. This has given me immense life in my grief at what I have sacrificed to pursue my academic career thus far. Second, Holy Trinity Reformed Episcopal Church in Chantilly, Virginia, for receiving me as I am and allowing me to belong with you in this season of life. Third, Kelby and Pip for our long, dearly loved and knowing friendship. You are salt and life and a reason for living in this world as I await the door beyond into the "farther up and farther in." You are home to me. Fourth, this book would not have been possible without the pastoral ministry of Justin Pearson and Kris Hassanpour who shepherded me in my Christian walk with the embodied practice of a concrete gospel, vulnerability, and laughter. You have been friends to me for many years, and I have watched, learned, and listened deeply from your preaching and way of life. I pray both of you will eventually return to ministry, as you spoke life and hope and love into this former post-Christian. Thank you.

Finally, two more thanks are in order. First, many thanks to Sam Jones for the cover art for this volume. His artwork is something I have come to love every "Inktober," and he graciously agreed to do the cover art for this volume. Second, thank you to my doctoral supervisors and examiners, who worked with and saw potential in what is chapter 2. I pray this book fulfills the examiners' desires to see what that chapter was pointing to. Again, I must thank my supervisors, David Cheetham and Nicholas Adams, for their silent acknowledgment of my other pursuits beyond my doctoral work. This is a fruit of my labor under you, even if it is not directly related to my doctoral research. Thank you.

Introduction

Imagine a world where popular culture re-enchants, resources, and rescripts the possibilities of belief through the power of its imaginative portrayals to present more credible and desirable options for belief than the Christian church. Imagine a world where what we believe is no longer exclusively cognitive or explicit but implicit within the very messages that we consume. Imagine a reality where what remains of Christianity and its message in late modern culture is embedded and distorted within the messages and imaginations of popular culture. If you can imagine this—and see this in our world—it implies the reality that we live, believe, and are shaped by an imagined realism. An imagined realism is where what we can imagine in a virtual reality can be imagined as actually real. This imagined realism entails a "virtual actuality"—which is when the conceptions of the imagination represent, reflect, and refer to something "real" about our actual reality when our beliefs are taken in and shaped by the messages found within the imaginations of popular culture. These messages in popular culture offer virtual representations and recitations of reality that in turn shape actual, real-world beliefs—that is, it is when *what* we believe and *imagine as* believable in the real world are informed by the messages of popular culture.

But an imagined realism also refers to both the reality that: (1) the religious or theological messages found within popular culture distort real-world beliefs, and yet they have the power to enchant the imagination with alternate visions of what is possible to believe; and that (2) those messages often leave behind Christian faith, doctrine, and life while latently reflecting implicit Christian themes and traces that still structure a post-Christian imagination. But when virtual and actual realities blur into one another, there is the creation of a simulacrum. Jean Baudrillard argues that the process of simulation is a movement of reference from something substantially and sacramentally

1

real, to its distortion, then to its reduction to the mere appearance of reality, and finally to a simulation that has no reference to any substantial reality.[1] A simulacrum is sustained when something actual is simulated through virtuality, where its actuality is distorted into the virtual, and then distinctions between virtual and actual worlds blur to the point of confusion over the question of what we refer to when we ask: "What is reality?"[2] As an example found on the internet illustrates: the actual reality is a pumpkin, the distortion is pumpkin pie, its reduction to appearance is a pumpkin spice latte, and its simulation is pumpkin creamer. So, what does this have to do with the notion of "post-Christian"?

If we begin to examine popular culture as something that simulates religious ideas, what it begins to reveal are contours and messages of what matters most to us, of what we can become, of the echoes of our longings, and of images that allow us to imagine our world in ways that move *beyond Christianity—all the while echoing its resonances and latencies*. This idea of moving beyond Christianity while yet echoing its resonances is exactly what this book articulates as post-Christian religion. This book argues that popular culture is a medium that reflects a turn in contemporary culture and imagination toward recitations of post-Christian theology. It does so through a hermeneutical method applied to objects of analysis in popular culture. As such, this book's subtitle is "theology through exegesis" to imply that we can only construct a post-Christian theology through the practice of pop cultural exegesis.

The exegetical method in biblical studies typically starts with analyses of the background context or frameworks of a book of the Bible—including cultural, historical, social, and political settings in which the book was written, alongside nuances of authorship, authorial intent, and dating of the text. Then it offers exegetical analyses of the book and passages in question through what is called the grammatical interpretation of the text. Finally, the third stage of biblical exegesis ends with the application of the text to our daily world. Another layer to biblical exegesis is the contribution of Hans-Georg Gadamer to philosophical hermeneutics, which (a) nuances between what is called exegesis and eisegesis, (b) emphasizes the reality that there is no neutral way to approach a text because everyone carries inescapable presuppositions or biases when we interpret a text, and (c) that from this, we all carry with us our interpretations and are embedded in historical traditions that shape how we approach a text.[3]

This book adopts this methodology and applies it to popular culture to reflect on post-Christian religion and articulate a post-Christian theology. This Introduction and part I offer the "Theoretical Frameworks" of this book to set the stage for whom and to whom this book is written, the cultural and historical context in which the objects of analysis are situated, and a methodological theory that approaches post-Christian religion in popular culture by reflecting on popular culture through the lenses of both a theology of cultural theory and the consumption of popular culture as an analogy for a post-Christian scriptural canon. Chapter 1 starts part I of the book by offering an introduction to the pop-culture "texts" that this book analyzes through an analysis of whether popular culture can represent a post-Christian canon that reflects on the problem of consumption for the possibilities of belief. Chapter 2 follows with a continuation of themes found in chapter 1, but focuses more on a theory that explicates the "consumptive poetics of belief." Chapter 2 offers a theoretical analysis of how the consumption of popular culture poetically informs the possibilities of belief.

Part II follows with three methodological approaches that are put into practice through theological-cultural exegesis. These methodological approaches are re-enchantment, resourcement, and rescription and are applied and interpreted through three "texts": the Marvel Cinematic Universe (MCU), *The Lion King*, and the show *Lucifer*. These chapters are not so much theoretical but rather demonstrate the methodological practices of three hermeneutical frameworks used throughout this book for theological interpretation. As such, while one can state the method, it is better to display what the theory or method looks like by putting it into practice. Thus, while part I offers theoretical frameworks of the book, part II puts into practice three hermeneutical methods through the practice of interpretation.

In turn, both part III and part IV analyze several texts in popular culture to illustrate a theme in post-Christian religion and theology. The first post-Christian theme developed in part III is the problem of modernity, particularly in what it prophesies (a) in the futurity of what the imagined ends of modernity can be through David Mitchell's *Cloud Atlas* and the Wachowski's film adaptation of the book (chapter 6), and (b) in the wake of the Black experience through the films *Black Panther* and *Wakanda Forever* (chapter 7). The second post-Christian theme developed in part IV is the human condition, which redefines the Christian problem of sin with the post-Christian problem of *brokenness*. This is first explored in chapter 8 through the traces and echoes of God, sin, and brokenness in the secular doxologies of three hit musical artists (Machine Gun Kelly, Halsey, Linkin Park) that have defined twenty-first-century music (or at least several sentiments of the millennial experience). Then, chapter 9 explores brokenness in the popular television show, *Shameless* (the American version) to explore what the systemic logic and effects of brokenness look like through the lens of the American urban poor (as displayed through the show's *bildungsroman* of the Gallagher family). Finally, the conclusion (part V) offers less of a practical application than a constructive proposal of the post-Christian theological messages found across the exegetical threads of this book.

In short, this book develops a theology through exegesis by interpreting how post-Christian religion and theology are recited in popular culture. It does so through an analysis of what constitutes a post-Christian canon in popular culture and a theory of the consumptive poetics of belief. These theoretical approaches set the stage for exegetical analyses of the Marvel Cinematic Universe, *The Lion King*, *Lucifer*, *Cloud Atlas*, *Black Panther* and *Wakanda Forever*, Machine Gun Kelly, Halsey, Linkin Park, and *Shameless*. Its examination of each of these popular cultural "texts" or "scriptures" articulates ways of rethinking Christianity and what implicit messages of post-Christian theology are being recited in late modern, twenty-first-century popular culture.

A MAP OF THE BOOK

If popular culture mediates messages and contents of religious beliefs via the virtual simulations of belief found in what we consume, then it is important to ask whether we are actually talking about "religion" or not. Granted, while several of the items examined throughout this book refer to real-world religions, this book is attuned moreover to religious sensibilities, theological messages, and religious/theological imaginations found within twenty-first-century popular culture. That is, this book is not so much concerned with *explicit* religion—the statements of what people believe or practice in a late modern, post-Christian world. Rather, it is more concerned with the *implicit* religion found within popular culture—the sentiments, sensibilities, and attitudes that shape how popular culture imagines the world and the possibilities of belief. While explicit religion refers to theological doctrines and institutional structures and practices that shape organized religion, implicit religion, by contrast focuses on the subtle messages, resonances, and echoes of religion and God found within everyday life and practice.

Parts of this book address the implicit religious sensibilities and beliefs found in the echoes of popular music, film, and television. Other parts of this book work out how popular culture utilizes religion to shape what consumers may find believable. And yet, the conclusion draws these threads of implicit religion together to show how the examination of religious sensibilities and resonances in popular culture can articulate an explicit proposal of what constructive post-Christian theological messages are reciting to us as true. It argues that popular culture's constructive post-Christian theological messages recite echoes or latencies of Christian messages that: (a) wrestle with issues of dehumanization, suffering, brokenness, and poverty; (b) rescript (post-)Christian theological virtues as love, longing, insistence, and endurance; and (c) hint at the traces of religion and belief that are resourced throughout the analyses of this book.

While part I analyzes theoretical frameworks surrounding canonization and consumption, part II analyzes three methodological approaches—re-enchantment, resourcement, and rescription—to problematize and paint a picture of how popular culture imagines post-Christian belief and its tensions with, and indebtedness to, Christian belief. Chapter 1 problematizes both the possibilities of popular culture as giving shape to a post-Christian canon and how the consumption of popular culture shapes the possibilities of belief. This gives shape to chapter 2, which analyzes how popular culture re-enchants belief through the consumption of the mythic imagination by advocating for an imagined realism. Chapter 3 analyzes how the MCU problematizes the notion of "re-enchantment" through critical analyses of how it imagines late modernity as "post-disenchanted," that is, as a world fundamentally shaped by disenchantment, yet re-imagining the world as also enchanted. Chapter 4 deconstructs an inter-religious resourcement in *The Lion King*: questioning whether it is morally necessary in a post-Christian culture for Christians to watch *The Lion King* because of its dual recitation of Christian inclusivism and religious pluralism. Chapter 5 analyzes how the television show *Lucifer* offers a theological rescription of Christian theology and how it alters and reflects the theological imagination of God and the Devil in a post-Christian culture.

Parts III and IV analyze post-Christian manifestations and imaginings of love, brokenness, dehumanization, and suffering. In part III, chapters 6 and 7 address the systemic, historical problems of modern dehumanization and suffering found in the futurity and wake of modernity through the films *Cloud Atlas*, *Black Panther*, and *Wakanda Forever*. Chapter 6 argues that *Cloud Atlas* prophesies the ends of modernity as a strategically dehumanizing secularized eschatology—but tactically counters dehumanization through the power of love. Chapter 7 analyzes arguments and silences made in my original chapter on *Black Panther*—which appears in the forthcoming *Theology and Black Panther*—by arguing that *Black Panther* and *Wakanda Forever* illustrate how Black humanity remembers its history to endure in the wake of Black suffering and experience.[4] Then, in part IV, chapters 8 and 9 analyze doxologies of brokenness in popular music and the systemic issues of poverty in *Shameless* through analyses of how Christian notions of sin are rescripted as brokenness. Through a doxological analysis of Machine Gun Kelly, Halsey, and Linkin Park, chapter 8 pays attention to the despairing, broken cries for love and redemption through the echoes of an absence theology in post-Christian culture. Chapter 9 offers an analysis of the systemic nature of sin and poverty in *Shameless* via an assist from the work of Pierre Bourdieu to illustrate a sociological, religious, and theological portrait of the structures and dispositions of sin in urban poverty.

Chapter 10 (part V, the conclusion) explicitly addresses the post-Christian theological messages found throughout the exegetical analyses of the book.

It argues that these explicit post-Christian theological messages are found in the implicit religious sensibilities and feelings recited within twenty-first-century popular culture. It emphasizes how post-Christian theology goes beyond Christianity, yet carries a Christian latency that is attuned to the sensibilities and cries of post-Christian religiosity in popular culture. As such, the conclusion offers a proposal that draws together implicit religious themes of post-Christian religion in popular culture into an explicit post-Christian constructive theology that pays attention to the messages and the contextual problems and promises of post-Christian theology.

APPEAL, BACKGROUND, AND FRAMEWORKS

Throughout this book, several discourses and definitions ought to be clearly stated at the forefront in how they are used. These deal with a particular historical-cultural-generational appeal and setting in which this book is situated, the methodological ideas applied throughout the book, and the background discourses that shape and contextualize the book.

First, it is relevant to nuance the difference between how post-Christian and non-Christian are used throughout the book. "Post-Christian" is used throughout this book to refer to what it means to leave behind Christianity as a cultural framework and plausibility structure, while yet coming to terms with and wrestling with what it means to leave Christian plausibility structures behind. This means post-Christian entails a historical indebtedness to Christianity. Or rather, that post-Christian is used where Christianity has historically held cultural sway and power. By contrast, this book typically uses the phrase "non-Christian" to refer to Asian or non-Western forms of religious faith and philosophy that do not have historical origins in Christianity. As such, non-Christian in this book refers to cultural, social, historical, religious, and philosophical frameworks that do not originally presuppose Christian plausibility structures that have shaped the contours of Western history and culture since the Middle Ages. This implies that while "non-Christian" refers to the lack of Christian plausibility structures, "post-Christian" refers to the latent effects of Christian plausibility structures in the twenty-first-century West.

The Twenty-First Century Generational Appeal

This book is a situated reflection on the contours of the possibilities of religious belief at the turn of the twenty-first century, and particularly, but not exclusively, reflects on pop cultural trends of the first two decades of the twenty-first century in which many millennials came of age, in which Gen X became established, and in which Gen Z became aware of the issues in the world as they grew up into adolescence and early adulthood. Because of this historical moment in which these generations are situated, this book offers important reflections on those religious ideas expressed in popular culture that tap into these generational experiences, moods, and sensibilities.

This book is written by a millennial born at the beginning of the last decade of the twentieth century. It reflects interests, concerns, and experiences that I have observed or found problematic for the millennial generation. That said, what is examined throughout this book should still find resonance with both Generation X and Generation Z. Gen X will recognize and take seriously the warnings about the promises and problems of modernity and technology found in chapter 6. They will also, I think, find delightful the irreverent offensiveness of the analyses in chapters 5 and 9 while also recognizing the resignation to its normativity found in their adult lives. Gen Z will recognize the concern for human dignity found in chapters 3 and 7 that try to wrestle with the reality of giving voice to minorities and those voices often not heard in dominant White patriarchal discourses. Gen Z, like Millennials, will also recognize sentiments of wrestling with the inadequacy of cliché theological answers to problems found within organized religion in chapters 5, 8, and 9. Both Gen X and Gen Z may also find resonances with the millennial experience found in chapter 8. Gen X may see in chapter 8 a part of their experience of the hopelessness and meaninglessness of life from their youth, while Gen Z may see an instance of how music may reflect potential answers to the problems they feel trapped in and without answers to. Even so, chapter 8 reflects at its core not only millennial sensibilities but also how millennials may wrestle with these problems in ways that do not declare an absolute answer to the problem while also sitting in the emptiness and ennui of the experience with those who suffer in it.

When it comes to chapters 3, 4, and 5, there may be a broad swath of generational responses. The appeal of the MCU over the last two decades has captured the attention of large portions of the world. And yet the arguments will situate its presentations of critical discourses about issues around the continued relevance and role of religion in contemporary Western society. In this sense, it may be easily relevant to each generation. The issue raised in chapter 4, however, may not be relevant, or even strange as to why it would matter, to the concerns of non-religious Gen Zs, partly because the original version of *The Lion King* debuted several years before Gen Z began. However, the issues it raises about religious pluralism and Christian inclusivism are still relevant for both those in older generations and Christians aware of the debates about religious pluralism at the turn of the millennium. This is because it touches on central issues of the continued relevance of Christianity and how it relates to non-Christian religions. Chapter 5, however, may find relevance for each generation as it reflects and rescripts notions of evil, an ever-present problem to the human imagination, through an irreverent depiction that challenges traditional understandings, while proposing alternate ways of understanding how we may imagine the nature of God, the Devil, and angels and demons.

Background Discourses

Because this book is situated primarily at the beginning of the twenty-first century, this also implies that there are several background traditions or discourses that shape the assumptions of this book. Each of these is tied intimately to one another and also reflects something of the millennial experience. Gen X may recognize how they lived through the shifts toward a postmodern culture. Millennials may recognize how the trends in postmodernism became normative in their own lifetimes. Gen Z may recognize how much of the postmodern world is assumed and unquestioned because by the time of their birth or coming of age, these forces had already become established as hallmarks of late modern culture.

These shifts in the generation's experiences of postmodernity are characterized by a shift from the postmodern to the late-modern. Using Zygmunt Bauman as a way of expressing the shift from postmodern to late modern, I think of this transition as when "the postmodern perspective is transformed from being a *reactive stance*, flinching from the unbelievable claims or intolerable demands of modern bureaucracies to being a *proactive force* that shapes how individuals construct their lives, identities, and relationships."[5] These proactive forces are not only for issues of social justice and gun violence but are also for Black rights in an unjust society, and for women's, gay, and trans rights. Each of these is not only a proactive force for a more just and equitably distributed society but also tactics that subvert the totalizing strategies of (white, patriarchal) modernity. Another side of the late-modern is typified as including sociological structures geared toward globalization and the pluralization of belief (along with the decline of participation in religious institutions), the rise of digital consumerism over industrial productivity, and the rise in both economic flourishing and a growing gap of economic inequality.[6]

If we turn to analyze what we mean by "postmodern," according to Dennis Smith, for Zygmunt Bauman, postmodernity is characterized by three interrelated tropes: postmodernity is a perspective, a habitat, and a process.[7] The postmodern perspective "is permeated with a sense of the ambivalence of existence, the contingency of events and the insecurity of being" marked by a skepticism about modernity and its promises.[8] A postmodern habitat, by contrast, happens when the ambivalence of the postmodern perspective becomes the dominant worldview. However, the process of postmodernity is more complex. It is marked by the structural transformations that altered capitalism from an industrial-producer society to a digital-consumer society; the tensions between the global and the local; the polarization between the rich and the poor, and the right and the left; the doubting of metanarratives; and the disillusionment of modern security found within the sovereignty of state, culture, and military.[9] Postmodernity is the product of modernity's goal to determine and control, set limits, and create parameters of security through the state, public sphere, and economy. But postmodernity transformed this into a consumer society—the postmodern is created and produced by the very means eclipsed in its formation in the modern.[10] Within the framework of postmodernity, postmoderns find themselves living in an age of uncertainty ushered in by the transformation from a modern to a postmodern society.

Furthermore, linked to the background discourses of postmodernism and its normative assumptions in late modernity is also the growing (re-) awareness of religion in the Western world, that is, postsecularism. The arrival of the postsecular is when we begin to be aware of and ask after and about the enduring presence of religion after the normative structures of the secular are beginning to be questioned, debated, and rethought.[11] For modern Christians, a side effect of the Enlightenment project of critiquing religion as backward and superstitious was that it reduced religious belief to a cognitive assent to the contents of belief among Western Christians. But it also argues that religion was something of a personal, private choice that ought not to have a place in the democratic processes and the making of public policy.[12]

The challenges posed to the secular worldview by the postsecular are manifold, but at the very least: (1) they argue for a recovery of religious participation and embodiment through an emphasis on the affective dimensions of religious practice upon the lived experience of faith[13]; and (2) secularists must wrestle with the very real reality of the presence of religions in political processes and the creation of public policy—whether that comes from the visible awareness of Islam and the reality of religious terrorism since 9/11, the rise in populist political movements and their appeal to religious believers in the last decade across global political elections, or even the marriage between Christians with the American politics exemplified by the Moral Majority and the Christian Right since the 1980s.[14]

But what is important for us to consider is that the postsecular critique of the secular sheds light on the relationship between the sacred and the secular in ways that produce and create a pluralization and optionality of believing when the dominant voice of Christianity—and its plausibility structures over society, culture, and politics—has weakened. Peter Berger argued that par for the course in modernity, religious plausibility structures—those structures that support a religious sacred canopy (a set of religious structures that help us make sense of our world under the overarching authority and formative power of religion)—have weakened.[15] But how they weakened did not mean the full eclipse of religion or its demise. Even Berger had to recant his propagation of the secularization thesis when he realized three decades later that religion was still, and still is, a very real and live presence in our world. This means that the secular has to come to terms with the pluralization of religion in the late twentieth century.[16]

Charles Taylor and others have argued that since the 1970s, religion has exploded and adapted to new cultural, historical, intellectual, and social situations and conditions in ways that have produced cross-pressures and the fragilization of believing alongside secular and non-religious options.[17] This optionality is both fragmented and pluralized into a network of points of reference governed by the notion of authenticity. Authenticity, in turn, has shaped how post-Christians make sense of the world without the overarching power of religious authority or organized religion to determine what we believe.[18] In the post-Christian contexts in which the Western world now lives, religion is now optional and chosen.[19] Its optionality comes from the pluralization of religious options, possibilities, practices, and ideas. Its chosenness is a contrast to those inherited religions we may or may not have grown up in. Between religion's chosenness and optionality comes a plethora of ways in which we can imagine what is true and real, often governed by the balance between the credibility and desirability of both what makes sense to us and our life experiences and what we find desirable and comforting in what religion or religious ideas and practices offer us.

Finally, the relationship between Christianity and post-Christianity is something that warrants an emphasis: the word post-Christian includes the words "post" and "Christian." To be "post-Christian" means to be historically indebted to, culturally shaped in light of, and found in the aftermath of the eclipse of Christendom. The Christian background behind the idea of post-Christian is telling: post-Christianity has a Christian latency. The latent traces of Christianity will be found throughout this volume through the use of Christian theological doctrines, themes, and ideas. This latency of Christian theological doctrines, themes, and ideas will be used as an interpretive framework and will be applied to popular culture as a way to understand what post-Christian belief may look like *after* Christianity. To be "post-Christian" means both *to come after* Christianity and *to be indebted to* the inescapable *latencies* of Christianity. Arguably, the possibility of a post-Christian religion is situated in the West because the Western world has a legacy of Christianity that shapes the structures of the Western world, and because of this, certain parts of the West are arguably the only places in the world so far that could be characterized as "post"-Christian.

The Methodological Frameworks

This book works with three methodological frameworks that shape the possibility of articulating post-Christian religion in popular culture: re-enchantment, resourcement, and rescription. Each of these ideas comes from various discourses in Christian theology and emphasizes different angles that can be used to understand post-Christian religion.

"Re-enchantment" is an idea in theology and philosophy that has been used widely over the last several decades. When we talk about "re"-enchantment, a question may be raised: Why and what would we need to re-enchant? Behind the idea of re-enchantment is the idea of "disenchantment," which is a popular, though misused, interpretation of a term attributed to an early twentieth-century sociologist of religion, Max Weber, who posited the "demagification" of the world.[20] Whether we use "disenchantment" the way Weber used it or not, it has come to signify a largely unquestioned reality: modernity is imagined or presupposed as closed to God and transcendence. This is what Charles Taylor calls a "closed-world-structure," particularly to an "enchanted" world inhabited by the possibilities of, and porous interactions with, spirits, gods, and the supernatural.[21] Taylor argues that modern people are "buffered" and "invulnerable" from the reality, possibility, or effects of the supernatural.[22] These are all elements of what is typically imagined by the idea of "disenchantment." But to "re-enchant" our world after disenchantment—or what has been called "post-disenchantment"[23]—entails not only a renewed openness to the reality of transcendence, the effects of the supernatural in our world, and what it means to be human.[24] It also refers to the renewed possibilities of believing in a post-Christian context that imagines again what religious belief may look like, particularly after the dominance of the Christian sacred canopy and its plausibility structures have weakened—and how they transform in a pluralistic arena. To speak of the "re-enchantment of the possibilities of belief" means to articulate the possibility of believing when it is optional, contested, and pluralized in its potential amalgamations of expressions—not that belief has necessarily disappeared or that culture has ever been truly disenchanted (which implies the false idea that "re-enchantment" would mean a return of religion after a total eclipse where it was fully lost).

Another idea in Christian theology is the idea of "resourcement." This term is a calling card of the *Nouvelle Theologie* tradition of French Catholic theology in the mid-twentieth century, associated with the work of Maurice Blondel, Yves Congar, and especially Henri de Lubac, among many others.[25] This tradition was a major influence not only on the theology of Vatican II of the 1960s but also more recently on the Anglo-Catholic movement in theology called "Radical Orthodoxy," associated with the work of John Milbank, Catherine Pickstock, Graham Ward, and many others.[26] The Radical

Orthodoxy movement is more of a sensibility, a post-secular project in theology that seeks to baptize, critique, and re-and-out-narrate the secular through the resourcement of classical Christian theology, particularly the theologies associated with Saint Augustine, Thomas Aquinas, Christian Neo-Platonism, and to a lesser extent, the Romantic-idealists and Heideggerian tradition.[27] The idea of resourcement is also something implicit in the work of the religious pluralist and pioneer of inter-religious dialogue, Raimon Panikkar.[28] Resourcement is about drawing from traditional orthodox religious and theological sources of the past and of particular religious traditions to offer an alternative voice that generates and instigates a rethinking and renewal of issues in and of the failures of modernity and religion. But it is not just to paint the failures of modernity—it is also to paint an adequate, alternative vision of the world that pays attention to the human religious experience and classical theological articulations and expressions of God.

The third methodological idea this book works with is "rescription." Rescription refers to the idea of "rewriting," particularly the rewriting of authoritative literature or theology to fit the ordinary experience and expressions of lived belief displayed through the enacted practices of a particular faith community and/or tradition. Rescription is an idea used in the sociology of religion and in a subdiscipline of practical theology called "ordinary theology." Ordinary theology refers to the theological expression and articulations of God by an uneducated, non-academic, non-theological, or informally trained laity.[29] Rescription comes from the word "script" and implies the idea of "scripture" as authoritative literature. But "rescription" entails the rewriting of theology and authoritative expressions of God for a religious community or believer in ways that reflect not just the beliefs, but moreover the theology expressed through ordinary religious practice and language. This is why practical theology is the place where rescription is most often used, because it reflects on and articulates the theological *language* used in the religious *practice*. By starting with practice, rescription entails a process of articulating the implicit beliefs embedded and embodied in the very practices of a lived faith.

The challenge of rescription for the academically trained theologian or Christian believer lies in the potential for heresy. Theological orthodoxy refers to a right understanding of theological truth, something originally determined in the early Christian church by the Christian community and its practice and confession as it wrestled with both (1) problematic philosophical and theological issues that were deemed heresy through centuries of debate and (2) the community's commitment to articulate coherently, consistently, and faithfully its confessional beliefs in Jesus as LORD and the activity and presence of the Spirit as one with God the Father. Christians had to try to articulate the consistency of their theological belief in Jesus and the Holy

Spirit with Jewish monotheism, and this was done through the turn to Greek philosophy by the Early Church Fathers.

Each of these methodological considerations offers tools for interpreting post-Christian religion in popular culture. Re-enchantment allows us to glimpse the renewed visibility and engagement with religion in a late-modern context where we can begin to imagine again the possibilities of believing—whether they are Christian or not. Resourcement offers us a tool to tap into traditional religious traditions to help us make sense of post-Christian religion in popular culture. Rescription allows us to understand how post-Christian theology in popular culture alters and transforms Christian beliefs in ways that move beyond Christianity. Each of these tools can help us interpret and make sense of what post-Christian religious belief looks like in the aftermath of Christianity while moving beyond it in the popular cultural imaginings of the possibilities of believing.

AUTHORIAL INTENT AND THEOLOGICAL METHODS

This section offers both a disclosure of the authorial intent of the book and a methodological note on the theological method of the book. One may be wondering, "What point of view is this book coming from?" and "What is the author's intent for why this volume ought to be taken seriously by both Christian and post-Christian readers?" This volume is not primarily concerned with religious practices or theological orthodoxy. Nor is it primarily concerned with literary theory or media studies. Rather, this book illustrates a set of theological exegeses (interpretations) of what post-Christian theological and religious messages are being recited to and by us through our consumption of contemporary popular culture. It investigates what post-Christian religiosity and theology recite to us when we are informed by the consumption of popular culture and its implicit religious messages, representations, and simulations of what can be imagined as believable. Between re-enchantment, resourcement, and rescription, this book proposes a threefold methodology that can help us examine possible articulations of post-Christian religion and theology found within popular culture.

This book offers late-modern, post-Christian, constructive theological exegeses of popular culture. It paints a picture of what post-Christian religion may look like in light of twenty-first-century popular culture as a point of contrast to both modernity and Christian theology and religion. Its analyses interpret how popular culture imagines post-Christian religion through a plethora of genres of popular culture—from popular pop punk and alternative music to imaginative theological rescriptions found in television series, and from fantasy, fiction, and comics literature adapted to film to modern visions of humanity found within the films *Black Panther*, *Wakanda Forever*, and *Cloud Atlas*. Because the purpose of this book is to analyze and interpret how post-Christian theological and religious messages are imagined and recited in and through popular culture, this book intends to present *neither* a Christian critique of post-Christian religion *nor* a Christian critique of popular culture.

Rather, this book takes popular culture and post-Christian religion seriously *on its own terms* through an interpretive framework that constructively investigates the theological contents, contextual contours, and religious sensibilities of post-Christian religion found within the expressions and recitations of twenty-first-century popular culture. That said, the value and significance of this book for a Christian audience is, hopefully, that they can be more in touch with the sensibilities of a post-Christian world so that they may be better equipped to witness, minister, evangelize, and share life with post-Christians. There are points throughout this book of contact between post-Christian religion and how Christians may respond in love to post-Christians, as well as points that emphasize a call for Christians to wrestle with the implications of post-Christian pop cultural expressions and what that may mean for Christians engaging with a post-Christian world. On the other side, the value and significance of this book for its post-Christian audience is that it seeks to give voice to your experience, your sensibilities, and your struggles with religion, particularly Christianity. I hope this book mirrors your experience in ways that offer pathways not only of thinking through your experience in the contemporary world through the lens of post-Christian religion but also that you would consider (maybe again) what Christianity may offer you (albeit, I think this is dependent on both whether the Christian community adequately bears their presence with you throughout the contours of your everyday lives—and whether it presents a more desirable and credible gospel than it may have to you in the past).

I hope that both Christians and post-Christians alike may benefit from this book because it offers a constructive theological and religious interpretation of post-Christian religion that sympathetically listens to how popular culture portrays it, while also offering an instance of making explicit sense of the implicit post-Christian messages in popular culture. This book ought not to be the last of its kind, as there is so much more in popular culture that may and can be examined—even in different, critical directions away and apart from Christianity. This book is intentionally written by a Christian who has dwelled most of his life in a post-Christian culture and context. Because of this, I hope the reader will see themselves and their post-Christian experience alongside their indebtedness to the latency of Christianity that permeates throughout twenty-first-century popular culture.

NOTES

1. Jean Baudrillard, *Simulations*, trans. Paul Foss, Paul Patton, and Philip Beitchman, Fourteenth (USA: Semiotext[e], 1983); Jean Baudrillard, *Simulations and Simulacra*, trans. Sheila Faria Glaser (Ann Arbor, MI: The University of Michigan Press, 1994).
2. Gilles Deleuze, "The Actual and the Virtual," in *Dialogues II,* ed. Claire Parnet and Gilles Deleuze (Indianapolis, IN: Bloomsbury Academic, 2006), 148–159.
3. Merold Westphal, *Whose Community? Which Interpretation?: Philosophical Hermeneutics for the Church* (Grand Rapids, MI: Baker Academic, 2009).
4. C.f. Andrew D. Thrasher, "Wakandan Imaginaries of Black Identity: Wakandan Politics of Identity," in *Theology and Black Panther*, ed. Matthew William Brake, Kimberly Hampton, and Travis Harris (Forthcoming).
5. Dennis Smith, *Zygmunt Bauman: Prophet of Postmodernity* (Cambridge: Polity Press, 1999), 154.
6. Ole Riis and Linda Woodhead, *A Sociology of Religious Emotion* (Oxford: Oxford University Press, 2010), 175ff.
7. Smith, *Zygmunt Bauman*, 153–154.
8. This includes democracy, globalization, and the renewed visibility of religion. C.f. Graham Ward, *The Politics of Discipleship* (Grand Rapids, MI: Baker Academic, 2009), 37–158.
9. Smith, *Zygmunt Bauman*, 154–155.
10. Zygmunt Bauman, *Postmodernity and Its Discontents* (Washington Square, NY: New York University Press, 1997), 25f.
11. Hent De Vries and Lawrence E. Sullivan, *Political Theologies: Public Religions in a Post-Secular World* (New York: Fordham University Press, 2006); Talal Asad, *Formations of the Secular: Christianity, Islam, and Modernity* (Stanford, CA: Stanford University Press, 2003).
12. C.f. Jürgen Habermas, *The Structural Transformation of the Public Sphere: An Inquiry into a Category of Bourgeois Society*, trans. Thomas Burger and Frederick Lawrence (Cambridge, MA: The MIT Press, 1989); Nicholas H. Smith, *Charles Taylor: Meaning, Morals and Modernity* (Malden, MA: Polity Press, 2002), 227; José Casanova, *Public Religions in the Modern World* (Chicago, IL: The University of Chicago Press, 1994).
13. For example, the writings of James K. A. Smith: James K. A. Smith, *Desiring the Kingdom, Worship, Worldview, and Cultural Formation*, vol. 1, 3 vols., Cultural Liturgies (Grand Rapids, MI: Baker Academic, 2009); James K. A. Smith, *Thinking in Tongues*, Pentecostal Manifestos 1 (Grand Rapids, MI: Eerdmans Publishing Co., 2010); James K. A. Smith, *Imagining the Kingdom: How Worship Works*, vol. 2, 3 vols., Cultural Liturgies (Grand Rapids, MI: Baker Academic, 2013); James K. A. Smith, *You Are What You Love: The Spiritual Power of Habit* (Grand Rapids, MI: Brazos Press, 2016).
14. This is particularly exemplified in the writings of José Casanova and Jürgen Habermas. C.f. Jürgen Habermas, *An Awareness of What Is Missing: Faith and*

Reason in a Post-Secular Age, trans. Ciaran Cronin (Malden, MA: Polity Press, 2010); Jürgen Habermas, *Religion and Rationality: Essays on Reason, God, and Modernity*, ed. Eduardo Mendieta, trans. Eric Crump and Peter Kenny (Cambridge, MA: The MIT Press, 2002); José Casanova, *Public Religions in the Modern World* (Chicago, IL: The University of Chicago Press, 1994).

15. Peter Berger, *The Sacred Canopy: Elements of a Sociological Theory of Religion* (New York: Anchor Books, 1967).

16. Peter Berger, ed., *The Desecularization of the World: Resurgent Religion and World Politics* (Grand Rapids: William B. Eerdmans Publishing Company, 1999), 9–11.

17. Ruth Abbey, "Theorizing Secularity 3: Authenticity, Ontology, and Fragilization," in *Aspiring to Fullness in a Secular Age: Essays on Religion and Theology in the Work of Charles Taylor*, ed. Carlos Colorado and Justin Klassen (Notre Dame, IN: University of Notre Dame Press, 2014), 98–124.

18. Paul Heelas, *Spiritualities of Life: New Age Romanticism and Consumptive Capitalism* (Malden, MA: Blackwell Publishing, 2008); Paul Heelas, *The New Age Movement: The Celebration of the Self and the Sacralization of Modernity* (Malden, MA: Blackwell Publishers, 1996).

19. Charles Taylor, *A Secular Age* (Cambridge, MA: The Belknap Press of Harvard University Press, 2007).

20. Hans Joas, *The Power of the Sacred: An Alternative to the Narrative of Disenchantment*, trans. Alex Skinner (Oxford: Oxford University Press, 2021).

21. Tone Svetelj, "Rereading Modernity—Charles Taylor on Its Genesis and Prospects" (Boston, MA: Boston College, 2012), 395.

22. Taylor, *A Secular Age*, 303.

23. Marika Rose, "Machines of Loving Grace: Angels, Cyborgs, and Postsecular Labor," *Journal for Cultural and Religious Theory* 16, no. 2 (2017): 240–259, 243.

24. Indeed, as Michiel Meijer et al. argue, re-enchantment may be religious or non-religious, focusing on what it means to be human in light of the loss of, and openness to, transcendence. C.f. Michiel Meijer and Herbert De Vriese, "Introduction," in *The Philosophy of Reenchantment* (London and New York: Routledge, 2021), 1–14; Akeel Bilgrami, "Might There Be Secular Enchantment?" in *The Philosophy of Reenchantment*, ed. Michiel Meijer and Herbert De Vriese (London and New York: Routledge, 2021), 54–77.

25. C.f. Gabriel Flynn and Paul D. Murray, eds., *Ressourcement: A Movement for Renewal in twentieth-century Catholic Theology* (Oxford: Oxford University Press, 2012); Jürgen Mettepenningen, *Nouvelle Theologie—New Theology: Inheritor of Modernism, Precursor of Vatican II* (London and New York: T&T Clark, 2010); Hans Boersma, *"Nouvelle Theologie" and Sacramental Theology: A Return to Mystery* (Oxford: Oxford University Press, 2009).

26. C.f. John Milbank, *The Suspended Middle: Henri de Lubac and the Renewed Split in Modern Catholic Theology*, Second Edition (Grand Rapids, MI: William B. Eerdmans, 2005).

27. C.f. John Milbank, Catherine Pickstock, and Graham Ward, eds., *Radical Orthodoxy: A New Theology* (London and New York: Routledge, 1999); C.f. Andrew

D. Thrasher, *An Advaitic Modernity? Raimon Panikkar and Philosophical Theology* (Lanham, MD: Fortress Press, 2024), 111–139.

28. I am currently working on a three-volume project called *Dialogical Catalysts for the Christian Faith,* developing this, especially volumes 2 (on twentieth-century continental thought) and 3 (on Asian resourcements for Christian faith).

29. Mark Cartledge, "Ordinary Theology and the British Assemblies of God Doctrinal Tradition: A Qualitative Study," in *Explorations in Ordinary Theology*, ed. Jeff Astley and Leslie J. Francis (Burlington, VT: Ashgate, 2013), 107–116; Mark Cartledge, *Testimony in the Spirit* (Burlington, VT: Ashgate, 2010); Jeff Astley, *Ordinary Theology: Looking, Listening, and Learning in Theology* (Burlington, VT: Ashgate, 2002); Jeff Astley and Leslie J. Francis, eds., *Exploring Ordinary Theology* (Burlington, VT: Ashgate, 2013).

Part I

THEORETICAL FRAMEWORKS

Chapter 1

Consuming a Post-Christian Canon?

At the heart of post-Christian theological exegeses of popular culture found throughout this book are the questions of how popular culture may present answers to the questions of the human condition and how the consumption of popular culture can shape the possibilities of belief. This means that the consumption of popular culture is intimately linked to the notion of how popular culture can be understood as "scripture" that can articulate the theological themes and genres of a post-Christian canon. This chapter argues that this concept can be situated in the question of *what* messages popular culture presents and *how* those messages may legitimize the possibilities of believing in late modernity. First, this deals with both the question of canonization and whether we may read popular culture as scripture. Second, this deals with both the question of believability and what role the consumption of popular culture may have in informing what is possible to believe. This chapter sets out to examine both of these sets of questions and argues that popular culture can be read as a set of scriptures that can articulate theological and religious messages *and* inform the possibilities of believing in late modernity.

POPULAR CULTURE AS SCRIPTURE

In religious studies, scripture is a central point of reference by which to study religion—religious scriptures inescapably shape the study of religion as a textual source by which to understand the myths, ethics, and truths of religion. And yet, scripture is also something always interpreted by a community that finds these texts authoritative insofar as these texts can shape religious practice and belief. Kevin J. Vanhoozer notes that for Wilfred Cantwell Smith, "'scripture' is simply a way of talking about human practices vis-à-vis the biblical texts, rather than about the texts themselves."[1] As such, interpreting religious texts is closely linked to interpreting not just the nature of God, but also both human practices and their reflections of the human condition. For this book, popular culture can also be read as a religious text that reflects on the human condition and the consumptive practices of humanity in the contemporary world. To read these theological and religious messages in popular culture is the point of this book—it analyzes how popular culture recites religious and theological messages that reflect the human condition and the consumption of contents and contexts that shape the possibilities of religious belief.

As a way of analogy, Kevin J. Vanhoozer's understanding of the Bible as a theo-dramatic text and performance can be a helpful way to understand popular culture as a "scripture." Just as Vanhoozer argues that the Bible is "an authoritative script" to be intellectually assented to and interpreted as a "live performance" of God's dramatic agency in human history, so also may popular culture be read as an authoritative script of a live performance of religious sensibilities and theological messages.[2] These sensibilities and messages can be interpreted as an authoritative script of what it means to be human and believe in the twenty-first century. Furthermore, just as the biblical canon is formative of what it means to covenantally practice what it means to be human in a relationship with God, popular culture reflects and presents messages about the human condition that both question the existence of God and moral norms, while also reflecting what life looks like and how it is practiced *without* traditional Christian beliefs in God or participation in institutional religion.

And yet, to interpret the religious and theological messages in twenty-first-century popular culture requires a canonical standard that may stand as a rule to understand how popular culture presents a script through which we may understand the shape and content of post-Christian religious belief and interpretive practice. (How) Are the texts analyzed throughout this book canonical for post-Christian religion and theology? What community do they represent? Arguably, the answer to the latter question is that they represent a late modern Western community—one in which the latencies of both modernity and Christianity linger as well as weaken when we begin to assume the normativity of the postmodern. To answer the former question, arguably this book sets out to show how popular culture not only expresses theological and religious messages and contents but also sets a standard for what it means to be human and believe in late modernity.

Are the texts analyzed in this book scripture? If we define scripture as an authoritative script that both reflects (on) the human condition *and* presents messages that form who we are, inform the contents of our beliefs, and transform how we understand reality, then yes, popular culture can be understood as scripture. Kevin Vanhoozer, arguing from a Christian theological position, states that "*to practice* sola scriptura *means to participate in the canonical practices that form, inform, and transform our speaking, thinking, and living—practices that the Spirit uses to conform us to the image of God in Christ.*"[3] And yet, to read twenty-first-century popular culture as a canonical script means to read it as a form of scripture that reflects on what it means to be human and believe in late modernity. Popular culture has the power to form who we are, inform us of what we believe, and transform how we see and understand reality. In this vein, popular culture may be read as scripture in ways that generate alternate ways of imagining and conceiving of both God and what it means to be a human person.

Throughout this book's exegeses of the post-Christian theological messages in popular culture, a helpful way of understanding how this can be done is to adopt Kevin Vanhoozer's notion of the dramaturge. Vanhoozer states that the dramaturge's "task is to study the playscript and prepare it for performances that truthfully realize its truth."[4] It is not only that most of the popular culture texts analyzed throughout this book were made, enacted, and/or directed by a dramaturge. It is also salient to remember that the dramaturge presents their understanding and recitation of religious and theological messages found in popular culture. In this sense, the role of this book is to read and interpret the implicit truths presented by the dramaturge through the popular cultural texts analyzed throughout this book. And so, which texts will be analyzed? And how may they analogously mirror the biblical canon? These two questions will be developed throughout the next two sections.

CONTEXTUALIZING THE TEXTS

In this section, the focus is to introduce the popular culture "texts" or "scriptures" this book analyzes. From chapter 2, several points of reference will shape the analyses found in the following chapters. First, it focuses on how secondary/virtual worlds and primary/actual worlds reflect two major theorists/theories that shape the analyses below. The notion of primary and secondary worlds comes from the literary reflections and criticism of J. R. R. Tolkien in his famous "On Fairy-Stories" and reflects on how the creation of fantasy worlds (secondary worlds/subcreations) is an expression of what it means to exercise what it means to be made in the image of God: God is the maker of the created, real-world (the primary world/creation), and humans are made in the image of God.[5] If God is a world-maker and humans are created in the image of God, then for Tolkien, the best expression of being human is to also create (secondary) worlds that reflect the image of their creator.[6]

Second, the notion of actual and virtual worlds hints at the legacy of Gilles Deleuze, Jean Baudrillard, and others who reflect on the idea of simulation. Simulation asks the question of what something refers to, of its substance, and responds in the negative. But moreover, it asks whether its reality is based on something divine, eternal, or infinite—or whether it is a simulation bound to finitude, nihilism, and this world. Simulation theorists will often vie for the latter answer, but with different sensibilities (Baudrillard saw it with nostalgia for what was lost, while Deleuze affirms this reality without any sense of loss). Third, the reader will see that many of the sources of popular culture are film and television adaptations and rescriptions of comics, fiction, and fantasy—emphasizing how popular culture mediates the written and drawn word through digital technology, acting, and green screens. Each of these hints at the reality that popular culture in the twentieth century not only finds resources in literature and the written word but also rescripts those sources to paint a picture and present messages that enchant the imagination in ways that subtly influence how we imagine religion.

When we turn to the remaining chapters, however, the focus of analysis shifts. Chapter 3 focuses on the Marvel Cinematic Universe (MCU), particularly Phases Three and Four at the turn of the third decade of the twenty-first century. Particularly, the films and television shows in the MCU that feature religion, the multiverse, time, and reality are under examination on how they imagine "re-enchantment"—such as the *Doctor Strange* films (2016, 2022), *The Eternals* (2021), *Ms. Marvel* (2022), *Thor: Love and Thunder* (2022), *Loki* (2021, 2023), *What If...?* (2021), *Moon Knight* (2022), *Avengers: Infinity War* (2018), and *Avengers: Endgame* (2019). One will notice the particular emphasis on Phase Four because it generates a plethora of ideas that make us wrestle with the intersection of religion, science, and technology.[7] Luckily, there is also a growing amount of scholarly literature to draw on at the intersection between religion and both the Marvel comics and the MCU.[8]

Chapter 4, however, is the one text analyzed in this book that does not date to the twenty-first century—other than its recent live adaptation: *The Lion King* (1994, 2019). This text is of particular importance because of its immense and long-lasting popularity across generations. It is the hallmark of one of the best and most successful Disney movies. It is a Disney classic that has captured the imagination through its popular soundtrack. But for this book, *The Lion King* also has subtle messages that present both Christian and non-Christian themes when it comes to reading the film through the lens of inter-religious resourcement. Chapter 4 presents a striking argument that should cause us to pause over several things: (a) the ambiguity of what *The Lion King's* theological message actually presents; (b) the moral implications (for Christians) or irrelevance (for post-Christians) of those messages; and (c) whether religious pluralism has had a lasting influence across the last three decades since *The Lion King* originally debuted. Arguably, the latter is no longer questioned but has been assumed into the cultural milieu of the late modern world, and the former two are contingent upon whether the discourse of Christian theology of religions is still relevant and for whom it is relevant.

Chapter 5 analyzes the popular show *Lucifer*, which is both an adaptation from the comics and writings of Neil Gaiman and a show that ran for six seasons across two networks (Fox, seasons 1–3, and Netflix, seasons 4–6). After Fox dropped the show, Netflix picked it up for another three shorter seasons. The focus of chapter 5 will primarily be on seasons 4 through 6, though it will reference and spoil things from most seasons, especially the ending of the show (spoiler alert!). But *Lucifer* plays an important role because it takes something with an immense, obscure, and dark history and rescripts it in irreverent ways that flip the script on how we can imagine and interpret God, Angels, Demons, biblical stories, and the Devil. This is an important text under purview because of its ability to imagine post-Christian theology in ways that may have a Christian latency in using its stories, but it does so in ways that are distinctly unorthodox from a traditional Christian perspective. While the power of *Lucifer's* rescriptions of God, Angels, and the Devil may not be as popular—and its subtly rescripted post-Christian messages—as other objects of the analysis presented here, it does shed important light on how we may imagine theology in a post-Christian context that may have lasting effects down the line.

Like chapter 5, chapter 6 focuses on a more (indeed the most) obscure text found in this book—both the book (2004) and film adaptation (2012) of *Cloud Atlas*. The Wachowski Sisters' film adaptation of David Mitchell's book is an interesting one, and it will be helpful to demarcate the discrepancies between the book and film. Both the book and the film bounce around between six different years in history: 1849, 1936, 1973, 2012, 2144, and 2346. The book is organized as a chiasm, presenting half of the story each from the 1849 story to the 2144 story. The center of the book/chiasm is the full 2346 story, and then the book presents the second half of each other story in reverse order (from the 2144 story down to the 1849 story). But the film bounces around these stories in confusing ways through an attempt to make sense of a book that seems impossible to adapt to film.

To understand the film, I recommend that the viewer watch it at least three times to make sense of the stories, time skips, and the underlying narrative. Some stories are strange and humorous, others stark and dark, and others hopeful (or idealistic). The book ends on a message that presents in 1849 what did not happen throughout the imagined historical narrative: that to imagine the world differently—without violence and the will to power—is an ideal hoped-for that takes active practice and participation.[9] The film's response to this was to see it as a single drop in the ocean, and the quippant response was "What is the ocean, but a multitude of drops?"[10]

Both forms of the text illustrate how the human drive for power and domination ruins the earth, and yet they both also demonstrate how love has the power to tactically subvert it, even if the smallness of those subversions is not enough to save the world from an ecological holocaust. Finally, the stark contrast between the film and the book is the relationship between Zachry and Meronym and how the 2346 story ends. In the film, they get married and are rescued and presumably taken to Mars or another off-world colony through Meronym's use of satellites on Hawaii. In the book, no rescue, marriage, or satellite use happens. The end of the 2346 narrative in the book entails the destruction through violence and sickness of two tribes—those tribes who retained their humanity. The book ends on a much more depressing note than the film does on the future of humanity.

Chapter 7 addresses some of the highest-ranking films in gross product on opening weekend—which is quite significant because of its representations of Black humanity—*Black Panther* and *Wakanda Forever*.[11] Chapter 7 addresses a critical reflection on the philosophical and historical silences found in a chapter I wrote in 2019 that will appear in the forthcoming *Theology and Black Panther*, but utilizes *Wakanda Forever* to illustrate further implications of my original chapter. With the immense popularity of *Black Panther* in both films and comics across time, the death of Chadwick Boseman (the actor who played T'Challa, the Black Panther), and the appeal of a Black superhero that bridges both African and African American experiences, it is pertinent to address the horrors of how the historicity and philosophy of Blackness developed as a modern phenomenon that prophetically calls the structures of modernity to come to terms with their complicity in dehumanizing Black humanity. This history is filled with suffering and grief, and yet a key component of the Black imaginary is remembrance, particularly remembrance of the past to help one live in the present and with the grief of the modern history of Black humanity. The afterlives of slavery and colonialism are very real and still immensely felt across the globe, and chapter 7 addresses the silences from my chapter in the forthcoming *Theology and Black Panther* because it fails to address the history and grief of this narrative.

Chapter 8, in turn charts the theological echoes found in three leading musical artists of the twenty-first century. Linkin Park has long been established as one of the most defining bands of the early twenty-first century—through hits like "In the End," "Numb," "What I've Done," and, more tragically, the suicide of its frontman Chester Bennington on July 20, 2017. The lasting effects of Linkin Park are also being felt with the recent twentieth anniversary re-release of their second studio album, *Meteora*, and the haunting cries of

Bennington in "Lost" that speak loudly of his early cries of pain that resulted in the taking of his own life years later.[12]

The haunts of Linkin Park are felt in other ways in the music of Halsey (Ashley Nicolette Frangipane), whose music cries out for love in the brokenness of unhealthy relationships. Halsey's music reflects the longings of the heart to be known and loved, yet speaks also of how broken love can be. In another way, the music of Machine Gun Kelly (MGK, or Colson Baker), especially in his pop-punk turn and collaborations with Blink-182 drummer Travis Barker, speaks of the anger, resignation, and brokenness of a world shaped not only by drugs and sex, but also by broken relationships and the healthy doubting of what it looks like to love, be loved, and belong to someone when we fear we are not lovable. MGK's music directly rejects God while still crying out to God in ways that reveal the musical talent to invoke something one doubts is real as something that still haunts our imagination—*as if we still want God to be there*. The echoes of an absent God are displayed all across the music of these artists, and they tap into a feeling, evoking cries for longing and love that find striking resonances in the millennial experience.

Finally, the turn in chapter 9 towards the American version of the show *Shameless* closes our exegetical exercises. *Shameless* ran for eleven seasons, and we saw several actors make their debut and grow up between 2011 and 2021. Starring William H. Macy as the patriarch of a white trash family in southside Chicago, we see his six kids grow up—raised not by their father or bipolar mother (who abandoned them), but by the eldest daughter Fiona (played by Emmy Rossum). Through drug addiction, alcoholism, COVID-19, racism, prison, the stark realities of unmedicated bipolar, the aspirations and destruction of a college career, and learning to love and cope in healthy ways, we see a family grow across eleven seasons. Some break, some disappear, and others die. Some we come to hate, and others we come to love. But underlying this story of a white trash Chicago southside family is not just the brokenness and the logic of poverty. It also presents the picture of what healthy love looks like when we grow into those we commit to. The point of chapter 9 is not to condemn the immorality or sexual licentiousness of the characters. Rather, the point of chapter 9 is to theologically take into account how love and brokenness are reflected in the logics of poverty through a sociological analysis of the *habitus* of urban poverty—all the while reflecting on how religion is viewed and used by the impoverished throughout the series.

Each of these popular cultural texts is an example of post-Christian scriptures that can be read to understand what it means to be human and believe in the twenty-first century. Each of them, except *Cloud Atlas*, and possibly *Lucifer*, reflects an immense level of popularity among the Western public and their consumption of these texts. While we will save an analysis of the consumption for later in this chapter, we must first ask the question of how these popular cultural texts reflect and mirror themes and elements of the biblical canon. While the next section is a bit speculative and analogical, the point of it is to shed light on the biblical latencies and likenesses of popular cultural texts to biblical genres so that they may be read as a post-Christian canon.

BIBLICAL AND POST-CHRISTIAN CANONICAL ANALOGIES

Do the popular cultural texts analyzed throughout this book reflect themes found across the biblical canon? Can they consist of a post-Christian canon, a rule or standard of measurement that analogically reflects themes found in biblical texts? Arguably, we can speculate that popular culture does indeed reflect certain elements and themes of the biblical canon. While the following may be a stretch, it will be worthwhile to analyze analogous connection points between contemporary popular culture and biblical texts because it will demonstrate how these popular cultural texts reflect canonical similarities to the biblical canon.

Jake Doberenz has written about an important link between reading biblical texts and cinematic universes. He argues that central to reading both canonical texts and cinematic universes are the background contexts in which they are produced and the Deutero-canonical material found in other literature or films that give shape and context to the meaning and impact of how to read canonical texts.[13] Arguably, this means that we must read twenty-first-century popular culture through the contexts of its history, culture, and so on. While that task is ultimately beyond the scope of this book, it is worthwhile to note both the latency of Christianity as well as the inescapable frameworks of modernity that shape twenty-first-century life. Furthermore, the postmodern normativity of both doubting modernity and religion plays an important role in shaping the conditions for belief and being human in late modernity.

But if we read popular culture after the pattern of biblical texts, what does this yield? Arguably, the MCU reveals a canon in and of itself. This can be analogous to reading portions of the Hebrew Bible together. Just as the Pentateuch, Nevi'im, and Ketuvim consist of canonical writings within a canon, so also may the MCU be read as a canon within a post-Christian canon. The MCU re-enchants religious ideas in a post-disenchanted context and in doing so, can be read as prophetically rescripting history with religious sensibilities that take into account the disenchanting effects of modernity. Likewise, *The Lion King* reflects the dual tension between reading it through both Christian and pluralistic eyes. This can be analogous to reading the Hebrew Bible through both Jewish and Christian eyes. Can Christians read *The Lion King* as presenting a Christian message in similar ways as Christians who read the Hebrew Bible as culminating in Jesus Christ? I think a case can be made for this. But on another level, can *The Lion King* be read through an alternate lens, just as the Hebrew Bible is read differently by both Jews and Muslims than by Christians? The point is to note that the lens *through* which we read texts shapes the interpretation of the canon.

In another sense, *Lucifer* presents alternate theological rescriptions of God and the Devil that reflect theological sensibilities that ask important questions: What is the nature of God, of the Devil, and of good and evil? While certainly, the biblical canon does not agree with *Lucifer* about the nature of God and the Devil, what both reflect is the reality that scriptures present to our imagination ways of thinking about God and the Devil—they present to us theological imaginaries that implicitly shape how we can imagine both God and the Devil, and good and evil. While *Lucifer* presents us with a theological imaginary that may reshape how we imagine and conceive of God and the Devil in the popular imagination, it also reflects post-Christian theological rescriptions that present theological understandings about divine beings.

Part III presents another analogous connection to the biblical canon—particularly with its emphasis on history and prophecy. *Cloud Atlas* and *Black Panther/Wakanda Forever* reflect on the issues of oppression, violence, and injustice across history that are analogous to the prophetic witness of the Hebrew Bible against Israel and the nations when they fail to keep the covenant through the oppression of the alien, the poor, and the weak. Just as Israel and the nations are condemned by the prophets across Old Testament history for their injustices, so also can we read the history of modernity through the lens of *Cloud Atlas* and *Black Panther/Wakanda Forever* in ways that prophetically challenge modern injustices and the abuses of the will to power.

Linked to this, part IV reflects certain elements found in the Ketuvim of the Hebrew Bible. Chapter 8 reflects a rescription of the Psalms. It presents the doxologies of late modernity in ways that reflect on the brokenness of humanity and lament the loss of God in the popular imagination. Chapter 9, however, offers a more complex picture. Certainly, it reflects on love in ways analogous to the Christian emphasis on agape, but through the lenses of poverty and brokenness. *Shameless* may be read as an analogous coming of age not just of the Gallagher family, but also of how people come to terms with brokenness and learn new, healthier ways of living in the world. Arguably, this reflects the Christian belief and acceptance of a fallen world that cries out for redemption. This fallen world is marked by systemic structures geared toward oppression that the oppressed may take advantage of but also strive to live beyond in the search for healthier ways of love and belonging.

These analogies show that while the popular culture's post-Christian canon presented here is not a one-to-one connection to biblical texts, it does show likenesses to themes found across the biblical canon. These post-Christian texts are canonical insofar as they reflect on the human condition and the content and shape of human belief in late modernity. These texts are canonical if we understand them to be wrestling with the latencies of Christianity as well as the problems of modernity that shape the possibilities of believing found among Western humanity in the late-modern contexts of a post-Christian twenty-first century. What these texts reflect, however, are not just canonical rules that give context to the possibilities of believing in late modernity. They also reflect post-Christian simulations of religion that reflect a Christian latency that goes beyond Christianity in its practical consumption of popular culture. A key element as to what constitutes a post-Christian canon is not only how it reflects the human condition, but also how what we consume in popular culture comes to inform the possibilities of belief.

THEORIES OF POST-CHRISTIAN RELIGION

Johan Roeland, Stef Aupers, and Dick Houtman argue that an underdeveloped thesis in Max Weber is how cultural discontents are not only generated out of the collapse of plausibility structures but also that it generates and stimulates "new pressures of cultural reconstruction" that not only do not necessarily abandon traditional religious and cultural ideas and beliefs but also that through that cultural reconstruction, beliefs become "less vulnerable to loss of plausibility."[14] They go further to state that "tradition and science have lost much of their authority and capacity to provide late modern selves with convincing explanations of what the world's processes 'really' mean and what the meaning of life actually is."[15] The problem of meaning is illustrated in Max Weber's "The Disenchantment of the World" where scientific modernity "can describe the world as it is" and articulates an "anti-metaphysical ethos" that makes "belief in a transcendent 'other-world' that gives meaning to 'this-world'" irrelevant.[16] And yet it still fails to provide an "inherent goal, [purpose], or meaning" and thereby, "this process evokes some existential uncertainties with respect to selfhood."[17] The role of popular culture, however, can play a role in the re-enchantment of our world through the practice of its consumption by spiritual seekers and religious consumers who are looking for ways in which to find meaning in a disenchanted world. The theories of Adam Possamai, Carole M. Cusack, and Emily McAvan help navigate this intersection between religion and popular culture.

Eileen Barker and Adam Possamai offer two definitions of "hyper-real religion" worth working with. First, Barker identifies it as implying that "simulacra are simulations that make no distinction between an object and its representation but which can be seen as more real than the 'real' and are, thus, 'hyper-real.'"[18] Second, Possamai defines it as referring "to a simulacrum of a religion, created out of, or in symbiosis with, popular culture" which inspires "believers/consumers."[19] In another sense, Carole M. Cusack defines "invented religions" as "exercises of the imagination that have developed in a creative (though sometimes oppositional) partnership with the influential popular cultural narratives of the contemporary West, particularly film and science fiction."[20] While Cusack's notion of invented religion is based in part on Possamai's notion of hyper-real religion (and Emily McAvan is working with both Cusack's and Possamai's notions of invented and hyper-real religions), the differentiation between them lies in the complex building blocks for each.

Possamai's hyper-real religion is a religious interpretation of Baudrillard's hyper-real simulacra applied to popular culture. While both McAvan and Cusack build on this, Cusack particularly focuses on how the hyper-real invents new religions based on popular culture. By contrast, McAvan brings us back to the bigger picture of the postmodern to identify how the relationship between popular culture and religion in the contemporary West is tied to postmodern conceptions of the sacred. McAvan argues that the "postmodern sacred" is situated between Lyotard's rejection of meta-narratives, Fredric Jameson's aesthetic theory of *pastiche*, and Baudrillard's hyper-reality and simulation. By situating how we imagine the sacred through unreal pop cultural texts with postmodern discourse, McAvan articulates how popular culture imbues the postmodern with re-imaginings of the sacred.[21] McAvan argues

> that the postmodern sacred is a paradoxical attempt at accessing spirituality, using symbols contained in explicitly unreal texts to gain a secondhand experience of transcendence and belief. This second-hand experience displaces the need for belief or real-world practice into a textual world, requiring little of its consumers. While they seem to suggest a desire for a magical world outside of capitalism, the wonder produced by these texts, however, is only temporary.[22]

Between these definitions of the relationship between popular culture and religion in the contemporary world, the problem of disenchantment is offered a series of solutions through the consumption of religion via its intertwinement with popular culture. As such, hyper-real religion, invented religions, and the postmodern sacred present the possibilities of re-enchantment in ways that tap into the postmodern consumer's concern for meaning and the subjective construction of beliefs.

Possamai's discussion of re-enchantment is enlightening because it is marked by the "move away from the over-rationalization of everyday life to re-enchanted forms of public and personal spaces."[23] This implies what

Possamai calls "an aestheticization of everyday life" where hyper-real religions offer re-enchantment narratives that simulate religion out of popular culture.[24] This may also entail how what we consume comes to re-enchant our imagination in ways that—through consumption—we may come to believe and understand our everyday reality less in terms of a spiritually dead mundane reality, and more in terms of a reality imbued with conceptions of the sacred shaped by what we consume. Cusack argues that for Possamai, "the shaping of [re-enchantment] narratives into subjective myths is . . . part of the process of individualistic cultural consumption."[25] These "subjective myths usually relate to the individual self" where spiritual seekers are at the center. Possamai articulates three ways in which spiritual seekers are motivated: as "illuminational" ("spirituality is an end in itself"); as instrumental ("where spirituality is 'a means to external ends'"); and as entertainment (a "spirituality directed to pleasurable ends").[26] The combination of individualism, consumption, and the combination of different religious and spiritual practices and beliefs is a standard practice in the West, "which advocates eclecticism as a form of consumerism."[27]

Possamai argues that there is a continuum between hyper-consumeristic religion on the one hand and hypo-consumeristic religion and fundamentalism on the other. The broad swathe between these poles is complex, but navigating them hinges on how religion and popular culture are perceived by the consumer between adherence to a religious tradition and the subjective choices of individual religiosity.[28] Possamai defines hyper-real religion as "a simulacrum of a religion partly created out of popular culture which provides inspiration for believers/consumers at a metaphorical level."[29] Possamai indicates that the implications of hyper-real religion have effects "on the spiritual consumer's subjective myth, but also on how they see themselves."[30] This implies that an individual's identity is constituted not only out of the real world but also out of the hyper-real where "the interactions between the field of fiction and the self" intertwine.[31] Possamai identifies three sub-types of hyper-real religion: (1) where consumers of popular culture use it to construct their own religion and beliefs; (2) where consumers dabble in pop culture to help explain and give depth to their beliefs—without forming their own religion; and (3) those religious or secular responses to religion in popular culture that oppose the construction or articulation of belief or religion from popular culture.[32] The relationship between popular culture and religion is defined by Possamai:

> Religion and popular culture co-exist intimately, and cannot be seen simply as a relationship of cause and effect. At times religion creates and regulates pop culture. Indeed, religious actors who express themselves in popular culture are also engaged in shaping popular culture, and in doing so, making possible

some experiences and denying access to others. It can take the form of using the content of popular culture to back up their religion, or it can take the form of censorship towards certain narratives. At other times, popular culture can shape the form and content of religion. Some people appear to practice religion/spirituality by creatively reusing the artifacts of contemporary mass-mediated culture . . . rather than following the meaning offered by religious institutions.[33]

From this, Possamai states that

the working assumption of popular culture is that it is a reflection of our society. The problem with this assertion is that the mirror is not always well-polished. Images might sometimes be distorted, but there will always be an element of truth in them. Popular culture is part of consumer culture and we can know people by what they consume.[34]

Furthermore,

consumer culture is the outcome of the massive expansion of the production of capitalist commodity. This outburst of the capitalist system has created a vast reservoir of consumer goods and sites for purchase and consumption to be "enjoyed" by the various classes of our society that are "in." This has led to the growing dependence on mass leisure and consumption activities.[35]

Possamai articulates two ways in which this has been understood: first, by the Frankfurt School as "the ideological and seductive manipulation of the masses by the dominant class."[36] Second by Michel de Certeau "as leading to more egalitarianism and individual freedom."[37] Following De Certeau in particular, Possamai argues that "we can think of consumers as active agents who create their own identity through consumption," where their religious and spiritual beliefs, as well as personal identity, are made up of a bricolage that mixes and matches "any disparate elements that may be at hand."[38]

Martin Geoffroy analyzes Possamai's re-interpretation of Baudrillard's hyper-reality as applied to religion and offers an account of Baudrillard as articulating a negative dialectic, characteristic of the Frankfurt School, of integral religion—which reads contemporary religious simulations via popular culture as unhooked from traditional religion.[39] As a nuance to Possamai's hyper-real religion—which draws on Baudrillard without talking about the "more real than real" dimensions of religion—Cusack articulates clearly how invented religions explicitly claim popular culture as a source for religion.[40] This allows not only the imagination to be a source of religion but also how popular culture can be a legitimizing source of meaning-making for spiritual seekers who practice the consumption of popular culture.

Possamai argues that for Baudrillard, the proliferation of mass media and communication results in a culture that

> is now dominated by simulations—these are objects and discourses that have no firm origin, no referent, no ground or foundation. In consumer culture, signs get their meanings from their relations to each other, rather than by reference to some independent reality of standard. Baudrillard's theory of commodity culture removes any distinction between objects and representation. In their place he pictures a social world constructed out of models or 'simulacra' which have no foundation in any reality except their own.[41]

Hyper-reality for Baudrillard entails a difficulty in distinguishing "the real from the unreal" where "hyper-reality—that is, a situation in which reality has collapsed—takes over."[42] What this implies is a virtual actuality, where the actual world is understood through the blurry lines of the virtual world—where the virtual world constitutes and shapes the religious and spiritual imaginings of the actual world. But a step must also be taken to understand how hyper-real religions imply the problem of the consumptive practices of belief. It is to this that we now turn.

THE PROBLEM OF THE CONSUMPTION OF POP-CULTURAL BELIEF

By this point, the reader may be wondering, what can popular culture reveal about what we believe? Why should we trust popular culture to reflect our beliefs? Is it not something controlled by the elite who cast their vision and control what we can imagine as believable? Is it not all a conspiracy to control the masses? These sensibilities are issued by both Theodor Adorno and Max Horkheimer's *Dialectic of Enlightenment* and are critically picked up, particularly regarding religious belief, throughout the writings of Michel de Certeau. Their pessimistic critiques of popular culture have certainly shaped the way religion and belief may be imagined in contemporary popular culture. Rather than dismissing these arguments, it is worthwhile to give an account of their ideas as a set of counter-arguments this book seeks to subvert. The contributions of Theodor Adorno and Max Horkheimer's *Dialectic of Enlightenment* have heavily influenced twentieth-century views of popular culture. But as Christopher Partridge has noted, their pessimistic despair and distrust of the elite's power over popular culture have largely been diffused in contemporary popular cultural discourses.[43] And yet it is worth analyzing their contributions and how this influences Michel de Certeau's application of their ideas to religious belief and faith.

Theodor Adorno and Max Horkheimer's contributions to the study of the "culture industry" illustrate important factors when we consider the role of popular culture and its ability to shape and manipulate what we can imagine as credible, desirable, and believable. They argue that when we consume popular culture, it is always already "imprinted" in advance with "the trace of the jargon" that the elites script, produce, and reproduce of what they want us to believe.[44] When we consume popular culture, then, we come to implicitly believe what the elites want us to believe, thereby shaping and manipulating the possibilities and assumptions of what we believe through what we consume. In turn, the work of art that the media produce represents and creates a simulated truth. The truths presented in popular culture not only reflect what is already there and dominant in the culture, but they also manipulate what we can imagine as true: the consumption of pop culture appeals to our aesthetic desires in ways that manipulate us into buying into the ideology not only of the elite or the culture but also of the implicit messages of what we come to believe through what we consume.

Horkheimer and Adorno's analysis of the culture industry paints a neo-Marxist, pessimistic analysis of how the culture industry is a systemic process, engendered by the Enlightenment, of mass deception by the totalitarian powers of modern politics and economics. Particularly, they show how culture is subverted into the advertisements of what the political and economic powers want us to know, desire, and believe. And yet the systemic organization of the culture industry not only carries messages of power but also of everyday people who not only buy into the messages organized by the state and economics to suppress/oppress them but because they continuously consume what the culture industry produces and reproduces, they also guarantee the efficiency of the system's ability to conform society to what the elites want. Or rather, our consumption of it alienates us from the ability to resist the messages of the elite because by consuming popular culture, we implicitly come to buy into and believe the ideology embedded within popular culture. These systemic structures of the culture industry imply a subtle but intentional manipulation of what we can imagine as truth so that we conform to the messages of what the system wants us to imagine as believable. But with the last of these, it is the work of Michel de Certeau that we find a wealth of material if we are to understand the power of popular culture to shape the (im-)possibilities of believing.

In the fracturing of Christian churches and the cultural certitude of the absence of God in ordinary life, Michel de Certeau argues that this process of emancipation from hierarchy and fundamentalisms of truth results in the reality that we are learning "from the past how a social group traverses the desertion of its beliefs and how it might profit from the conditions to which it is subjected in order to invent its liberty and plot out a space of movement."[45] That is, with the emancipation from the legitimating powers of the church over everyday life, we begin to wander in our beliefs, which become individuated and chosen for their desirability and ability to reflect our reality over their ability to satisfy our intellect and supply visions of how we can make sense of the world through them.

But for Certeau, in a spiritual marketplace, there is also a rampant devaluation of values.[46] He states:

> Right where it is compensated for and hidden, it reappears in a different form. Dogmas, knowledges, programs, and philosophies are losing their credibility; they are shadowless bodies that neither the hand nor the mind can grasp, but whose evanescence irritates or deceives the gesture that continues to seek them; they merely leave us, tenaciously, with the illusion of the desire to "hold them."[47]

Within this, the incredulity of belief leads to the inability to hold onto and legitimize truth. With the reduction of belief in "truth" into the legitimating powers of utility and desire in a spiritual marketplace, truth diffuses and subverts the [cultural] believability and its credulity.[48] De Certeau continues: "When stripped of its credibility and believability, believing is demoralizing and exploitative to those who still adhere to institutions through conviction. . . . They literally lose all sense of direction."[49]

In the absence of truth and representation, authorities and what is authoritative "no longer correspond[s] to the real geography of meaning."[50] In "becoming increasingly opaque, a marginalized life has no escape in our system of representations."[51] Luce Giard argues that for De Certeau,

> every representation articulates and makes manifest a conviction, which in turn provides a basis for the legitimacy of authority. At the point where belief no longer inhabits representations, authority is bereft of its basis and is soon deserted. Its power collapses, undermined from within.[52]

Across the Western world, whether rural or urban, Certeau argues that there is a population of "silent subjects" whose "convictions are no longer affiliations."[53]

Yet, in the marginalization and abstention of representation, reference, and belonging, there is still "a refusal of insignificance" in the very appeal to in*sign*ificance.[54] By appealing to the insignificance of life and belief, one is implicitly refusing to be insignificant. It means that one is signifying meaning in the opaque absence of meaning: in the absence of meaning, there is a signification of meaning. While De Certeau applies this logic to the violent struggle of life, it can also apply to the struggle with the mediocrity of life.[55] Putting a spin on Certeau, behind [mediocrity, passivity, and indifference], even if it is unaware of its real name, there is the desire to create a [life where we are left to ourselves]; there is a desire to organize the conditions of life in relation to reasons to live

where others make no demands on us.[56]

And yet, for Certeau, "beliefs are emerging that make a common design *possible*. Once it is spoken . . . [it] points [to] references, sources, a history, an iconography, in short, a construction of 'authorities'" that "creates heroes, prophets, and myths" that demystify "powers and ideologies."[57] Certeau goes further to state that "for every constructive desire . . . signs of recognition and tacit agreements about the conditions of possibility . . . need to be made."[58] In the creation of the social and cultural inheritance of the possibilities of popular cultural belief, each representation inaugurates "a new credibility at the same time that they express it."[59]

De Certeau goes further: "These nascent credibilities attest to what is most fragile, but also most moving and fundamental, in all social life."[60] These produce what De Certeau calls implicit "revolutions of the believable" that are often left silent. He says, rather, "more often, they are more modest in form and thus more formidable, such as inner movements; they produce displacement within affiliation; they surreptitiously reorganize received authorities; in a constellation of references, they happen to favor certain ones and extinguish others."[61] For the labor of acting in everyday life for the sake of society and its "reasons for living that belong to all and to each," De Certeau argues that "there is a need, among other things, to reconstitute in common language, and through a critique of traditional stereotypes and powers that have become unthinkable, circuits that make a reciprocal recognition *possible*."[62]

De Certeau's account of the credibility of belief links it to belonging in the aftermath of the loss of the representational truth. No longer do religious dogmas sway us to believe (though they can). De Certeau emphasizes the erosion of convictions, where the vestiges of faith ebb away from what we formerly questioned of what is possible to believe in light of a stronger absence of credibility that draws us beyond traditional religions.[63] In a post-Christian culture where believing in the Christian faith is no longer normative, believing is now constituted by a space where beliefs are individualized and articulated through simulated productions of meaning found within popular culture. De Certeau states that "today, it is no longer enough to manipulate, transport, and refine belief; its composition must be analyzed because people want to produce it artificially. . . . There are now too many things to believe and not enough credibility to go around."[64] However, De Certeau offers an account of how to recover the credibility of believing. This is done:

On the one hand, [by] the claim to be *speaking in the name of a reality* which, assumed to be inaccessible, is the principle of both what is believed (a totalization) and the act of believing (something that is always unavailable, unverifiable, lacking); and on the other, the ability of a discourse authorized by a "reality" to distribute itself in the form of *elements that organize practices*, that is, of "articles of faith."[65]

That is, the media and popular culture present to us the possibilities of both believing and making people believe. De Certeau states that with "the identification of the seen with what is to be believed" we find the possibilities of believing and making people believe through the referential system of symbolic mediation that popular culture and the media present to us as credible, desirable, and believable.[66] The simulacrum of belief becomes the new real in the absence of representational truth when the invisible becomes visible. When the real becomes visible through the narrated experiences and practices of consuming popular culture, it unveils the real's invisibility into the seeing as believing.[67]

And yet, through the contributions of De Certeau, Adorno, and Horkheimer, we can still offer another side to the power of popular culture to shape the possibilities of believing in late modernity. Consumptive practices embed within the imagination the implicit messages of what we consume, and these messages shape what becomes possible to imagine as believable. And yet, what we imagine *as* believable is filtered through two inter-independent tests: of credibility and desirability. The test of credibility asks whether what we imagine as believable makes sense. It includes a cognitive function in our ability to imagine what is possible to believe. The credibility test, however, is not determined by logical rationality alone. It is paired with the aesthetic desirability of what we *want* to believe is true.

Popular culture can illustrate not only the logical credibility of alternate worlds we may imagine as believable, but it can also can tap into our desires and our sensibilities, of what we *want* to be true. This means that what is believable is tied to the images and imaginations of popular culture's ability to illustrate, meet, and make sense of what we can believe through its ability to mirror and reflect sensibilities and sentiments of what we want to believe. Pop culture can alter what we imagine as believable because it mirrors and reflects sentiments and sensibilities already latent in culture. Pop culture reflects and alters what is already present in the cultural and religious sensibilities of the consumer alongside its ability to shape and manipulate what becomes possible to believe through the continual consumption of the implicit messages of what we consume.

This section raises important reflections about the intersection of religion and popular culture. While popular culture is no longer as controlled by the elites as it was in Adorno and Horkheimer's time, the elite distributes its messages and implicit beliefs via the very production of images and ideas that it *wants* us to believe. However, an important element of postmodernity is that the elite no longer holds totalizing control over what we consume in the West. This power now lies in the media and its producers. Yet it is also diffused in and through the consumption of the individuated literatures, imageries, and doxologies that reflect the religious heart of late-modern culture. What culture and society want to hear and see is perpetuated by the continuous simulations, alterations, and recitations of what they already believe. The subtle power of the media lies in its ability to reflect and resource what is already believed, while at the same time subtly rescripting those beliefs by introducing new elements and messages that re-enchant the possibilities of post-Christian believing. And yet these images, representations, recitations, and simulations of belief also reflect both messages that we believe *and* the problems that we are coming to recognize in late-modern popular culture.

CONCLUSION

This chapter has set out to ask the question of whether popular culture not only reflects and presents religious sensibilities and theological messages but also how popular culture may come to set a canonical standard that may shape the post-Christian possibilities of believing in a late modern culture. Each section of this chapter has illustrated that popular culture can problematize the possibilities of belief—in ways that both question traditional religion and generate the possibilities of rethinking what believing and the human condition look like during the twenty-first century. While this chapter has shown that popular culture can be read canonically, it also problematizes the consumptive role of popular culture in how it can simulate the possibilities of belief. It is this latter question that the next chapter focuses on and continues to reflect on the theoretical implications of popular culture and the conditions for belief in late modernity.

NOTES

1. Kevin J. Vanhoozer, *The Drama of Doctrine: A Canonical-Linguistic Approach to Christian Theology* (Louisville, KY: Westminster John Knox Press, 2005), 227.
2. C.f. Vanhoozer, *The Drama of Doctrine*, 236.
3. Vanhoozer, *The Drama of Doctrine*, 237. Original Italics.
4. Vanhoozer, *The Drama of Doctrine*, 247.

5. J. R. R. Tolkien, "On Fairy Stories," in *The Tolkien Reader* (New York: Random House, 1966), 33–99.

6. C.f. Austin M. Freeman, "Sins of the Imagination," in *Theology, Fantasy, and the Imagination*, ed. Andrew D. Thrasher and Austin M. Freeman (Lanham, MD: Rowman and Littlefield, 2023), 19–34; Josh Herring, "The Hero as God: An Exploration of Mormon Soteriology in the Fantasy Novels of Orson Scott Card and Brandon Sanderson," in *Theology, Fantasy, and the Imagination*, ed. Andrew D. Thrasher and Austin M. Freeman (Lanham, MD: Rowman and Littlefield, 2023), 155–175; U-Wen Low, "Cosmology as Agnostic Self-Actualization in Terry Pratchett's *Discworld*," in *Theology, Fantasy, and the Imagination*, ed. Andrew D. Thrasher and Austin M. Freeman (Lanham, MD: Rowman and Littlefield, 2023), 115–131; Andrew D. Thrasher, "Fantastic Inter-religious Resourcement in Robert Jordan and David Eddings," in *Theology, Fantasy, and the Imagination*, ed. Andrew D. Thrasher and Austin M. Freeman (Lanham, MD: Rowman and Littlefield, 2023), 133–153.

7. Even with its growing disillusionment among the Marvel bandwagon, I do not think nor have heard of people who dislike phase four because of religion. Rather, I have seen and personally heard the dissatisfaction with how messy the films, scripts, and acting have been.

8. C.f. Gregory Stevenson, ed., *Theology and the Marvel Universe* (Lanham, MD: Lexington Books, 2020); Jennifer Baldwin and Daniel White Hodge, ed., *Marveling Religion: Critical Discourses, Religion, and the Marvel Cinematic Universe* (Lanham, MD: Lexington Books, 2022); Michael D. Nichols, *Religion and Myth in the Marvel Cinematic Universe* (Jefferson, NC: McFarland, 2021).

9. David Mitchell, *Cloud Atlas* (New York: Random House, 2004), 508.

10. *Cloud Atlas*, DVD (Warner Bros. Pictures, 2012).

11. For the Domestic Box office, *Black Panther* ranks as the eighth highest-ranking film at $202 million and *Wakanda Forever* ranks as the thirteenth highest-ranking film at $181 million for opening weekend. C.f. https://www.the-numbers.com/box-office-records/domestic/all-movies/weekend/opening.

12. Linkin Park, *Lost*, Single (Los Angeles, CA: Warner, 2023).

13. C.f. Jake Doberenz, "Reading Religious Texts as a 'Cinematic Universe,'" *Popular Culture and Theology* (Blog) June 22, 2020: https://popularcultureandtheology.com/2020/06/22/reading-religious-texts-as-a-cinematic-universe/

14. Johan Roeland, SteF Aupers, and Dick Houtman, "Fantasy, Conspiracy and the Romantic Legacy: Max Weber and the Spirit of Contemporary Popular Culture," in *Handbook of Hyper-real Religions*, ed. Adam Possamai (Leiden and Boston: Brill, 2012), 401–422, 417–418.

15. Roeland, Aupers, and Houtman, "Fantasy, Conspiracy and the Romantic Legacy," 402.

16. Roeland, Aupers, and Houtman, "Fantasy, Conspiracy and the Romantic Legacy," 402.

17. Roeland, Aupers, and Houtman, "Fantasy, Conspiracy and the Romantic Legacy," 402.

18. Eileen Barker, "Preface," in *Handbook of Hyper-real Religions*, ed. Adam Possamai (Leiden and Boston: Brill, 2012), ix–xii, ix–x.

19. Adam Possamai, "Yoda goes to Glastonbury: an Introduction to Hyper-real Religions," in *Handbook of Hyper-real Religions*, ed. Adam Possamai (Leiden and Boston: Brill, 2012), 1–21, 1.

20. Carole M. Cusack, *Invented Religions: Imagination, Fiction and Faith* (Burlington, VT: Ashgate, 2010), 7.

21. Emily McAvan, *The Postmodern Sacred: Popular Culture Spirituality in the Science Fiction, Fantasy, and Urban Fantasy Genres* (Jefferson, NC: McFarland, 2012), 17.

22. McAvan, *The Postmodern Sacred*, 19; Opt. cit. in Carole M. Cusack and Venetia Laura Delano Robertson, "Introduction: the Study of Fandom and Religion," in *The Sacred in Fantastic Fandom: Essays on the Intersection of Religion and Pop Culture*, ed. Carole M. Cusack, John W. Morehead, and Venetia Laura Delano Robertson (Jefferson, NC: McFarland, 2019), 1–13, 5.

23. Adam Possamai, *Religion and Popular Culture: A Hyper-real Testament* (Brussels: Peter Lang, 2005), 103.

24. Possamai, *Religion and Popular Culture*, 104.

25. Cusack, *Invented Religions*, 128–129.

26. Cusack, *Invented Religions*, 129; Possamai, *Religion and Popular Culture*, 75–76.

27. Cusack, *Invented Religions*, 47.

28. Possamai, *Religion and Popular Culture*, 49.

29. Possamai, *Religion and Popular Culture*, 79.

30. Possamai, *Religion and Popular Culture*, 79.

31. Possamai, *Religion and Popular Culture*, 79.

32. Possamai, "Yoda goes to Glastonbury," 3–9.

33. Possamai, *Religion and Popular Culture*, 20.

34. Possamai, *Religion and Popular Culture*, 23.

35. Possamai, *Religion and Popular Culture*, 42.

36. Possamai, *Religion and Popular Culture*, 42.

37. Possamai, *Religion and Popular Culture*, 42.

38. Possamai, *Religion and Popular Culture*, 44.

39. Martin Geoffroy, "Hyper-real Religion Performing in Baudrillard's Integral Reality," in *Handbook of Hyper-real Religions*, ed. Adam Possamai (Leiden and Boston: Brill, 2012), 23–35.

40. Cusack, *Invented Religions*, 125.

41. Possamai, *Religion and Popular Culture*, 77.

42. Possamai, *Religion and Popular Culture*, 78.

43. Christopher Partridge, "Religion and Popular Culture," in *Religions in the Modern World: Traditions and Transformations*, ed. Linda Woodhead, Hiroko Kawanami, and Christopher Partridge, Second Edition (London and New York: Routledge, 2009), 490–521.

44. Max Horkheimer and Theodor W. Adorno, *Dialectic of Enlightenment: Philosophical Fragments*, ed. Gunzelin Schmid Noerr, trans. Edmund Jephcott (Stanford, CA: Stanford University Press, 2002), 101.

45. Luce Giard, "Introduction: Opening the Possible," in *Culture in the Plural* by Michel de Certeau, ed. Luce Giard, trans. Tom Conley (Minneapolis, MN: University of Minnesota Press, 1997), ix–xv, ix.

46. Michel de Certeau, *Culture in the Plural*, ed. Luce Giard, trans. Tom Conley (Minneapolis, MN: University of Minnesota Press, 1997), 5.

47. Certeau, *Culture in the Plural*, 5–6.

48. Certeau, *Culture in the Plural*, 6.

49. Certeau, *Culture in the Plural*, 8.

50. Certeau, *Culture in the Plural*, 9.

51. Certeau, *Culture in the Plural*, 9.

52. Giard, "Introduction: Opening the Possible," xii.

53. Certeau, *Culture in the Plural*, 9.

54. Certeau, *Culture in the Plural*, 10.

55. Certeau, *Culture in the Plural*, 10.

56. Certeau, *Culture in the Plural*, 11.

57. Certeau, *Culture in the Plural*, 11.

58. Certeau, *Culture in the Plural*, 11.

59. Certeau, *Culture in the Plural*, 11.

60. Certeau, *Culture in the Plural*, 11.

61. Certeau, *Culture in the Plural*, 12.

62. Certeau, *Culture in the Plural*, 14.

63. Michel de Certeau, *The Practice of Everyday Life*, trans. Steven Randall (Berkeley, CA: University of California Press, 1984), 178.

64. Certeau, *Practice of Everyday Life*, 179.

65. Certeau, *Practice of Everyday Life*, 185.

66. Certeau, *Practice of Everyday Life*, 187.

67. Certeau, *Practice of Everyday Life*, 186–187.

Chapter 2

The Consumptive Poetics of Belief

At its heart, popular culture simulates belief in imaginative ways that both keep religion alive and distort its reality—blurring the lines of belief between virtual and actual reality in ways that break down the explicit boundaries between them. This chapter articulates a theoretical approach by laying a foundation for what can be called "imagined realism." Imagined realism can be analyzed by examining how popular culture poetically re-enchants the possibilities of believing. As such, popular culture creates an imagined realism of belief where what we believe is imagined as possible through its formation via the practice of consuming popular culture. When we consume popular culture, it helps to re-enchant what is possible to believe in ways that are constituted by both actual religions and virtual simulations of religion. The interplay between actual real-world religions and virtual simulations of religion is generated through the consumption of the mythic imagination. The mythic imagination not only reveals what is possible to believe, it also informs what we *imagine* to be credible and desirable through its ability to shape our imagination. Thus, the consumption of the mythic imagination generates an explosion and proliferation of possible beliefs that play with the interaction between "as if" worlds and real-world religions.

This chapter begins with a working theory about the possibilities of believing and follows with an analysis of cultural consumptive practices. Then, it articulates the effects of defamiliarization—through analyses of simulation and recitation—and finally turns to show how the mythic imagination defamiliarizes religion and the secular through its re-enchanting effects on the possibilities of belief. Between the mediated simulations and re-enchantment of belief in the mythic imagination lies a virtual actuality of belief that marks an imagined realism: the blurring of boundaries between actual and virtual belief, between secular and religious traditions, where the interaction and formations of secondary and primary worlds can reflect, distort, and reimagine the possibilities of believing.

A WORKING THEORY ON THE POSSIBILITIES OF BELIEF

Michel de Certeau is famous for analyzing the problem of the incredulity of believing.[1] This chapter continues that analysis, but while Certeau's analysis is pessimistic about the possibilities for the credulity of believing, this chapter argues *for* the credulity and credibility of believing. It argues that believability in late modernity is shaped by whether we find the messages *recited* in popular culture, the media, and the mythic imagination desirable and credible, and hence, believable, or not. That is, the content we consume presents an imagined message about what is possible to believe. In turn, those messages are filtered through whether we find them credible and/or desirable and this interplay creates the possibilities of belief.[2] This creates a plethora of possible messages of what we may find believable, and yet it also draws upon our desires and reflects ideas that we already implicitly hold. The interaction between the credibility and desirability of what we find believable is inescapably shaped by the messages of what we consume (figure 2.1).

Furthermore, it is not only about what we consume in popular culture that shapes the possibilities of belief. Popular culture is always already presenting messages that we already find believable. Using an analogy of a mirror that

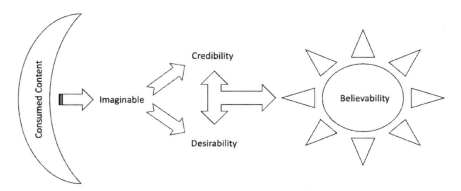

Figure 2.1   Pop-Cultural Processes of Believing.

reflects, alters, and distorts our desires, our beliefs, and our commitments and motivations, Bruce David Forbes argues that popular culture reflects

> only a portion of our realities, interests, values and desires [which] are reflected back to us, with a selectivity that is influenced by the personal perceptions and intentions of the creative forces behind popular culture. . . . If popular culture reflects values we already hold, that reflection also serves to reinforce our values and deepens our commitments to them.[3]

This means that the more we consume various messages from popular culture, the more we find them believable and the more we conform our beliefs to the messages presented to us in what we consume.

What we consume in popular culture, the media, and the mythic imagination has the power to enchant our imagination and shape what is possible to believe. The mythic imagination and the power of popular culture can re-enchant and simulate the possibilities of believing in late modernity. Furthermore, the consumption of popular culture and the media *re*-presents and simulates religious themes through the ideas of resourcement and rescription. Popular culture resources traditional religious themes in and through its rescription of them through the messages of what the media wants us to believe. What we consume in everyday life enchants the possibilities of believing in ways that what we can imagine as believable in late modernity is dependent upon the content and subtle religious themes and tropes presented to us and hidden within popular culture, the media, and the mythic imagination. With this background theory in mind, we can now turn to an analysis of the consumptive cultural practices of belief.

CONSUMPTIVE CULTURAL PRACTICES OF BELIEF

At the intersection of religion and popular culture, the discipline of cultural studies plays an important role in describing the consumptive and formative practices and manifestations of belief. And yet, it also underlies a sociological analysis where belief is not only subtly simulated but also recited by the media in ways that reveal the simulacra of our ultimate concerns. Consumptive practices not only reveal mediated methods of simulated belief but also subtly control what we find or deem believable through the mediated messages they invoke. To describe the consumptive cultural practices of belief, it is crucial to examine cultural and sociological theories—stemming from the Frankfurt School[4] and Zygmunt Bauman[5]—to understand the pop cultural simulation of belief through participatory practices in what the media recites to us as believable. Underlying each of these is the shift from a modern, industrial-productive society to a technological-consumerist society and the culture of postmodernity. With the advent of industrialization and the accumulation of wealth, leisure time and activities were produced and society was technologically transformed into a culture of consumerism.

This consumerism, Bauman argues, is marked by a highly individualized consumer paradise where many people are excluded based on social, economic, and cultural capital.[6] And yet, Bauman's sociological analyses of consumerism collapse, according to Alan Warde, along three lines of failure: (1) Bauman fails to appreciate and nuance the interconnection between state and market; (2) Bauman fails to nuance self-identity in social groups around cultural capital; and (3) Bauman fails to appreciate the notion of belonging as an interpersonal dimension of a consumer's belonging to social groups.[7] Within a consumer society, the cultural practices and accumulations of wealth produce various forms of cultural production and new religious concerns.

And yet, the crossings between religion/theology and popular culture highlight not only a sociological problem but also a pessimism in cultural analysis. According to Christopher Partridge, Theodor Adorno and the Frankfurt School[8] retained a Marxist pessimism toward popular culture (or rather, mass culture)—characterized by a culture industry that produces goods to inhibit social change by convincing "the masses that this is the way things are and this is the way they should be."[9] This is done subtly by the elites in an attempt to control the masses. While there was a shift away from the Frankfurt School's pessimism that began in the 1960s[10] —when the media began to be unhooked from state control—the complex relationship between the market and the state produced a much more nuanced and complex vision of reality in the twenty-first century. This is because what we find believable in popular culture is now subtly influenced by the elites but unhooked from direct state control. Furthermore, popular culture now has the power to create new visions of reality and simulations of belief among the masses.

Partridge also invokes a theological problem: that religious ideas within popular culture do not deal with religious or theological realities. Rather they imply a deceptive religious superficiality where, according to disenchantment, the "myths and images of the divine [in popular culture] lack divine potency. [Adorno] saw a vibrant religious culture being replaced by a 'pseudo-culture' which, in turn, supported a pseudo-enchantment."[11] And yet, Partridge articulates how popular culture raises striking philosophical and religious questions about the nature of reality: popular culture invokes religious and philosophical questions about reality that are then reflected within the simulations of popular culture. In this case, the simulations of religious and philosophical ideas within popular culture not only distort reality with a pseudo-enchantment, but they also re-enchant our world by playing with reality in ways that produce a hyper-reality through the transmission between primary and secondary worlds—a virtual actuality. Religion and religious ideas are played with—simulated—in popular culture and they creatively re-enchant our imagination in ways that play with what we find and deem possible to believe.[12]

With the production of film and television and the transition from print to digital media, not only is there a proliferation of new images, values, and nuances to what matters most to us, but the very reality of advertising and the accumulation of knowledge is mediated by the gatekeepers of truth: the media. The media *shape* our desires, values, and concerns and *reflect* our cultural and religious imaginaries.[13] The reflection of our beliefs within the cultural consumerism of a late-modern society is shaped by the media's ability to shape our beliefs. Moreover, the media shape what we imagine of our world and how it functions, and this is the formative role the media play in constituting, shaping, and reflecting our ultimate concerns.[14] Within this framework, popular culture plays a crucial and undeniably important role in informing us of not just what we/to believe, but also that the media play a role in articulating the credibility of belief through the recitation of the stories we are told and tell ourselves about the reality we believe.[15]

Within this framework, Jeffrey Mahan calls us to understand the "porous boundary and creative tension between the seemingly secular and seemingly religious."[16] Moreover, Elaine Graham calls us to examine and understand culture as a theological reflection of human *poeisis*. Through the intersection between concrete cultural practices and how we imagine God, and how we express what it means to be human, "culture, both as a world of meanings and world of practices and material artifacts, thus holds the potential to disclose more about ourselves as human beings, and provides the sources and resources whereby we can contemplate fundamental and ultimate realities."[17] Graham states that in locating religiosity within the cultural expression of lived experience,

> culture and cultural practices thus figure as essentially both the product of, and the context for, human *being, making, and imagining*. This in turn, engenders new insights into the very nature of theological discourse itself, effecting a shift from theology as *doctrine* or belief, to theology as *practice*: and thus, an opportunity to conceive of theological reflection as one of the activities by which human beings build worlds of meaning and significance, and experience themselves as creative, moral, and purposeful beings.[18]

Examining further theological reflection upon popular culture, Graham argues that the theological turn to culture reveals something of our humanity and potentially of God. If "talk about God" is to a large extent a human activity, the work of the human imagination, then the fruits of our cultural imagination will be an arena within which God will be revealed.[19]

Just as popular culture has the power to help us make sense of the world, Graham argues that the turn to culture in theological study reflects a shift to understanding cultural practices as embodying implicit cultural beliefs that inform and constitute meaning and identity. Indeed, following Mahan, to examine cultural practices reveals the porous boundaries between religion and spirituality and secular ordinary life. The focus on the poetics and *poiesis* of cultural practices reveals via theological reflection the implicit beliefs found within the pop cultural practices of everyday life.

And yet, the cultural poetics of belief and theological imagination also highlight a defamiliarizing effect in everyday life. Pop cultural theological reflection produces not only reflections of what matters most to us but also the creative interplay between secular and religious traditions that generate the possibilities of both re-enchantment and simulation. Popular cultural poetics of belief do not only reveal something of human religious concerns and theological reflections. They also open us to the creative imaginings of the possibilities of believing through the simulations of believing. These simulations of believing provoke us to imagine the possibilities of believing in new and creative ways, blurring the lines between virtual and actual reality. It is to the simulation and recitation of belief that we now turn to understand the defamiliarizing effects of popular culture's ability to simulate belief through its recitations of what we imagine as *possible* to believe.

SIMULATIONS AND RECITATIONS OF BELIEF

The previous section argued that pop cultural consumption invokes sociological, cultural, and theological problems that can enchant and simulate the possibilities of belief through the power of the imagination. But this section articulates the defamiliarizing effects of simulated and recited belief. It does so by describing the disillusionment of belief through an analysis of the simulacra of belief, its credulity, and its virtuality. Each of these analyses describes how simulations of belief are unhooked from traditional religious theological positions. Or, rather, through the analysis of simulacra and simulations of a virtual reality, this section demonstrates how the porosity of belief is repetitiously reflected in a storied, or recited, society.

A central theme in our contemporary imaginary is Jean Baudrillard's idea of the simulacra of reality. Kelton Cobb states that according to Baudrillard, the postmodern era has witnessed the end of the naïve belief that signs, language, and images refer to reality, the end of the idea that, as a mirror reflects an original, we represent reality as it actually is, to some degree of accuracy, through symbols we use to speak about it.[20]

Surveying Baudrillard's analysis of the movement away from representational reality to the simulacrum,[21] Cobb describes the four stages as a movement from reflection and representation to its distortion and then its *"absence of a basic reality."*[22] The final step is one, "of estrangement of image from reality" where we realize

> that words and images bear no relation to any reality whatsoever; words and images reflect only other words and images. All the images that surround us are nothing more than reflections of other images; all of the symbols reflect only other symbols. All of our images and symbols are copies for which no original ever existed. This is pure simulation, the simulacrum, for which belief in any original was always an illusion; we have attained a level of culture in which all images, all representations, are copies of copies. . . . There is no originary ground or foundation for our simulations. There is no reality out there in light of which to measure the veracity of our representations of it.[23]

Within the simulacrum of reality, we have moved via the simulations of the real into a groundless copy of copies of a hyper-reality by which

> the human intellect has been striving all this time through its image-making to produce simulacrum that is even better than the real thing could ever have been. And we are finally at the point where it has become apparent, according to Baudrillard, that our simulacra do not reflect any originals, but just other images. Our world is a hall of mirrors, images imitating images.[24]

Baudrillard locates the simulacrum as the hyperreal which is diffused of its substance and representational reference. The hyperreal becomes a sign that has eclipsed its reality in its deferring into an imaginary that blurs the lines between the real and the imagination. The hyperreal is the simulacrum of reality's simulation of a virtual reality produced out of itself as unhooked from representations or images of the real.[25]

Alongside Baudrillard's conceptions of the simulacrum, Gilles Deleuze argues that the original process of simulation emerges as repetition and difference of things or beings that are both actual and virtual. According to Claire Colebrook, for Deleuze, "We only realize virtual potentialities after they have been actualized. We never see the virtual or the power of simulation itself; we see created beings but not the process of becoming of which they are actual effects."[26] For Deleuze, according to Colebrook, the actual and virtual worlds are not dualistic. Rather, the actual world is found in the simulacrum of copies that are reflected in the virtual world. This produces masks and false images of itself, distorting the actual world's reality through its copies, manifestations, and creations in the virtual world. The repetition and difference create the simulacra as other than itself—reflecting its becoming actuality through its virtuality of performance.[27] Colebrook states:

> Jean Baudrillard argues that media culture has reduced everything to surface images with no reference to the real. Deleuze's notion of the simulacra both resists the nostalgia that would not want to go back to a time when life was "more real" *and* rejects the idea that we now live in a postmodern world of mere images with no real causes. For Deleuze, the simulacrum or image is real, and life is and always has been simulation—a power of production, creation, becoming, and difference.[28]

For Deleuze, the simulacrum is *real* and not a mere copy because it *is* what it takes on: "It imagines or projects what it is not (yet). It simulates: becoming other than itself through the very power of a life which is always more than itself."[29] Within this framework, the virtuality of reality blurs the reality of the image into and as a means of its reproduction through the simulations of its reality. At its heart, the hyperreality of virtual reality is not only reproduced through its simulations but even more so, what we imagine of reality is indeed its absence—or rather the absence of a sacramental reality that it would imitate and reflect through its representations of the real.[30] In a late modern setting, the hyperreality of the simulacrum and the virtuality of reality eclipses any metaphysical grounding onto the real and thereby implodes upon itself as the real. It is in this implosion of (its) reality that Graham Ward argues that the secular is collapsing in on itself. Ward argues that the implosion of the secular "comes about through internal processes, forces, or principles which no longer regulate the immanent order but overshoot it."[31] At the heart of the simulacra of a virtual, hyper-reality is not only the implosion of the secular but also precisely the implosion of how we imagine reality and the possibility and credibility of belief.

Kelton Cobb states that

> there is a gathering disillusionment with the promises of material consumption, with the ideology of consumerism itself. This disillusionment has been deferred longer than Marx anticipated, due to the genius of marketers who learned how to harness the power of commodity fetishism and to insert brands into the sockets of our lives that were once filled with religious symbols and icons.[32]

Furthermore, Douglas Kellner argues that

> Baudrillard interprets modernity as a process of the explosion of commodification, mechanization, technology, and market relations, in contrast to a postmodern society, which is the site of an implosion of all boundaries, regions, and distinctions between high and low culture, appearance and reality, and just about every other binary opposition maintained by traditional philosophy and social theory. Furthermore, while modernity could be characterized as a process of increasing differentiation of spheres of life . . . , postmodernity could be interpreted as the process of dedifferentiation and [its] attendant implosion.[33]

Baudrillard argues that while information defers, collapses into, and devours the signification of meaning, it does so in its negation and implosion of communication and sociality. The negation and implosion of reality simulate a meaningless hyperreality through its deconstruction of meaning for mass society. This deconstruction of meaning comes through the defamiliarizing structurization of the "medium" in playful, manipulative, and subversive ways.[34] This defamiliarizing structurization of the medium simulates the emptiness and recreation of meaning as the media simulates its meaning as a simulated message that subtly shapes and influences what we deem believable through the messages of our participation in what consumptive practices reveal as meaningful to us.[35]

The messages of the media are themselves simulations of belief that invoke both the distortion and representation of what we can imagine as believable. The more we listen to them, the more they become believable. But their power of enchantment may not necessarily be theological—even while it remains fundamentally religious insofar as we consume and believe what the message tells us to imagine *as* believable.[36] The medium of the message then implodes the meaning in its "absorption of one pole into another," blurring and erasing distinctions and oppositions between the medium and the real.[37] Thus what we find believable in the message of the medium distorts the difference between what we deem real—between what we can imagine and what we believe to be true.

If the postmodern implosion and simulacrum of reality are marked by the eclipse of reference, representation, and sacramentality, this implies that the conditions for belief are rooted in the very absence of a divine representation. Belief and absence become equivocal in this schema, wherein belief vies for credibility in the very absence of reference to a divine reality in the simulations of the real. The implosion of the processes of simulation not only entails its collapse from within. Belief also implodes upon itself in the absence of its credibility precisely because its credibility is simulated in the very stories and myths that we believe to reflect and shape our reality. Within this framework, the credibility of belief becomes something recited and simulated through faith and yet ungrounded through its very repetition.

Graham Ward, commenting on Michel de Certeau, says that today we are a "recited society." De Certeau states that "our society has become a recited society in three senses: it is defined by stories (*récits*, the fables constituted by our advertising and informational media), by *citations* of stories, and by the interminable *recitation* of stories."[38] Ward goes further to state that "in a recited society people believe what they see and what they see is produced for them; hence [simulations of] created belief" that is

> based upon citing the authority of others. Thus, the production of a simulacrum involves [reciting what people believe], but without providing any believable object. In a recited society there is a multiplication of pseudo-believers promoted by a culture of deferral and credit.[39]

Furthermore, Baudrillard describes the simulacra of communication as a lure to which a myth is attached. This belief in the myth is both believed and marked by disbelief in it as an excess. Belief as such becomes enigmatic and ambivalent.[40] Moreover, Cobb argues that the power of the media to disseminate and communicate ideas implies the colonization of truth and knowledge. Within this framework, the media become the gatekeepers of belief, truth, and knowledge—where what we imagine as truth and what we believe as real is determined precisely through the media's ability to choose what to communicate and disseminate to us as believable.[41] This implies that truth is mediated through the very modes in and by which we imagine our reality: through the recitation of its virtuality. If truth is mediated in, by, and through its virtuality and the recitation of stories that re-enchant our imagination, then this implies that truth is a virtual simulation of the real. Truth is marked by a hyper-reality that only becomes credible when the stories it tells us are believable. However, these truths must be taken in faith, for they speak not of an absolute truth or reality. Rather, they speak to the truth of a reality we believe as credible, precisely because it copies truths about reality through the playful telling and recitations of the stories that produce what we imagine as believable and move us to believe through their reflection of what we *already* imagine as believable.

MYTHIC RE-ENCHANTMENT

If simulations of belief entail through recitation the possibilities of believing, what we find in the mythic imagination are the defamiliarizing forces of re-enchantment. While the previous section highlights the negative effects of pop-cultural simulations of believing, this section highlights its positive effects—drawing out how simulated beliefs produce the possibilities of believing through the ability to imagine and transform belief via virtual actuality. This section demonstrates through the mythic imagination of fantasy and comics how they imagine the possibilities of believing in late modernity. Taking two genres of literature-adapted-to-film—comics/superheroes and fantasy—what we find in the mythic imagination are potentially[42] positive imaginings of what is possible to believe in the recitations of the simulacra of virtual reality.

Within the mythic imagination found in comics and fantasy, we find key examples of religious rescription and religious resourcement. If religious rescription entails the playful (and distortive) re-writing of religious sources and ideas to articulate new views of the religious or theological imagination, then religious resourcement entails tapping into and unveiling of religious and theological themes and tropes found throughout the recitations of popular culture. While religious rescription and resourcement entail the re-mythicization of religious themes in the poetic re-enchantment of belief, what becomes clear is that they do so through the mythic imagination as a way of re-enchanting our religious and cultural imaginaries of belief.

Comics and fantasy display key cultural reference points that serve three religious functions: (1) they bring people together; (2) they recite, rescript, and retell religious myths and narratives; and (3) they re-enchant our imagination with the possibility of believing. By bringing people together around shared, common loves, people sometimes form religious communities around the creation of secondary or imagined worlds where we can imagine differently our own world. In these "subcreations" (as Tolkien would call them), we find underlying myths and narratives that imagine an alternate take on our own world: distorting and revealing something true about our world through the mythic imagination. Furthermore, the imagination enchants our world with the possibility for belief in ways that produce a virtuality of belief that helps to re-mythicize and rescript our primary world while also simulating through the secondary world the image of the primary world. The secondary world reflects and mirrors the primary world in significant ways. The primary world is a simulated source for the secondary world, yet the secondary world can play with, shape, and transform how we imagine (believe in) the primary world.

The mythic imagination brings people together in the articulation of shared loves that form communities and common knowledge and beliefs. For example, consider the Trekkies and their determinations of *Star Trek* canon,[43] the expressions of Black experience, identity, and theology within the film *Black Panther*,[44] the powerful role *Lord of the Rings* and *Harry Potter* have played in re-enchanting our world with religious themes,[45] or even the Marvel and DC cinematic universes with their rescripting nearly a century of comics and superheroes.[46] Each of these examples of popular culture implicitly shapes what we believe and informs us of what to think or believe. Moreover, they reflect and rescript our primary world cultural and religious imaginaries in ways that simulate through the believability of secondary worlds the "virtual actuality" of primary world possibilities of believing.

The process of "virtual actuality" has two steps: (1) it both distorts and misleads, and transforms and re-mythicizes, primary world beliefs *into* the narratives and myths of the secondary world; and then (2) re-veils, hides, simulates, and re-presents primary world beliefs back into the primary world *through* the narratives and myths of secondary worlds. This means that the possibilities of belief are shaped by a movement from primary world beliefs into the beliefs of the secondary worlds, and then beliefs move *through* secondary worlds *back into* the primary world—producing a virtual actuality of belief—a simulated hyper-reality of belief that we imagine as possible, believable, and true. It creates through "as-if-worlds" the renewed possibilities of believing after they have been simulated back into the primary world: opening our primary world again to the hyperreal, trans-mythicized possibilities of believing through the very power of what we imagine as believable—as informed *by* the content of the primary world simulated *through* the imagination of secondary worlds while passing *back into* the imaginaries of primary worlds.

The consumptive practices of the mythic imagination simulate the possibilities of believing—of re-enchantment—in a disenchanted world. The sacralization of belief works through the imagination in ways that produce the possibilities of believing. And the imagination is rescripted through consumptive practices. If comics and fantasy are not only read but also displayed in authorized versions through film, they have the power to rescript what we find possible to believe as true. They can alter not only written forms of the imagination but also the images of the imagination. Through the recitation of a story, they have the power to make the imagination virtually real: a simulation of the imagination that we can see. If "seeing is believing," a nuanced interpretation entails that the consumption of images through the medium of film dis-plays a message that we are taken in by and find and deem believable through the very play of a secondary world's imagination upon what we find believable in our primary world. Christine Hoff Kraemer and A. David Lewis argue that

> comics function religiously in a way that has considerable overlap with film. Both sometimes express traditional religious narratives and values to inspire or reinforce an existing religious practice. In both film and comics, images create

opportunities for emotional engagement and can provide a sense of immersion or participation. Both mediums convey narratives that function as modern myths, providing secular and religious audiences with ideological stories that help them to articulate ethical positions and form individual and collective identities. Film and comics also share an overlapping community of consumers, some of whom gather at festivals or conventions for ongoing discussions of the favored works.[47]

Kraemer and Lewis argue that the cultural relevance of comics displays a religious tension with modernity in that it produces a hyper-reality displayed through comics' imaginative recreations of religious, historical, social, and cultural tropes and themes. They state that

> the narratives of popular culture, therefore, are up for grabs to be used by anyone seeking to create meaning. Comics fandom may constitute a hyper-real religion in that it provides ritual practices, community, mythological narratives, and beliefs (though perhaps not a systematic theology) to comics readers.[48]

This demonstrates the reality that popular culture resources and rescripts the mythic imagination in the creation of a hyper-reality that both reflects and distorts the religious dimensions of a primary world while yet re-enchanting our imagination and forming communities constituted by common loves and passions.

Likewise, fantasy re-enchants our imagination, drawing us away from the modernizing processes of disenchantment and into subcreated worlds that symbolically reflect our own world while simultaneously articulating mythic rescriptions of belief. J. R. R. Tolkien defines the imagination as marked by a difference in the degree of image-making. Tolkien argues that the distinction between degrees of the imagination is determined by (1) how we perceive the image and grasp its implications, as well as (2) how it expresses imaginatively the vividness and strength of the image's inner consistency in articulating a reality. This implies that the mythic imagination is an art that links the imagination to the articulation of a subcreation.[49] Tolkien and C. S. Lewis both adhered to an aversion to the distorting effects of allegory.[50] And yet allegory remains necessary for the creation of the subcreations of the fantastic imagination. Or rather, the subcreator remains responsible for presenting the symbolism of the primary world as allegorically reflected within the secondary world. This is done by unpacking the archetypical dynamics of religion within the mythic imagination.

For Tolkien, these archetypes include both the dynamics of fall, mortality, and the machine and the storied recitation of fantasy's ending in eucatastrophe.[51] Tolkien argues that the Christian archetypal image-making of the subcreation is patterned after religious ideas (and their distortion: of fall, death, and domination) along with the happy ending after overcoming great evil. Both rescript the primary and secondary world with sacramental narratives and myths that simulate religious symbolism. In doing so, the mythic imagination not only resources religious symbolism from the primary world into the secondary world, but it rescripts religious myths and narratives within the fantastic sub-creation back into the primary world. The rescription of religious myths and narratives highlights the re-enchanting powers of the fantastic imagination. Tolkien states that

> enchantment produces a secondary world into which both designer and spectator can enter, to the satisfaction of their senses while they are inside; but in its purity, it is artistic in desire and purpose. Magic produces, or pretends to produce, an alteration in the primary world.[52]

Within the secondary world of the imagination, we not only see its symbolic patterning after the primary world but also the implicit belief in the reality of the subcreation. The willful suspension of disbelief is a mark of fantasy's ability to re-enchant our imagination in ways that we may begin to believe as we recognize the allurements and "dramatic and symbolic attractions" of imagined subcreations.[53] Through the production of the secondary world, our imagination is not only enchanted by the willful suspension of disbelief, but just as our imagination is enchanted, it gives us the ability to imagine our world differently. The mythic imagination allows us to re-enchant our world and recognize how the imagination copies or reflects the images it recycles and re-scripts *as* we experience the mythic imagination. In turn, the mythic imagination re-enchants the possibility *for* belief in ways that produce a religious imaginary that remains open and porous in its reception of the possibility of transcendence.

At its heart, the mythic imagination *imagines* worlds and alternate realities that *play* with the concrete realities of everyday life and experience. But the mythic imagination does not only re-enchant the world through the imagination. It also re-enchants our imagination in ways that *play* with religious themes or tropes by recreating, re-mythicizing, and rescripting theological and religious concepts and realities. The mythic imagination also creates worlds that reflect amalgamations of religious ideas that resource religious themes in fantastic and cohesive ways as it re-enchants our religious imaginaries with theological imitations and imagined subcreations. At its heart, fantasy and superheroes demonstrate not just imagined myths, but through the consumption of these myths, they re-mythicize the possibilities of belief with visions of reality that trans-mythicize, rescript, and resource our religious imagination through the interplay between the primary and secondary worlds' virtual actualities of belief.

This section has argued that popular culture plays a defamiliarizing role in re-enchanting our imagination. Through re-mythicizing religious themes, popular culture plays with our beliefs, re-imagines religious belief within new historical contexts, and re-enchants our religious imaginaries in ways that open us to the defamiliarizing tensions between what we believe and what we imagine as believable. It is to these defamiliarizing tensions between belief and the imagination in the consumptive practices of popular culture that we turn to next.

DEFAMILIARIZING BELIEF THROUGH POPULAR CULTURE

Ole Riis and Linda Woodhead summarize two assessments of the postmodern condition. On the one hand, culture fragments into commercialized superficiality in the overproduction of images that simulate fantasies, desires, and dreams of authenticity and self-satisfaction. On the other hand, postmodern culture opens us to diversity and new possibilities for self-articulation, freeing us for self-determination in the dissolution and implosion of boundaries in everyday life. This includes the possibility of enchantment in the "creative blurring of boundaries."[54] They go further to state that

> commercialized dream-worlds are often inspired by religious traditions and have parallel mythic functions, though the new myths do not refer to any specific community as a source of an obligatory set of values. Individuals are not just passive recipients or victims of cultural manipulation, but active consumers and co-producers of postmodern culture. They select and reinterpret symbols according to their own preferences.[55]

Riis and Woodhead describe how the process of globalization in late modernity simulates a variety of symbolic resources of cultural communication and religious ideas. While they argue that these symbolic resources simulate a "pervasiveness of religious themes and symbols," they also argue that this does not indicate a return or revival of religion.[56] Rather they argue that people

> do not confuse the religious or magic universes of the books or films with "reality", and do not feel a moral commitment to their program. Religious symbols . . . present an alternative to the "real" world. This "as-if-world" presents to us topics and dystopias that form templates for comparing features of the everyday

world and the known social system . . . the mythical "as-if-worlds" do not convince because of their seeming realism but because they evoke genuine emotions, in a way that non-religious alternatives fail to do.[57]

This emotive evocation of belief is something "mirrored" as described by Bruce David Forbes: "'We' make something popular when it touches a chord within us, perhaps expressing our assumptions and values, or portraying our yearnings, or providing moments of escape."[58] It is in the emotive evocation of belief that Riis and Woodhead find the relevance of religion in late modernity. It is referenced through the individual's choice (of what) to believe. They are clear that the mythic imagination does not blur the lines between the mythic and the actual, nor does it imply the return or revival of religion. And yet, Riis and Woodhead underestimate the power and effects of simulated beliefs. The power of popular culture's ability to simulate belief through re-enchantment and the mythic imagination defamiliarizes virtual and actual reality, primary and secondary worlds—blurring them into distortions found only in a virtual actuality. This is not a break from reality where we confuse the virtual world as actually real in the sense that we are no longer experiencing the actual world. Rather, it is where we experience the actual world insofar as it is informed by the virtual world. It is a defamiliarizing inter*play* of simulations between the virtual and the actual—invoking, evoking, and simulating through the mythic imagination creative possibilities and imaginings of belief that reflect both our own primary, actual world, and the simulated virtuality of secondary worlds *into* one another. It is in this virtual actuality that belief is imagined and understood as (im-)possible in all its creative possibilities. The power of simulated, recited belief and the mythic imagination opens us to the trans-mythicized possibilities of believing in late modernity where believing remains in tension with how we imagine the possibilities of belief in a virtual actuality.

The ability of popular culture to simulate belief is powerful. It is powerful precisely because of its ability to defamiliarize us of, from, and to belief. Popular culture can draw us into a defamiliarized space between religion and the secular. It defamiliarizes us from both, making each strange as we wander between them largely without belonging solely to one or the other. Between the secular and the religious, popular culture helps us to imagine the possibilities of believing. It both opens and closes us to the possibility of believing in God. It opens us again to imagining belief in a secular society. It re-enchants our imagination and stimulates our intellect to believe in the possibility of God in renewed and rescripted ways through the transmission of recited beliefs between primary and secondary worlds. And yet it also distorts, even in its ability to tap into what matters most to us, religion and religious beliefs through its simulations and recitations of mythical stories.

Take for instance *The Lion King* and Robert Jordan's *The Wheel of Time*. *The Lion King* simulates the religious ideas of dharma, harmony with nature, and messianism. It articulates a pluralistic simulacrum where the story of *The Lion King* both evokes a re-enchantment of our religious sensibilities through its powerful recitation of those religious ideas *and* blurs the line between religions in ways that distort the truth of singular religious traditions. Indeed, the story of *The Lion King* both hides religious ideas in musical, storied imagery—making them believable and credible in imagined ways—and distorts traditional religions into a cohesive story that synthesizes a hidden, pluralistic, religious imaginary. The imagination as such propagates a message, a rescription, and a resourcement of religious ideas that blur the lines not only between religions but also between the religious and the secular. *The Lion King* blurs the lines between the religious and the secular precisely through its hidden religious imaginaries, distorting and re-enchanting our imagination as to what is implicitly believable through the medium of its message.

Furthermore, Robert Jordan and Brandon Sanderson's epic fantasy *The Wheel of Time* also distorts not only the boundaries between religions and religious ideas but also helps us to imagine the credibility of a pluralistic belief system through the imagination. *The Wheel of Time* blurs the lines between Abrahamic messianism and Indian reincarnation, between myth and history, and between magic and neo-Confucian and Daoist notions of the Taiji through the story of its fantastic sub-creation. But what *The Wheel of Time* does most notably is imagine the possibility of a cohesive pluralistic system of religious ideas in its fantastic subcreation that combines religious ideas that do not go together in primary world religious systems.[59] Like *The Lion King*, *The Wheel of Time* imagines a world where religion enchants the imagination in hidden and subtle ways, simulating through the imagination the possibilities and credibility of pluralism.

But between both *The Wheel of Time* and *The Lion King* also lies in their mythic imagination the defamiliarization of belief. Both distort primary-world religious ideas in ways that simulate the possibility of cohesive religious beliefs that are systematically irreconcilable in the primary world. The picking and choosing of what we want to believe is now warranted in a virtual actuality because it plays with and imagines an alternate reality where the medium subtly provokes us to believe. The subcreation of religious beliefs through the mythic imagination opens us to the possibilities of rethinking and imagining religion in renewed ways. In doing so, it both defamiliarizes traditional religions through the mythic imagination—*both* blurring the lines between what is imagined and real *and* hiding in plain sight religious ideas that subtly re-enchant and play with our imagination the possibilities of belief in late modernity—*and* defamiliarizes the secular through the process of re-enchanting the imagination—opening us again to the possibility and credibility of belief in a world where the religious is contested as a viable option in our secular world.

CONCLUSION

Popular cultural poetics of belief open us through the defamiliarization of consumptive practices to the renewed possibilities and the credibility of belief precisely through how we imagine religion through the religious simulations of the mythic imagination. Popular culture defamiliarizes traditional religions and the secular through its ability to both re-enchant the imagination *and* simulate the possibilities of belief through its recitations of what we may imagine believable in a world marked by virtual actuality. That is, popular cultural poetics of belief not only re-enchant but also mirror our imaginings of religious beliefs. They evoke in us something that the secular fails to do, and yet they also invoke in our imaginations the (distorted and veiled) continuation of religious ideas and sensibilities that inform the possibilities of what it means to believe.

The mythic imagination opens us back to the possibilities of believing and the enchantment so central to pre-modern religiosity. And yet, it also defamiliarizes us from traditional and institutional religion, allowing us to imaginatively create anew our beliefs based on a wealth of religious symbolism and ideas. Moreover, through the very simulations of beliefs, dream worlds, and as-if-worlds of popular culture, they re-enchant and imaginatively create new possibilities of belief where the lines between the secular and the religious blur into one another. In doing so, these secondary worlds both help us imagine our primary worlds anew and make the primary world more intelligible. This chapter has offered a methodological and theoretical approach to resourcing the possibilities of believing through an analysis of popular cultural poetics of believing. In doing so, it offers methodological insights into the possibilities of re-enchanting post-Christian imaginaries of religious beliefs in ways that point out how popular culture both simulates renewed possibilities of religion as well as distorts traditional religion. To explore this, the remainder of the book will put into practice, interpret, and apply the theories found within this chapter. First, it will put into practice the notions of re-enchantment, resourcement, and rescription in part II. Then in part III, it will play with the literary genres of apocalypse and prophecy. Moreover, part IV will conclude the exegetical practice through an analysis of the human condition. To wrap things up, part V will offer a constructive post-Christian theology that draws on these exegetical practices. Thus, the remainder of this book constructs a post-Christian theology that is developed through popular cultural exegesis.

NOTES

1. Michel de Certeau, *The Practice of Everyday Life*, trans. Steven Randall (Berkeley, CA: University of California Press, 1984), 177–189.
2. C.f. Diagram 3.1.
3. Bruce David Forbes, "Introduction: Finding Religion in Unexpected Places," in *Religion and Popular Culture in America*, ed. Bruce David Forbes and Jeffrey H. Mahan, Third Edition (Berkeley, CA: University of California Press, 2017), 1–24, 6.
4. C.f. Kelton Cobb, *The Blackwell Guide to Theology and Popular Culture* (Malden, MA: Blackwell Publishing, 2005), 45–51; Jean Baudrillard, *The Consumer Society: Myths and Structures*, Revised Edition (London: SAGE, 2017).
5. Zygmunt Bauman, *Work, Consumerism, and the New Poor*, Second Edition (Maidenhead: Open University Press, 2004); Zygmunt Bauman, *Freedom* (Milton Keynes: Open University Press, 1988), 19–98; Zygmunt Bauman, *Legislators and Interpreters: On Modernity, Postmodernity and Intellectuals* (Cambridge, MA: Polity Press, 1987), 149–187; Zygmunt Bauman, *Thinking Sociologically* (Oxford: Blackwell, 1990), 195–213; and Zygmunt Bauman, *Intimations of Postmodernity* (London: Routledge, 1992), 49–53, 97–98, 197–198.
6. C.f. Alan Warde, "Consumers, Identity and Belonging: Reflections on Some Theses of Zygmunt Bauman," in *The Authority of the Consumer*, ed. Russell Keat, Nigel Whiteley, and Nicholas Abercrombie (London and New York: Routledge, 1994), 58–74, 65; and Russell Keat, Nigel Whiteley, and Nicholas Abercrombie, "Introduction," in *The Authority of the Consumer*, ed. Russell Keat, Nigel Whiteley, and Nicholas Abercrombie (London and New York: Routledge, 1994), 1–19, 8.
7. Indeed, Warde analyzes Bauman's theses on consumption—(1) that the state is to blame for the inadequacies of the market, (2) that self-identity as a consumer remains inadequately morally responsible and pessimistic, and (3) that belonging as a goal of consumerism ties us and our identity to the market and a particular class—and demonstrates their inadequacies. C.f. Warde, "Consumers, Identity and Belonging: Reflections on Some Theses of Zygmunt Bauman," 58–74.
8. C.f. Peter Thompson, "Marxism," in *The Oxford Handbook of Atheism*, ed. Stephen Bullivant and Michael Ruse (Oxford: Oxford University Press, 2013), 293–306, 301.
9. C.f. Christopher Partridge, "Religion and Popular Culture," in *Religions in the Modern World: Traditions and Transformations*, ed. Linda Woodhead, Hiroko Kawanami, and Christopher Partridge, Second Edition (London and New York: Routledge, 2009), 490–521, 507.
10. Partridge, "Religion and Popular Culture," 508.
11. Partridge, "Religion and Popular Culture," 508.
12. This idea of 'play' comes from Jean-Jacques Suurmond, in "The Church at Play: The Pentecostal/Charismatic Renewal of the Liturgy as the Renewal of the World," in *Pentecost, Mission, and Ecumenism: Essays on Intercultural Theology*, ed. Jan A. B. Jongeneel, et al. (Frankfurt: Peter Lang, 1992), 247–259, 249–250.

13. C.f. Gordon Lynch, *Understanding Theology and Popular Culture* (Oxford: Blackwell Publishing, 2005), 43–68; C.f. For analyses of digital media: John C. Lyden and Eric Michael Mazur, eds., *The Routledge Companion to Religion and Popular Culture* (London and New York: Routledge, 2015), 41–182.

14. C.f. Cobb, *The Blackwell Guide to Theology and Popular Culture*, 7.

15. Jeffrey H. Mahan, "Reflections on the Past and Future of the Study of Religion and Popular Culture," in *Between Sacred and Profane: Researching Religion and Popular Culture*, ed. Gordon Lynch (London and New York: I.B. Tauris, 2007), 47–62.

16. Mahan, "Reflections on the Past and Future of the Study of Religion and Popular Culture," 62.

17. Elaine Graham, "'What We Make of the World': The Turn to 'Culture' in Theology and the Study of Religion," in *Between Sacred and Profane: Researching Religion and Popular Culture*, ed. Gordon Lynch (London and New York: I.B. Tauris, 2007), 63–81, 80.

18. Graham, "'What we Make of the World': The Turn to 'Culture' in Theology and the Study of Religion," 66. My italics.

19. Graham, "'What we Make of the World': The Turn to 'Culture' in Theology and the Study of Religion," 76.

20. Cobb, *The Blackwell Guide to Theology and Popular Culture*, 63.

21. Jean Baudrillard, *Simulations*, trans. Paul Foss, Paul Patton, and Philip Beitchman (USA: Semiotext[e], 1983), 11–12; Jean Baudrillard, *Simulations and Simulacra*, trans. Sheila Faria Glaser (Ann Arbor, MI: The University of Michigan Press, 1994), 3–7: Baudrillard traces the divine simulacra to theological presence masked in a representational sign that is subsumed by the simulation of the real into the emptiness of its referential. The four steps to simulacra move from the theological/sacramental signification to masking it as an evil appearance to playing as an appearance that becomes a simulation.

22. Cobb, *The Blackwell Guide to Theology and Popular Culture*, 63.

23. Cobb, *The Blackwell Guide to Theology and Popular Culture*, 63.

24. Cobb, *The Blackwell Guide to Theology and Popular Culture*, 64.

25. Baudrillard, *Simulations and Simulacra*, 1–3.

26. Claire Colebrook, *Gilles Deleuze* (London and New York: Routledge, 2002), 99.

27. Colebrook, *Gilles Deleuze*, 100.

28. Colebrook, *Gilles Deleuze*, 101.

29. Colebrook, *Gilles Deleuze*, 101.

30. Graham Ward, "Michel de Certeau's 'Spiritual Spaces,'" *The South Atlantic Quarterly* 100, no. 2 (2001): 501–517.

31. Graham Ward, "Introduction: Where We Stand," in *The Blackwell Companion to Postmodern Theology*, ed. Graham Ward (Malden, MA: Blackwell Publishers, 2001), xii–xxvii, xvi.

32. Cobb, *The Blackwell Guide to Theology and Popular Culture*, 9–10.

33. Douglass Kellner, *Jean Baudrillard: From Marxism to Postmodernism and Beyond* (Stanford, CA: Stanford University Press, 1989), 68.

34. This "medium" is the media: insofar as images pass through the media, the media becomes the medium for re-enchantment, disillusionment, and recitation of what a society finds and deems believable. It is a "defamiliarizing structurization" because it both defamiliarizes us *from* reality through the structures that organize what we understand and find believable *within* reality. As such, it defamiliarizes us from the real through its simulation of a hyper-reality, opening us to the possibility of a simulated belief. It also remains a structurization that is both structuring and structured in the vein of Bourdieu: it is both a structure that actively shapes (subjective) reality and it is a structure that is (objectively) established within our cultural, social, economic, symbolic, and religious understandings of the real.

35. Baudrillard, *Simulations and Simulacra*, 80–82.

36. Here I am underlying this in terms of James K. A. Smith's Bourdieusian interpretation of Paul Tillich's ultimate concerns—which can be secular or religious because what matters most to us is displayed in our practices. C.f. James K. A. Smith, "Secular Liturgies and the Prospects for a 'Post-Secular' Sociology of Religion," in *The Post-Secular in Question: Religion in Contemporary Society*, ed. Philip S. Gorski et al. (New York and London: New York University Press and Social Science Research Council, 2012), 159–184.

37. Baudrillard, *Simulations and Simulacra*, 82–83.

38. Certeau, *The Practice of Everyday Life*, 186.

39. Graham Ward, "Introduction," in *The Certeau Reader*, ed. Graham Ward (Malden, MA: Blackwell Publishers, 2000), 1–14, 6–7.

40. Baudrillard, *Simulations and Simulacra*, 81.

41. Cobb, *The Blackwell Guide to Theology and Popular Culture*, 39.

42. As Austin Freeman points out, the imagination is not always theologically Christian in its imaginings. The sins of the imagination are grounded in a distinctly Christian reading of fantasy: where our imagination can reflect Christian content and patterns in the mythic imagination or can reflect a sinful imagination that distorts our imagination away from a Christian vision of what we create and imagine of reality. C.f. Austin Freeman, "Sins of the Imagination," in *Theology, Fantasy, and the Imagination*, ed. Andrew D. Thrasher and Austin Freeman (Lanham, MD: Rowman and Littlefield, 2023), 19–34.

43. Michael Jindra, "It's About Faith in Our Future: Star Trek Fandom as Cultural Religion," in *Religion and Popular Culture in America*, ed. Bruce David Forbes and Jeffrey H. Mahan, Third Edition (Berkeley, CA: University of California Press, 2017), 223–241.

44. C.f. Matthew William Brake, Kimberly Hampton, and Travis Harris, eds., *Theology and Black Panther* (Lanham, MD: Rowman and Littlefield, Forthcoming).

45. C.f. Douglas Estes, ed., *Theology and Tolkien*, 2 vols. (Lanham, MD: Rowman and Littlefield, 2023); Taylor J. Ott and Shaun Brown, eds., *The Theological World of Harry Potter* (Lanham, MD: Rowman and Littlefield, Forthcoming).

46. C.f. Gregory Stevenson, ed., *Theology and the Marvel Universe* (Lanham, MD: Rowman and Littlefield, 2020); Roshan Abraham and Gabriel McKee, eds., *Theology and the DC Universe* (Lanham, MD: Rowman and Littlefield, 2023); Ben Saunders, *Do the Gods Wear Capes? Spirituality, Fantasy, and Superheroes* (London

and New York: Continuum, 2011); B. J. Oropeza, ed., *The Gospel According to Superheroes: Religion and Popular Culture* (New York: Peter Lang, 2005).

47. Christine Hoff Kraemer and A. David Lewis, "Comics/Graphic Novels," in *The Routledge Companion to Religion and Popular Culture*, ed. John C. Lyden and Eric Michael Mazur (London and New York: Routledge, 2015), 210–227, 212.

48. Hoff Kraemer and Lewis, "Comics/Graphic Novels," 211.

49. J. R. R. Tolkien, "On Fairy Stories," in *The Tolkien Reader* (New York: Ballentine Books, 1966), 68–69.

50. J. R. R. Tolkien, *The Silmarillion*, ed. Christopher Tolkien, Second Edition (New York: Del Rey, 2020), xv–xvi; Michael Ward, *Planet Narnia: The Seven Heavens in the Imagination of C.S. Lewis* (Oxford: Oxford University Press, 2008), 30–32.

51. Tolkien, "On Fairy Stories," 85–86; Tolkien, *The Silmarillion*, xvi.

52. Tolkien, "On Fairy Stories," 73.

53. David Jasper, *"The Pilgrim's Regress* and *Surprised by Joy,"* in *The Cambridge Companion to C. S. Lewis*, ed. Robert MacSwain and Michael Ward (Cambridge: Cambridge University Press, 2010), 232–233.

54. Ole Riis and Linda Woodhead, *A Sociology of Religious Emotion* (Oxford: Oxford University Press, 2010), 177.

55. Riis and Woodhead, *A Sociology of Religious Emotion*, 179–180.

56. Riis and Woodhead, *A Sociology of Religious Emotion*, 189.

57. Riis and Woodhead, *A Sociology of Religious Emotion*, 190.

58. Forbes, "Introduction: Finding Religion in Unexpected Places," 5–6.

59. This is the underlying point of my chapter in *Theology, Fantasy, and the Imagination*. C.f. Andrew D. Thrasher, "Fantastic Inter-religious Resourcement in Robert Jordan and David Eddings," in *Theology, Fantasy, and the Imagination*, ed. Andrew D. Thrasher and Austin M. Freeman (Lanham, MD: Rowman and Littlefield, 2023), 133–153.

Part II

METHODOLOGY THROUGH PRACTICE

Chapter 3

Marveling Re-enchantment?

Part I laid out theoretical frameworks for how popular culture and religion are shaped by the postmodern cultural consumption of belief. That is, to believe in late modernity is to be shaped by the cultural frameworks and messages of what we consume. Furthermore, what we consume has effects on what we find desirable, credible, and believable, often constituting a pastiche or bricolage of religious beliefs and practices for individual consumers/believers. Popular culture comes to shape the possibilities of believing in ways that constitute what it means to believe in late modernity. Chapter 2 stated three methodological approaches through which to understand how late modern consumptive believing comes to use traditional religious beliefs and ideas in ways that move us beyond traditional religious beliefs, particularly Christianity. These three post-Christian methodological approaches are re-enchantment, resourcement, and rescription. The chapters in part II demonstrate how each of these is put into practice through analyses of the Marvel Cinematic Universe (MCU), *The Lion King*, and *Lucifer*. While the following two chapters will focus on how *The Lion King* deconstructs inter-religious resourcement and how *Lucifer* rescripts traditional Christian theology, this chapter analyzes the question of (re)-enchantment and how the MCU re-enchants the late modern cultural imagination.

This chapter argues that the MCU re-enchants the imagination when we begin to pay attention to the tensions between metaphysical conceptions of reality presented in the MCU alongside the critical, deconstructive questions of whether it is right to appropriate and give voice to, while distorting, the religious voices of the marginalized and the oppressed. It does so in ways that resist traditional religious conceptions of reality while also giving thought and expression to how we can think about reality in alternate ways. Furthermore, it develops how the MCU thinks critically about post-disenchantment through the problems of science, magic, technology, and the use of available mythologies. Each of these is framed by the question of whether this is re-enchantment or whether it is, as I argue, a characterization of late modern post-disenchantment. This chapter begins and ends with this question, and between it are analyses of both how the MCU imagines a reality in ways that can enchant the imagination and how we can problematize the MCU's use of available mythologies through a critical deconstructive reading of its resourcement and rescription of available myths.

THE PROBLEM OF DISENCHANTMENT

"Have we ever been disenchanted?" I often hear this question and often hear contradictory answers to this question. Some will say "no" because of the perpetual fascination with magic, the supernatural, and the continued belief in the power of spirits or the Holy Spirit to heal, curse, and have effects in the natural world.[1] Others will say "yes" because modern world structures are no longer determined or shaped by religious structures: the modern notions of the nation-state, public sphere, and market economy of a direct access society have flattened the need for a vertical relationship with God that was mediated by the church.[2] The question of disenchantment is marked by how we define disenchantment in both the spheres of quotidian life as well as in the differentiated spheres of modern imaginaries. And yet, how we wrestle with this problem is based on how we define enchantment, disenchantment, re-enchantment, and post-disenchantment.

The question of enchantment goes back at least a century with Max Weber posing the term *"entzauberung"* which is often translated as disenchantment. Hans Joas offers a sustained, critical analysis of what Weber meant by *"entzauberung"* and how he used it.[3] Joas begins his analysis with the linguistic origins of the word and then articulates how philosophers through the mid-twentieth century used the word. Variously, it connotates "being lifted from a spell" or "to dispel myths" and their power to enchant us.[4] How *entzauberung* has been used to mean disenchantment has come to connote however, a modern historical process of disbelieving in the spiritual and the differentiating effects of the modern world from the power of religious structures. However, rather than define *entzauberung* as disenchantment, Joas argues through thorough analyses that a better word for how Weber used the word was "demagification." However, according to Joas, tied to demagification for Weber, *entzauberung* also has connotations of detranscendentalization and desacralization.[5]

To translate *entzauberung* as disenchantment is a mistranslation because it more accurately can be translated as the historical processes of "demagification," "desacralization," and "detranscendentalization." Furthermore, the term belies an irony: many of those proponents of disenchantment at the turn of the twentieth century were remarkably interested in the occult, magic, and superstitious.[6] Hans Joas argues that the historical processes of modernity are marked by the turn away from the belief in, or the reality or power of, magic (demagification). It is also characterized by the movement away from both belief in the sacred and how the sacred captures how we make sense of our ordinary, mundane lives—as such it entails how the ordinary world is stripped of the sacred (desacralization). This in turn leads to detranscendentalization where the notion of transcendence is eclipsed and rejected by the turn to pure immanence.

Joas' analysis of Weber's understanding and use of *entzauberung* follows Weber's own shift in the conscious use and adoption of the word as a catch-all for his understanding of the historical processes that have led to modernity. But when *entzauberung* means demagification, according to Joas, this is tied to Weber's reading of magic as having a subjective instrumental meaning, which throughout historical processes, has led to the gradual disbelief in the power of magic. While Weber traces this to the Ancient Hebrews in the Old Testament and across global history (often problematically), it is especially clear when it comes up against modernity's rationalizing processes found in the Enlightenment and modern science. According to Joas, Weber understood the demagification of the world to be tied to the intellectualism of the world, where human beings rationalize their beliefs and fascination with magic in an attempt to understand and systematize the world through rational, instrumental reasoning.[7]

And yet, enchantment is often defined by Charles Taylor as the belief in spirits, demons, angels, God, gods, and Satan. These, in turn, have the power to influence and shape the human psyche. Taylor argues that enchantment presupposes the notion of a porous self where the spiritual has the power to affect and seep into who we are and shape and empower us with spiritual energies and influences. By contrast, Taylor argues that the modern self is buffered and invulnerable to these spiritual energies and entities. In that sense, yes, we are disenchanted from believing in a world where the effects of spiritual realities no longer shape human identity, psyche, or social imaginary.[8] But we must also ask, *who* is enchanted? When we talk of the modern subject, they carry with them a way of looking at and experiencing the world as closed to the supernatural and thus are disenchanted. The hallmark of disenchantment is disbelief in the power of spiritual realities to have effects on the natural world.

The way we define our world as enchanted or disenchanted is an important starting point because how we define them will determine how we imagine the notion of "re-enchantment." If we are already enchanted in the sense of believing in the power of God or the gods to act in the world or sense something meaningful in the experiences of ordinary life, then there is no need for "re-enchantment." However, if we are speaking of the modern social imaginary which presupposes a closure to transcendence, magic, and the sacred, then clearly the question of re-enchantment holds great significance. But what does "re-enchantment" look like in the second sense, where the sacred still has relevance to a modern *disenchanted* world? Does this mean a return to a medieval world where everything in the world makes sense through its participation in the sacred? Does it mean that the power of Christianity ought to shape our world again in the sense that it did across the Latin Middle Ages?

The answer to both of these questions is no. Both Christendom and the notion of participation in the sacred have not only lost their allure for many in the West because of the faults and complicity of Christendom in the Inquisition, the Crusades, and witch hunts, but they are also contested in our contemporary world because of how fragmented and pluralistic the Western world is today. The pluralization of both religious traditions, sects, and denominations, and secular formations of how we make sense of gender, race, and religion in a public sphere, do not allow the space for a universal, absolute, institutional, or unnuanced notion of Christianity that closes the door to the modern issues of human rights, equality, freedom, and justice tied to these perspectives.[9]

But when we speak of re-enchantment, we must also nuance between those who do not presuppose the closure to the spiritual realities acting in the world—whether they do so or not—and those who, in ordinary language, speak of the sublime, a sense of something more or meaningful in our ordinary lives. The question of re-enchantment in both of these situations presupposes both secular and religious modes of imagining the world as enchanted—and this is the space for post-disenchantment. When we speak of re-enchantment, we are primarily speaking of the structures in which religious belief may have a place in secular modernity. But when we speak of re-enchantment in terms of how we may imagine enchantment in a world that presupposes disenchantment, it may be proper to speak of, following Marika Rose in her coining of the phrase, "post-disenchantment."[10]

Paul Cloke, et al. argue that Marika Rose's notion of "post-disenchantment" implies "co-constitutive forces of disenchantment and enchantment at work in late capitalist societies."[11] The notion of post-disenchantment challenges the idea that we live in a disenchanted world that can only be solved by "a process of 're-enchantment'."[12] By contrast, Rose argues that post-disenchantment

> recognizes not only that we can no longer evade the persistence of magical thinking and practices, but also that the entangling networks which constitute

contemporary capitalism function as a system of technological re-enchantment, a secular reiteration of the kinds of structures of power and dominion which characterized the enchanted universe of classical Christian thought.[13]

The question post-disenchantment poses is especially whether there can be not only religious or Christian re-enchantment, but also whether secular enchantment is possible.[14] Cloke, et al. argue that

> to some extent, secular re-instatement of enchantment leans on the capacity of the postmodern to restore to the world what modernity had denuded of it; a reinvigoration of initiative and authorship of action, and the right to give meaning to and construe narratives counteracted a de-spiritualized and de-animated model of the world in which the capacity of the subject has gone missing.[15]

While post-disenchantment is not a one-to-one correlation to re-enchantment, it does invoke certain themes and issues bound to the notion of re-enchantment. While re-enchantment implies both the turn to structurally de-differentiate modern secular structures and the turn to imagine the world as enchanted, post-disenchantment implies the concern for imagining the world as enchanted while still presupposing the differentiation between religious and secular structures as an unresolvable problem in which we must live between the tensions. That is, while re-enchantment presupposes a return to enchantment in both how we imagine the world and the effectual de-differentiation or resacralization of the world, post-disenchantment presupposes that any turn of re-enchantment must wrestle with the effects of disenchantment as here to stay. Post-disenchantment takes disenchantment seriously and is something that any form of re-enchantment must take into account. Post-disenchantment deters any idealism where the return of religion is unnuanced and absolutist. Rather, post-disenchantment articulates the realism of re-enchantment as living in the tension between enchantment and disenchantment in our everyday world.

As a case study for this, we may look at Phase Four's *The Falcon and the Winter Soldier* and the opening scenes of *Wakanda Forever*. Both are examples from within the MCU where Western powers are wrestling with the realities of enchantment in a post-disenchanted context. In the MCU, the secular political structures have been confronted with magic, aliens, and superhuman powers. They must also wrestle with the realities of several billion people returning after the blip. And yet, they search for Vibranium throughout the world in their hunger for power. What we find here is a secular reality that is confronted with enchantment and searches for a way to master it through technology. *The Falcon and the Winter Solider* is especially a case where secular world structures wrestle with the aftershocks and effects of powers beyond human control. The opening scenes of *Wakanda Forever* are of both Wakanda and Talokan protecting their Vibranium from Western powers. The search for Vibranium is a Western (and White) response to things beyond their control. As Willie James Jennings argues, Whiteness is marked by mastery, control, and domination.[16] Both *The Falcon and the Winter Solider* and *Wakanda Forever* display a White response and sensibility to things beyond their control: *"We must be able to control it, and that means obtaining the means by which we can do so!"* The confrontation with magic, aliens, and powers beyond our control, and the attempt to technologically control it, are central aspects by and through which the MCU reveals the contours of post-disenchantment. And yet how the MCU enchants the imagination is something that must be both articulated through analyses of its mythic imagination as well as critically examined through its problematic rescription and resourcement of traditional religions. It is to these that we turn to for the remainder of this chapter.

MARVELING ENCHANTMENT

Does the MCU enchant the imagination? If it does, how does it do so? This section argues that the MCU enchants the imagination and how we imagine religion in ways that speak to a complex account of the supernatural, the sacred, and magical power. This is done through analyses of divine hierarchies, the infinity stones, and space, time, and reality in the multiverse of the MCU. Let us turn to each to examine how they can "enchant" the imagination.

Divine Hierarchies

Austin Freeman has argued that the MCU and Marvel comics display a hidden Neo-Platonism in their hierarchies of the divine.[17] Freeman defines the "fundamental impetus [of Neo-Platonism] was the reconciliation of the problem of the One and the many, which led to the positing of many gradations of being between absolute spiritual unity and the multiplicity of the observed physical world."[18] Freeman ranks the divine hierarchy in Marvel in ways that correlate to Neo-Platonic hierarchies, though with nuance, especially regarding the place of the demiurge.[19] The way Freeman analyzes this hierarchy, from the lowest to the highest, reflects through the imagination how to make sense of divine hierarchy in Marvel as not only resourcing Neo-Platonism but re-enchanting how we may imagine religion in the MCU. While Freeman offers an amazing analysis and account of this hierarchy, I want to expand upon it to reflect on higher forms of life and civilization across the MCU.

The MCU includes multiple species and civilizations that reflect humanoid characteristics. In the case of the Skrulls and Kree, to Xandar and the

Sovereign, the MCU enchants the imagination not so much with religion or the supernatural, but moreover with the belief in extraterrestrial beings. The central concern of S.H.I.E.L.D. is to protect the Earth from the supernatural dangers out in the universe and those present here on Earth. Throughout the first several seasons of *Agents of S.H.I.E.L.D.*, we see Agent Coulson try to make sense of being brought back to life, the rise of the Inhumans, and the ramifications of the terrigen crystals infecting those of Kree descent across the world. While the Mutants have only begun their appearance in the MCU, what is clear about the Inhumans and the Mutants is that they have enhanced powers that go beyond normal human powers. Here we see the bottom of a hierarchy that is not yet divine, but still very (super)human.

When we turn to examine the first level of the divine hierarchy in Freeman's analysis, the MCU has expanded upon a variety of "Cosmic Gods" that we have been exposed to since the publication of *Theology and the Marvel Universe* at the end of the third phase of the MCU. We have been exposed not only to Thor and the Asgardians but also to the Ice Giants, of which Loki is a descendant, as well as figures like Bast and Kukulkan in the religions of Wakanda and Talokan, who make an appearance in *Thor: Love and Thunder*. In *Thor: Love and Thunder,* we also find several other cosmic gods, particularly the appearance of Zeus and his son Hercules, alongside Gorr the God Butcher. Key to interpreting the nature of the cosmic gods throughout *Thor: Love and Thunder* is especially their moral ambiguity concerning their devotees. Do the gods care about mortals and those who worship them? This is the moral problem that both Thor confronts at the Assembly of the Gods and the formerly pious Gorr the God Butcher seeks vengeance for in his attempt to rid the universe of the Cosmic Gods.

When we turn to Freeman's second ranking of a divine hierarchy in Marvel, we find that the Celestials come to play a central role, which Freeman correlates to the Neo-Platonist demiurge. We see the Celestials in several places throughout the MCU, particularly in Knowhere (a mining colony based on the remains of a Celestial), the father of Star-Lord (Ego the Living Planet), who tries to absorb all of creation under his consciousness, and especially with Arishem the Judge in *The Eternals*. We see throughout the film *The Eternals* that Arishem had sent his immortal servants to destroy the deviants to allow the populations of humans to grow across the earth so that a maximum capacity will allow the birth of a new Celestial, Tiamut.

While Freeman works from the comics, his insights have played out in the MCU as well, when he states that "the Celestials use human history as a grand experiment, manipulating evolution on a universal scale in order to perfect creation. They modify human-kind, giving it the genetic potential to create both mutants and superheroes."[20] Thus, when the Eternals defy their purpose against Arishem and transform Tiamut into stone (adamantium?), Arishem comes to judge the Eternals who remained on Earth. What role the Eternals play in the rest of the MCU we are yet to see as of the time of this writing in January 2024. Like the hypercosmic gods of Love, Hate, Order, and Chaos, we have yet to see much in relation to the roles of Eternity, Infinity, Death, and Oblivion as correlations to the Neo-Platonic World Soul in the MCU. Nor have we seen much of the Living Tribunal or The One Above All.[21] But how the MCU integrates the Watcher in *What If . . . ?*, and Loki and the One Who Remains in *Loki*, involves figures that do not easily fit into the divine hierarchy in Freeman's analysis.

While the Watcher plays a role in watching and not interfering, in the multiverse, we see in season one of *What If . . . ?* a crisis that forces him to bring the Guardians of the Multiverse together to trap Killmonger with one multiverse's Ultron to keep him from destroying all life across the multiverse. (This was done through a spell by one multiverse's Dr. Strange who tries to transgress an Absolute point.)[22] When it comes to He Who Remains in *Loki*, it is clear that he is not divine, and yet his control of time across the multiverse displays an important power in holding his own variants across the multiverse at bay. With the death of both He Who Remains and of the Conqueror, what is to come of the Kang Dynasty hints at a massive cosmic war that may shatter our conceptions of time and reality across the multiverse in the MCU.[23] What role Loki will play in determining the multiverse is yet to be known in the MCU.[24] How time is imagined across the multiverse is an important point of reflection on the basic components and powers of the universe. It is a reflection on the power of the Infinity Stones that we turn next.

Reflections on the Powers of the Infinity Stones

The power of the Infinity Stones across the first three phases of the MCU is astounding. They have the power to: (a) destroy planets, as Ronan tried to accomplish with the Power Stone in *Guardians of the Galaxy, Vol. 1*; (b) control minds and create artificial intelligence with the Mind Stone in both Ultron and Vision across *Avengers* and *Avengers: Age of Ultron*; (c) create wormholes across time with the Space Stone for the invasion of Thanos' Chitauri in the first Avengers film alongside Loki's deviant escape from Iron Man in *Avengers: Endgame* and capture by the Time Variance Authority (TVA) at the beginning of season one of *Loki*; (d) Thanos altering reality to create a flourishing planet as a place of retirement at the beginning of *Avengers: Endgame*, and, in *Avengers: Infinity War*, Thanos' deception of the Guardians of the Galaxy with the Reality Stone so that he could learn where the Soul Stone was kept; (e) manipulate time and bind Dormammu's timelessness to time with the Time Stone in *Dr. Strange* and, in *Avengers: Infinity War*, reverse time so that Vision dies twice so that Thanos can capture the

Mind Stone; and (f) more mysteriously, bind to those we love and sacrifice, the Soul Stone remains a mystery yet intimately reflects the power of love as we see in both *Avengers: Infinity War* and *Avengers: Endgame*. When all the powers of the Infinity Stones are combined, Thanos has both the power to commit utilitarian genocide by wiping out half the population of the universe and the unactualized potential to double the resources of the universe (which is the Falcon's critique of Thanos in *The Falcon and the Winter Soldier*).[25]

The power of the Infinity Stones is immense and rivals the power of the Living Tribunal. And yet, we also learn in *Loki* that the Infinity Stones are both essential elements of the universe manifested in stones with the power of each element—but trivial when located in the TVA. In the TVA, Infinity Stones have no power and are mere rocks collected for Casey's fancy collection. Furthermore, we see that there is a multiplicity of Infinity Stones because of the multiverse and the Time Variance Authority's control over the Sacred Timeline. As such, the power of Infinity Stones has both the power to reshape all of reality and tap into the elemental forces of the multiverse, as well as become trivial trinkets with no power in the TVA. But what the Infinity Stones represent as elements of universal forces is worth reflecting more on.

The power to alter reality, manipulate time, control the mind, warp space, destroy worlds, and the mystery of love as elemental forces in the Infinity Stones is worth a cause for reflection. The Reality Stone (or the Aether in *Thor: The Dark World*) allows its wielder the power to alter reality, create illusions of reality, and deceive others about what is real while still presenting the deception as truly real. This power, I believe is largely untapped by Thanos because the magnitude of the power to augment reality is dependent on the expansive ability of the imagination. What is imaginable can become reality with the Reality Stone. The Time Stone is arguably one of the most significant and subtle of all the Infinity Stones. Dr. Strange's astute understanding of it when applying it to bind Dormammu to a time loop, and his unique ability to predict alternate futures with it, implies that, again, the ability to *imagine* its capabilities allows Dr. Strange a powerful ability that subtly transcends Thanos' brutal use of it to bring back the Mind Stone and kill Vision a second time.

As hinted at through Dr. Strange's use of the Time Stone, the Mind Stone allows its wielder to control the minds of others as well as understand the mysteries of grief, as Vision states to Wanda in a memory found in *WandaVision*: "What is grief, if not love persevering?"[26] When it comes to the Space Stone, we see it grants its user the ability to transcend the laws of time and space and travel across the universe in seconds. The ability to transcend the laws of space is unique among the Infinity Stones because it breaks how we understand space and time: if I can move through infinite space in seconds, this breaks any normal conception of how much time we have until someone arrives. Usually, we would know that it takes A amount of time to go between points X and Y, but with the ability to warp through space, this means that the temporal anticipations of space are circumvented and become irrelevant.

The Power Stone grants the wielder the ability of immense power and energy and can only be touched by those who belong to divine descent or higher beings like the Titans. It contains the power to destroy and, in the wrong hands, could lead to the devastation of entire worlds and civilizations. The untapped mystery of love in the Soul Stone implies a connection between love and sacrifice in ways that to wield the power of the Soul Stone, one must sacrifice what one loves. For its power, the demand is "A soul for a soul." We see Clint and Natasha fighting to sacrifice themselves for one another in ways that present a stark contrast to Thanos relentlessly throwing a struggling Gamora from the cliff. But even with Thanos' warped love for Gamora—how agonizing it is to sacrifice those we love! And yet, as we moved into Phase Four of the MCU, we saw that the powers of the Infinity Stones, while great, become irrelevant when we reflect on the relationship between time, space, and reality in the multiverse—to which we now turn.

Time, Space, and Reality in the Multiverse

Throughout *Avengers: Endgame*, the first seasons of *Loki* and *What If...?*, *WandaVision*, *Dr. Strange 2: Multiverse of Madness*, and *Antman and Wasp 3: Quantumania,* there are significant advances in how we can understand time, space, and the multiverse. We see the beginnings of mind-altering conceptions of time, space, and reality, especially across *Dr. Strange* and *Avengers: Infinity War*. But what we find at the end of Phase Three and throughout Phase Four are imaginative presentations of time travel, predestination, the multiverse, and the quantum realm. While the first two particularly play with our conceptions of time, the latter two play with our conceptions of space and reality. Let us examine how each of these plays out across the MCU.

When we examine the MCU's play with time, two central problems arise. First, if time travel is possible, is time a continuum or a loop? Second, if all of our actions are part of a predetermined sacred timeline, where is the space for free will? The first question can be intuited from *Avengers: Endgame* and *Loki* as a seeming contradiction. While Tony Stark figures out how to time travel, he is adamant that all of the Infinity Stones must return to their original timelines. Here, we see Tony unknowingly adhering to the laws of the TVA. But when we see that the Ancient One is surprised at the Hulk's request for the Time Stone and that Dr. Strange gave it up in his own timeline, we see an implicit contradiction that leaves us a problem if time is a continuum rather than a loop. If time is a loop, then the Ancient One, before the events in *Dr. Strange,* had already given the Time Stone to the Hulk, and we are left to assume that this is a silent but revealed backstory behind *Dr. Strange* during the Chitauri invasion of New York in the first *Avengers*.

But the contradiction that seemingly lies in the idea that time is a continuum must be maintained by the TVA. In *Loki*, we find out that there is a sacred timeline that must be protected at all costs, and also that it was all predetermined by the One Who Remains until the threshold was crossed. What *Loki* seemingly implies is that time is marked by a predetermined continuum, and yet if that continuum is predetermined to allow the remaining Avengers to time travel to recover the Infinity Stones, then why would it not allow the possibility of a time loop? Yet the problem this raises is if this time travel looped back as a circular loop that comes back to the origin without continuing into the future beyond the events of *Endgame*. This is not the case as the story continues throughout the MCU, even while the story is no longer predetermined by He Who Remains. This implies that the time traveling in *Avengers: Endgame* is a loop that successfully fulfills the predetermined path set by the TVA by returning the sacred timeline to its intended course. This means that the Avengers' time-traveling was a loop that was not only intended but a predetermined part of the continuum of the sacred timeline.

We also see in season one of *Loki* that his predetermined timeline was to follow the course we see across the first three phases of the MCU. When Loki uses the Tesseract to escape capture from the Avengers, he breaks his predetermined course along the sacred timeline. Throughout *Loki*, we see Loki allying himself with both the TVA and Sylvie at various points, and throughout the show, we see the fault lines in blindly following the TVA's propaganda. By the end of the first season, we learn that the Time-Keepers are machines created by He Who Remains to judge those who transgress the TVA and the sacred timeline. Throughout the show, we see Sylvie's rebellion against the TVA and ultimately against the predetermined timeline of He Who Remains. All of Sylvie's and Loki's attempts to kill He Who Remains fail until the threshold is crossed. That is when He Who Remains does not know what will happen. He had created the TVA and the sacred timeline to protect it from his own variants, who in their own ways can manipulate and control time. Only he (and Loki?) can keep his variants in check and paints himself as a quirky and seemingly benevolent predeterminer of time because of this.

But the question of predestination becomes a nail when it comes up against free will. Loki learns that all of his life—what it was and what it was to become—was predetermined to be a useless sacrifice in an attempt to save his brother and the universe from Thanos. Loki's anger is apparent at the triviality of his death, and cries out for meaning against the meaninglessness of his life. And yet, behind this anger is the cry for free will that Sylvie so masterfully manipulates in her ability to survive, as all the variants of Loki are so skilled to do. Sylvie's anger against predestination leads her to kill He Who Remains, even while Loki cautions her against it because he recognizes the potential for greater danger to come if He Who Remains is dead.

When we turn to examine the relationship between space and reality in the multiverse in *What If . . . ?*, *WandaVision*, *Multiverse of Madness*, and *Quantumania*, we also see several puzzles worth reflecting on. While *What If . . . ?* and *Multiverse of Madness* deal explicitly with traveling across the multiverse, *WandaVision* plays a preparatory role for *Multiverse of Madness*, and *Quantumania* plays a role in understanding the Quantum Realm as an alternate realm beneath all realms. *WandaVision* appropriately provides the link between the end of Phase Three and the beginning of Phase Four by presenting the development of her magical powers in relation to her grief. *WandaVision* follows the stages of her grief over having lost Vision through the alteration of reality in the fictional town of Westview, New Jersey. This alternate reality hints at her ability as the Scarlet Witch to alter reality, who is prophesied in *Multiverse of Madness* to destroy or rule the multiverse. Her search throughout the *Multiverse of Madness* for her children is a desperate attempt in the madness of grief for love and to be a mother. Wanda's altering of reality to fit her vision of reality is an immense power, one governed by the madness of love and grief.

But what the *Multiverse of Madness* brings to the table alongside *What If...?* are the first tangible articulation of the multiverse in the MCU. While it is left ambiguous at the end of season one of *Loki* as to whether He Who Remains governed the Sacred Timeline of the entire multiverse, season two seems to suggest that he did. Underlying this is the possibility that there could be multiple timelines across the multiverse that are maintained by the Sacred Timeline. And yet, after having crossed the threshold where He Who Remains does not know what will happen over time, what this entails are the possibilities of incursions across the multiverse. In *Multiverse of Madness*, we learn that incursions have the potential to destroy the fabric of reality and the multiverse as they converge on one another. (This is especially illustrated at the TVA in season two of *Loki*). In *Multiverse of Madness*, the purpose of the Illuminati was to protect the multiverse from incursions. Hence, when Dr. Strange gains access to the Darkhold instead of the Book of Vishanti, he not only opens his third eye to dark magic but becomes an ally against incursions across the multiverse in the closing scenes of *Multiverse of Madness*.

What If...? in turn presents a vision of the multiverse as observed by the Watcher, who realizes that in one universe, Ultron was successful against the Avengers and ultimately wiped out all sentient life from that universe. Upon realizing the existence of the multiverse and the existence of the Watcher between the multiverses, Ultron then penetrates beyond his universe and begins expanding his intent to destroy all life across the multiverse. In season one of *What If... ?*, it is the Watcher's efforts to bring together the Guardians of the Multiverse that ultimately defeat Ultron through Dr. Strange's spell to capture the struggle for control over the Infinity Stones between Ultron/Zola and Killmonger.

When it comes to *Quantumania*, what we find are alternate ways of imagining space within the quantum realm. Janet Pym's long survival in the quantum realm and her friendship-turned-fight against the Conqueror are revealed in *Quantumania* as the transition into Phase Five of the MCU. Though the second season of *Loki* can (and has) take(n) us in a different direction, the end of *Quantumania* teases for us the idea that the variants of Kang are set to conquer the multiverse through their ability to control time. The spatial and temporal distortions in the quantum realm are significant, as the passing of time and space in the quantum realm differs from that found in the multiverse. Hank Pym's ants develop a sophisticated civilization across thousands of generations, while the same amount of time for Hank, Scott, and the others is only several days. The quantum realm transforms how we understand reality in the MCU because it is a world unbounded by the normal conceptions of time and space we find in the multiverse. It is no surprise that the Kangs sent the Conqueror to the quantum realm in exile—he could not interfere with their plans to conquer the multiverse.

Dr. Strange: the Multiverse of Madness, *What If... ?*, and *Quantumania's* presentation of the multiverse significantly expands not only the divine hierarchy in the MCU, but also how we understand time, space, and reality across the multiverses. *What If. . . ?* expands our understanding of time and space because it implies that there is some sort of divine figure outside of time and space who watches the happenings in the multiverse. *Multiverse of Madness* expands our understanding of reality because it opens the door to an infinite number of universes where the possibilities in one universe may find their expression in other universes. Our conceptions of time and space are both transformed in *Quantumania* with the quantum realm as a world beneath all worlds. Each of these illuminates how the MCU expands how we imagine time, space, and reality through its development of the multiverse. If this section has analyzed how the MCU enchants how we imagine reality, then the following section makes a shift in understanding the post-disenchanted reality of the MCU by critically examining the deconstructive role of decolonization in the MCU.

MARVELING CRITICAL POST-DISENCHANTMENT

As a starting point in a critical analysis of post-disenchantment, we can examine the relationship between magic and science in the first three phases of the

MCU. In the confrontation between magic and science, the MCU has demonstrated a subtle tension, and yet one where the scientific worldview remains central. When Eric Selvig and Dr. Strange are confronted with magic, they cannot reconcile magic with their scientific imaginary, "so they widen their worldview to accept a nonscientific framework."[27] Lisa Stenmark offers an analysis to show that this does not decenter the scientific worldview, but rather sees science and magic as coexisting together. And yet, these are not parallel frameworks or realities: these are "never fully realized and instead, the boundaries of science are expanded in such a way as to redefine magic in terms of science."[28] Stenmark argues that in the MCU, "magic is not magic; it is a primitive form of science."[29] Stenmark continues:

> Although the concept of magic has the potential to challenge our understanding of science, and its relationship with religion, as well as the colonial ideologies that are intertwined with it, this potential is never fully realized in the MCU, largely because magic is subsumed into science—that is, instead of using the concept of magic to problematize the idea of science, the MCU just repeats the historical trick of moving the goalposts to claim magic as a *kind* of science.[30]

This means, according to Stenmark, that

> the suggestion that multiple frameworks could coexist is never realized, not because of the existence of a superior scientific framework, but because of the need to reduce all reality and experience to a single framework which, in this context, is necessarily scientific.[31]

My own arguments, drawing on the comics, show that another way of looking at science and magic in the MCU is to see them in terms of Aristotle's understanding of actuality and potentiality: magic is not only a primitive form of science but is the end of all science, even if we have not yet actualized its potential.[32] As Michael D. Nichols succinctly states, in the MCU, "magic is merely science that has not yet been understood."[33]

As a way of rethinking the relationship between science and magic in the MCU, adding into the mix the question of technology for the Wakandans allows us to see another, decolonial, side to the relationship between science, magic, and technology. Lisa Stenmark's reflection on the Afrofuturism of Wakandan technology, magic, and religion offers helpful contextualizations of the complex relationship between the (de-)colonial logic of science, technology, and magic. She states:

> Wakanda represents a reimagined past, an Africa that was never colonized, which provides an opportunity to imagine what Africa might have been, and could be still. Wakanda is a technologically advanced society, which disrupts

the Eurocentric narrative of progress in which technology is distinctly non-Western, combining elements of technology, magic, and religion.[34]

Stenmark notes that the power of Wakanda comes from the fictional imagining of an alien Vibranium. This problematically means that Wakandan Afrofuturism is not a cultural production, but rather stems from something alien to Africa.[35] And yet, Stenmark notes that

> unlike magic in the MCU, which decentered science without challenging the narrative of progress, Afrofuturism in the MCU critiques the narrative of progress, but does not decenter the primacy of a scientific and technological worldview: Wakanda is civilized *because* of its advanced technology (alien or not).[36]

Here we see a problem of decoloniality posed by imagining a world wherein Africa was not colonized. In this imaginary, Wakanda plays a central role in decentering Western globalizing power and control because of Wakanda's possession of Vibranium and the technological power this allows them. And yet, I think we have to pause and reflect on the problem of technology in ways that generate problems of decolonialism. George A. Dunn and Jason T. Eberl follow Martin Heidegger's analysis of technology to show how the question of technology is not just about the anthropological activity and the instrumental use of technology, but also about the essence of technology as an inescapable *gestalt* (enframing destiny) that drives our lives.[37] Clarifying this, Dunn and Eberl state that

> technology is not just a set of hyper-efficient means to achieve our goals, nor it is just an assembly of mechanical parts fitted together to perform some task. Most essentially, technology is a particular way of interpreting and ordering the world, in which the whole of nature presents itself to us as ... a vast storehouse of raw materials and energy waiting to be [used] by human beings.[38]

This is especially illustrated through *Wakanda Forever's* depiction of Western powers searching the world for Vibranium and trying to steal Wakandan Vibranium. While T'Challa had promised to share Wakandan resources and technology with the world, after his death, his mother, Queen Ramonda, (rightly) realized that Western powers could not be trusted to use this technology responsibly in ways that would lead to the betterment of humanity rather than the aim to create weapons of mass destruction in an attempt to wield power and control. Just as the Black Panther comics present the White Western world as power-hungry and greedy for domination and control, so also does *Wakanda Forever* present the same in Western powers' attempt to steal Vibranium for military ends and uses. Here we see that the problem of technology comes to the fore as a central problem in the MCU.

But there is also another decolonial problem linked to post-disenchantment. When Dr. Strange meets the Ancient One, Rhiannon Grant and Jo Henderson-Merrygold argue that we find a confrontation between the dominating representation of White Protestant, Christian, middle class, and that of an Eastern religious, feminine, and monastic representation. They state that "the world of the Ancient One needs translating but teases us with the prospect of confronting assumptions, although ultimately it consolidates rather than undermines those presuppositions."[39] This is particularly displayed in how the Ancient One is perceived through Western eyes toward Eastern Orientalism. Add into the mix the rescription of the Egyptian God Bast and the Hindu God Hanuman for the Wakandans, and the problem for Grant and Henderson-Merrygold is not only with orientalism, religious representation, and gender. The problem is also with the lens through which they are viewed and represented—ultimately through the lens of Western, White, American, Christianity.[40]

Furthermore, the problem of decoloniality is raised by both Stenmark and Bauman and Khan as an issue that they doubt the MCU will resolve. Stenmark is doubtful whether the transformative role of living in the tension between two worlds will be actualized in the real world, especially when that is the MCU's world of the multiverse.[41] Bauman and Khan are doubtful whether the MCU will offer multiple interpretations of the world through the "'hidden voices' within dominant modern, Western traditions, as well as the multiple worlds, histories, and voices outside of modern, Western traditions" because of the tendency to repeat neoliberal globalizing trends of colonialization.[42] And yet, how Phase Four has addressed this tension between neoliberal globalization and the tension between living in two worlds is especially illustrated in the show *Ms. Marvel*.

Ms. Marvel presents a tension of living between worlds in significant ways through the lens of a Muslim American with ancestral roots both historically rooted in the partition of India and religiously rooted in the rescriptions of the pre-Islamic (and Islamic) belief in Jinn. But what is presented in *Ms. Marvel* is also a doubling of identities. Kamala Khan is an American of Pakistani descent. And yet, Pakistan was only formed in 1947 with the partition of India. *Ms. Marvel* presents not only the complexity of what it means to be a Muslim American but also the complex identities of South Asians and their shattered history found within the partition of India. *Ms. Marvel* presents the aftereffects of the Partition of India in ways that are still felt today across India and Pakistan in the tense relationships between various religious traditions in India, particularly between Hindus and Muslims. The confusion seen at the train station during the partition is significant because it illustrates how families were uprooted from their traditional homes and separated from one another during the violence and confusion of the era. The doubling of identities in *Ms. Marvel* illustrates not only the aftereffects of the partition of India and decolonization but also the racial and religious prejudices against Muslim Americans since 9/11.[43]

In *Ms. Marvel*, the mythology is presented to us in the form of the Islamic tradition. Kamala Khan is a descendant of a Djinn, who are believed in the Islamic tradition to be spirits created out of fire and who can be good or evil. Throughout *Ms. Marvel*, we learn that these Djinn are trying to return to their own plane of existence through the use of a magical bracelet. However, it is revealed that the bracelet opens the door to another realm and that if it does, the collision between these planes of existence will destroy the world. Furthermore, in *Moon Knight*, we also see another mythology, particularly Egyptian mythology, with its representations of Taweret (the Goddess of Women and Children), who guides Spector and Grant to the Field of Reeds, and Khonshu (the Egyptian God of Time, the Moon, and Vengeance) fighting against Ammit, the Egyptian God of Divine Retribution, who has foreknowledge of whose scales will reveal whether their good or evil deeds outweigh one another. Between these gods and more, the actions of the Egyptian gods are primarily enacted through their avatars, who wield the powers of the god that they serve.

When it comes to *Wakanda Forever*, we are introduced to an alternate Mesoamerican myth with the belief in the feather-serpent god, Kukulkan. When Spanish conquistadors came across the ocean, several Mesoamericans prayed to their God, who showed them a magical herb, like that found in Wakanda, whose powers come from the fictional Vibranium. This time, the MCU plays with Mesoamerican myths and ties them into colonial history, where Namor is named as the one who is without love when he slaughters Spaniards after seeing their abuse of Mesoamerican peoples. In *Thor: Love and Thunder*, we also see the Assembly of the Gods, where we are exposed to their unworthiness in their moral ambiguity and unconcern for those who worship them. Adam Barkman and Bennet Soenen offer key reflections on the unworthiness of the gods within the MCU. Through Thor's comment on Gorr the God Butcher's statement about the unworthiness of the gods, Barkman and Soenen succinctly state:

> First and foremost, Thor is not just referring to Mjolnir in his evaluation of the gods as unworthy. They are unworthy of worship and love from the mortals who so revered them. Second, Thor is not declaring the gods unworthy because of their ontological status as gods. He is declaring them unworthy because of the ethical framework that developed from their ontological status. Their being

gods is not what makes them unworthy, but the pride and selfishness that develops from their being nearly ageless and nearly omnipotent is what makes them unworthy.[44]

The ethical nature of the gods in the MCU, then, is that they are unworthy of worship. And yet what the MCU appropriates from various mythologies across world traditions is a remarkable level of awareness of the hidden voices across the world. Moreover, we must also question whether these hidden voices are seen through the lens of Western orientalism. Arguably, while *Dr. Strange* does present seemingly subversions of Western science under the mystic arts, what we find there is rather that magic is subverted under a scientific worldview. But when we turn to these hidden religious voices found in Phase Four of the MCU, we begin to see the voices of decolonization more vividly. Whether this is done through the visibility of prejudices against Muslim Americans and the unaddressed scars of the partition of India and Pakistan in *Ms. Marvel*, or even the recovery and rescription of Egyptian and Mesoamerican mythologies in *Moon Knight* and *Wakanda Forever*, we see that the visibilities of these hidden voices are inevitably shaped by and wrestle with the lasting effects of Western colonialism.

Are they presented through Western eyes? Of course. They are films generated out of Disney—a Western phenomenon. But they also present to the West those hidden voices and mythologies that have been silenced by Western Christian colonialism. By giving greater visibility to these traditions and mythologies, what the MCU offers are imageries of re-enchantment in a world that has often been presupposed as disenchanted. Does this lead to more problems through its cultural/religious appropriation and how they can enchant the Western imagination? Yes. I think what it also presents are critical reflections on Western culpability with colonialism and its lasting effects on the global world. But underneath this is also the reality that enchantment must wrestle with the reality of colonial disenchantment and its silencing of the other for a dominant White, Western, Christian vision. To be enchanted in a post-disenchanted world means to wrestle with the contextual problems of our post-colonial world in ways that shed light on the aftereffects of colonialism in addition to the greater visibility of those religions silenced by Western history.

MARVELING THE MYTH OF ENCHANTMENT

Throughout this chapter, the focus has been to locate the role of enchantment in the MCU. It raised the question of disenchantment and whether the West has indeed been disenchanted from an enchanted worldview, whether it needs to be re-enchanted, and what that means in terms of post-disenchantment. And yet, underlying these analyses is an underdeveloped silence: the role of myth and how it is used in the MCU.

Michael D. Nichols locates the role of religious myth in the MCU "along the lines of worldwide mythic and religious narratives [which] also serves as a new iteration of commentary on ancient human concerns."[45] Nichols argues that the mediation between the sacred and the secular, God and humans, through what Ben Saunders calls the "impossible synthesis" has no easy answers, because superheroes play a role in a society wrestling with the "questions and dilemmas and issues that have perennially plagued humanity."[46] Some of these issues are of "justice, identity, and good versus evil" as well as "the problem of death"—the focus of Nichols' argument throughout his study of the MCU.[47]

As a definition of myth, Nichols states that "myths can be understood as narratives, cultures, or traditions considered sacred, dealing often with the origins of rituals, social structures, moral codes, and other timeless concerns of the human condition."[48] Furthermore, he argues that "mythic, religious, and literary traditions have always been enmeshed in webs of dialogue, borrowing and interaction, laterally between one another and diachronically with older traditions."[49] Nichols continues:

> Mythic and religious traditions throughout history have always dwelt in overlapping contexts and appropriated terms, piecing together new significations and structures from what came before. . . . The MCU has both echoed previous mythic forms . . . , but also re-envisioned these older forms into new situations, adapting ancient myths and questions for modern times and audiences.[50]

In addition, Andrew Tobolowky argues that "the difference between thinking about myth in terms of what is 'traditional' and what is 'available' is that what is traditional is a group choice. What is 'available' is what seems to an individual to *be* available."[51] He argues that even those who reinvent stories are bound in some sense to a tradition—not so much as "where we are, and when we are, but also *who* we are."[52] As the narrative construction of an available myth is shaped by the individual, so also may it become a source for both the self and canon. The available myth opens the door for not only the construction of individual beliefs but also to the constructive rescription of religious canons that must hold the tension between traditional canons and the rescriptions of canon that shape the possibilities of believing.

Furthermore, these possibilities of believing can shape how we imagine our world in unique ways that are shaped by individual religious beliefs. The individual nature of religious beliefs can be supported through the MCU because it offers "us, as viewers, a multitude of templates for how we could navigate these forms of questions and challenges in our lives and communities."[53] But the nature of individuated religion is not something that excludes the mystery of the transcendent. The MCU holds open the space for mystery in ways that may not point to God, but it does hold open the space through which we can imagine anew what it means to believe after disenchantment. Both Whitney Bauman and Imran Khan, and Jennifer Baldwin emphasize holding open to the mystery and hope in unknown spaces. Bauman and Khan emphasize that this holding open to the space for mystery allows a vibrancy of life to emerge, live, and breathe, while Baldwin holds open the space for the experience of mystery, following William James.[54]

The MCU holds open this space in ways that problematize the role of religion in a disenchanted world. To hold open the space for mystery is to hold open the space through which who we are and what we believe are constructed and constituted by what we consume. When we consume the MCU, we are exposed to subtle problems of decolonialism through both the subversion of magic into a scientific worldview and how technology shapes how we imagine our identities in inescapable ways. We are also exposed to the way the MCU imagines the divine, power, and the multiverse in ways that enchant the imagination with alternate ways of understanding the real world.

Whether this world is actually or virtually real is not the question. Rather, the question is how this world imagines enchantment in actually virtual ways—the way the MCU blurs our imagination and opens the possibilities of enchantment in a world that must struggle against its closure and the legacy of the effects of modernity. Marveling post-disenchantment must wrestle with the legacies of modernity, the effects of the West across global history, and the contextual conditions that shape the constitution and construction of both religious beliefs and individual identity in the aftermath of modernity. What myth do we believe? I think we ought to marvel at what the MCU opens up as to the myth of enchantment. The marvel of the MCU's myth of enchantment is that it holds open the space for enchantment and reimagining our world in ways that guard against naïve assumptions of re-enchantment while also holding open the need to question and doubt what enchantment looks like in a post-disenchanted world.

NOTES

1. I am thinking in particular of both Pentecostalism and African Traditional Religions here, as well as some friends I have who believe in and practice witchcraft and paganism.

2. C.f. Charles Taylor, "Modes of Secularism," in *Secularism and Its Critics*, ed. Rajeev Bhargava (Delhi: Oxford University Press, 1998), 31–53.

3. Hans Joas, *The Power of the Sacred: An Alternative to the Narrative of Disenchantment*, trans. Alex Skinner (Oxford: Oxford University Press, 2021), 110–153.

4. Joas, *The Power of the Sacred*, 114–116.

5. Joas, *The Power of the Sacred*, 113, 141.

6. C.f. Joas, *The Power of the Sacred*, 113; Jason A. Josephson-Storm, *The Myth of Disenchantment: Magic, Modernity, and the Birth of the Human Sciences* (Chicago, IL: The University of Chicago Press, 2017).

7. Joas, *The Power of the Sacred*, 119.

8. C.f. Charles Taylor, *Modern Social Imaginaries* (Durham: Duke University Press, 2004); Charles Taylor, *Dilemmas and Connections* (Cambridge, MA: Harvard University Press, 2011).

9. C.f. Eduardo Mendieta and Jonathan VanAntwerpen, eds., *The Power of Religion in the Public Sphere* (New York: Columbia University Press, 2011). I not only think William E. Connolly's notion of bicameral faith helps us learn to live in the agonistic tension with difference, but I also think Raimon Panikkar's notion of "Christianness" is a helpful framework for learning how to live as a Christian in a pluralistic world without absolutizing our faith and enforcing it over others. C.f. Raimon Panikkar, "Trisangam: The Jordan, The Tiber, and the Ganges: The Three Kairological Moments of Christic Self-Consciousness," in *Christianity: A Christophany*, Opera Omnia III.2 (Maryknoll: Orbis Books, 2015), 3–26; William E. Connolly, *Pluralism* (Durham, NC and London: Duke University Press, 2005), 22, 27, 31.

10. Marika Rose, "Machines of Loving Grace: Angels, Cyborgs, and Postsecular Labor," *Journal for Cultural and Religious Theory* 16, no. 2 (2017): 240–259.

11. Paul Cloke, Christopher Baker, Callum Sutherland, and Andrew Williams, *Geographies of Postsecularity: Re-envisioning Politics, Subjectivity, and Ethics* (London and New York: Routledge, 2019), 69.

12. Cloke, et al., *Geographies of Postsecularity*, 69.

13. Rose, "Machines of Loving Grace," 243; opt. cit. in Cloke, et al., *Geographies of Postsecularity*, 69.

14. C.f. Akeel Bilgrami, "Might There Be Secular Enchantment?" in *The Philosophy of Reenchantment*, ed. Michiel Meijer and Herbert De Vriese (London and New York: Routledge, 2021), 54–77; Akeel Bilgrami, "Secularism: Its Content and Context," in *Secularism, Identity, and Enchantment*, ed. Akeel Bilgrami (Cambridge, MA: Harvard University Press, 2014), 3–57.

15. Cloke, et al., *Geographies of Postsecularity*, 18.

16. Willie James Jennings, *After Whiteness: An Education in Belonging* (Grand Rapids, MI: William B. Eerdmans, 2020).

17. C.f. Austin M. Freeman, "Gods Upon Gods: Hierarchies of Divinity in the Marvel Universe," in *Theology and the Marvel Universe*, ed. Gregory Stevenson (Lanham MD: Rowman and Littlefield, 2020), 157–172.

18. Freeman, "Gods Upon Gods," 158.

19. Freeman, "Gods Upon Gods," 158.

20. Freeman, "Gods Upon Gods," 161.

21. Freeman, "Gods Upon Gods," 162–163.

22. An Absolute point is a rule across all multiverses as something that cannot happen. For Dr. Strange, this is to be with Dr. Christine Palmer.

23. This is mere speculation at the time of this writing, as *Secret Invasions* has just premiered the day of writing this, and *Kang Dynasty* and *Secret Wars* are several years down the line.

24. By the time of finalizing this chapter (January 2024), Jonathan Majors has been fired from Disney and they have begun planning the pivot to Dr. Doom. And yet, it is too early to tell how the MCU will make this transition.

25. For the Utilitarianism of Thanos, C.f. Tim Posada, "The Gospel According to Thanos: Violence, Utopia, and the Case for a Material Theology," in *Theology and the Marvel Universe*, ed. Gregory Stevenson (Lanham, MD: Rowman and Littlefield, 2020), 71–83.

26. "Previously On," Streaming, *WandaVision* (Burbank, CA: Disney+, February 26, 2021).

27. Lisa Stenmark, "Science and the Marvel Cinematic Universe: Deconstructing the Boundary Between Science, Technology, and Religion," in *Marveling Religion: Critical Discourses, Religion, and the Marvel Cinematic Universe*, ed. Jennifer Baldwin and Daniel White Hodge (Lanham, MD: Lexington Books, 2022), 143–158, 151.

28. Stenmark, "Science and the Marvel Cinematic Universe," 151–152.

29. Stenmark, "Science and the Marvel Cinematic Universe," 152.

30. Stenmark, "Science and the Marvel Cinematic Universe," 152.

31. Stenmark, "Science and the Marvel Cinematic Universe," 152.

32. Andrew D. Thrasher, "Modern Re-enchantment and Dr. Strange: Pentecostal Analogies, the Spirit of the Multiverse, and the Play on Time and Eternity," in *Theology and the Marvel Universe*, ed. Gregory Stevenson (Lanham, MD: Rowman and Littlefield, 2020), 221–233.

33. Michael D. Nichols, *Religion and Myth in the Marvel Cinematic Universe* (Jefferson, NC: McFarland, 2021), 22.

34. Stenmark, "Science and the Marvel Cinematic Universe," 153.

35. Stenmark, "Science and the Marvel Cinematic Universe," 153.

36. Stenmark, "Science and the Marvel Cinematic Universe," 153.

37. George A. Dunn and Jason T. Eberl, "'I See a Suit of Armor Around the World': Tony Stark's Techno-Idolatry and Self-Sacrificial Love," in *Marveling Religion: Critical Discourses, Religion, and the Marvel Cinematic Universe*, ed. Jennifer Baldwin and Daniel White Hodge (Lanham, MD: Lexington Books, 2022), 3–18, 8–9.

38. Dunn and Eberl, "'I See a Suit of Armor Around the World'," 10.

39. Rhiannon Grant and Jo Henderson-Merrygold, "Old Gods in New Films: History, Culture, and Religion in *Black Panther*, *Doctor Strange*, and *Thor: Ragnarök*," in *Marveling Religion: Critical Discourses, Religion, and the Marvel Cinematic Universe*, ed. Jennifer Baldwin and Daniel White Hodge (Lanham, MD: Lexington Books, 2022), 67–85, 74.

40. Grant and Henderson-Merrygold, "Old Gods in New Films," 80.

41. Stenmark, "Science and the Marvel Cinematic Universe," 154–155.

42. Whitney Bauman and Imran Khan, "Religion, Science, and the Marvel Universe: Reimagining Human-Earth Relations," in *Marveling Religion: Critical Discourses, Religion, and the Marvel Cinematic Universe*, ed. Jennifer Baldwin and Daniel White Hodge (Lanham, MD: Lexington Books, 2022), 159–177, 160.

43. C.f. John McDowell's chapter in Marveling Religion on the logic of terrorism across the MCU since 9/11: John C. McDowell, "Marveling at Captain Danvers, Or, What is So Super About Our Heroes?: Contesting the Identity Politics of Self-Other," in *Marveling Religion: Critical Discourses, Religion, and the Marvel Cinematic Universe*, ed. Jennifer Baldwin and Daniel White Hodge (Lanham, MD: Lexington Books, 2022), 197–215.

44. Adam Barkman and Bennet Soenen, "The Worthiness of Thor," in *Marveling Religion: Critical Discourses, Religion, and the Marvel Cinematic Universe*, ed. Jennifer Baldwin and Daniel White Hodge (Lanham, MD: Lexington Books, 2022), 87–100, 96.

45. Nichols, *Religion and Myth in the Marvel Cinematic Universe*, 2.

46. Nichols, *Religion and Myth in the Marvel Cinematic Universe*, 13–14.

47. Nichols, *Religion and Myth in the Marvel Cinematic Universe*, 14.

48. Nichols, *Religion and Myth in the Marvel Cinematic Universe*, 8.

49. Nichols, *Religion and Myth in the Marvel Cinematic Universe*, 161.

50. Nichols, *Religion and Myth in the Marvel Cinematic Universe*, 161.

51. Andrew Tobolowsky, "The Thor Movies and the 'Available' Myth: Mythic Reinvention in Marvel Movies," in *Theology and the Marvel Universe*, ed. Gregory Stevenson (Lanham, MD: Rowman and Littlefield, 2020), 173–186, 180.

52. Tobolowsky, "The Thor Movies and the 'Available' Myth," 180.

53. Daniel White Hodge and Jennifer Baldwin, "Preface: Marveling Religion: Visual Culture as a Common Tongue," in *Marveling Religion: Critical Discourses, Religion, and the Marvel Cinematic Universe*, ed. Jennifer Baldwin and Daniel White Hodge (Lanham, MD: Lexington Books, 2022), vii–xviii, xiii.

54. Jennifer Baldwin, "'Open Your Eye': Psychedelics, Spirituality, and Trauma Resolution," in *Marveling Religion: Critical Discourses, Religion, and the Marvel Cinematic Universe*, ed. Jennifer Baldwin and Daniel White Hodge (Lanham, MD: Lexington Books, 2022), 179–194, 188; Bauman and Khan, "Religion, Science, and the Marvel Universe," 170.

Chapter 4

Deconstructing Inter-Religious Resourcement in *The Lion King*

The Lion King is one of the most beloved films within the world of Walt Disney. This film is rich with religious symbolism and offers important insights into the problem of whether Christians ought to engage with religious pluralism. Often, Christians have an aversion to religious pluralism because pluralism tends to say that all religions are equally salvific. And yet, what happens when both Christian and pluralistic messages are presented beside one another in the same story? This is explored throughout this chapter by problematizing the popular idea of religious pluralism and giving it more complexity. This chapter argues that *The Lion King* presents to Christians a moral problem through a deconstruction of its implicit inter-religious resourcement of a multiplicity of religious ideas from Christian and non-Christian traditions.

How do Christians reconcile the reality that *The Lion King* is both an example of inter-religious resourcement and of Christian inclusivism? *The Lion King* presents both a pluralistic message that resources multiple religious traditions *and* a Christian message that includes these traditions with a capacious sense of the fullness of Christian truth as it can be found in other religious traditions. This creates a moral problem for Christians: Ought Christians to read *The Lion King* as presenting an inclusive Christian message when it is also presenting a resourcement of inter-religious ideas found in non-Christian religions? Thus, this chapter deconstructs the problem as something the Christian must wrestle with and defers the problem as something that must be held together in tension for the Christian: Christians can read *The Lion King* as presenting both a Christian and pluralistic message. The problem that remains is whether the Christian ought to engage with it when it does both.

This chapter argues that *The Lion King* can be read religiously through an analysis of the concept of righteousness throughout the story of *The Lion King*. *The Lion King* is a work of inter-religious resourcement that draws on Asian and African ways of viewing the world, along with Abrahamic religious focuses—especially messianism. But it is also a work that focuses not on contrasting absolute truth claims between religions, but rather on how it presents *both* a pluralistic resourcement of belief that re-envisions the concept of righteousness through the synthesis of a plurality of religious ideas *and* a Christian capaciousness or fullness to include inter-religious resourcements of the idea of righteousness into Christianity's ability to include truths from other religious traditions.

By drawing upon various religious sources, this chapter argues that *The Lion King* reflects a pluralistic syncretism of the concept of righteousness. It also articulates how the film can be read as propagating a Christian capaciousness to include truths from other religious traditions. However, this chapter concludes by articulating a moral dilemma of how we imagine religion in a post-Christian context. By questioning what we deem as *truth* in a contested post-Christian and pluralistic society and culture, this chapter argues that *The Lion King* opens Christianity to the problem of pluralism and deconstructs it in ways that question how Christianity remains relevant in a post-Christian, pluralistic context.

Structurally, this chapter is organized as a chiasm. The center of the chapter is where the religious messages of *The Lion King* are recited. Its recitations of inter-religious resourcement offers an analysis of righteousness that moves through multiple religious ideas found in the narrative and plot of *The Lion King*. Working out from the center, the chapter offers parallel analyses of the two ways of reading *The Lion King*—as a Christian capaciousness and as a pluralistic simulation of truth. Bookending the chapter are the parallels of the introduction and conclusion which lay out for Christians the moral problem that remains when we deconstruct an inter-religious reading of *The Lion King*.

TWO WAYS OF READING *THE LION KING*

This chapter argues that *The Lion King* can evoke two ways of reading how it imagines truth through its inter-religious resourcement. One way of reading *The Lion King* may be through a pluralistic resourcement and synthesis of religious truths, and the other, as Christian capaciousness or fullness to include non-Christian religious truths. By reading *The Lion King* in two ways, this chapter argues that it problematizes truth through an advocation for, and resourcement of, both pluralistic and Christian messages.

The first way of reading *The Lion King* is that it creates such a pluralistic *simulacrum*—an imagined reality that both reflects and blurs the lines between the real and the imagined—that we come to see as representative of our world.[1] Jean Baudrillard's conception of the simulacra implies four steps as we move from theological to nihilistic perspectives on the truth of reality. If the first step invokes the sacramentality of reality (its symbolic invocations of a religious reality), the second step is a turn that distorts the representation of the image of truth in reality. The third step involves the appearance of truth without substance, which leads to the fourth stage: the disappearance of reference to truth and actual reality in the simulation of a virtual reality. These simulations distort what we deem as true, real, and believable, and in *The Lion King*, they present a virtual reality that blurs the lines between religious traditions and their conceptions of truth and reality.

In *The Lion King*, this pluralistic simulation of a virtual reality displays an inter-religious resourcement—the practice of focusing not on the *equality* of religions, but rather by appealing to the discipline of inter-religious resourcement where inter-religious ideas and expressions of faith are tapped into to portray a pluralistic image of reality. *The Lion King* envisions a world, not in which all religions are equal, but rather, in which various religious teachings coalesce to offer ways of shaping our imagination and explaining our world. Inter-religious resourcement in *The Lion King* simulates how we may imagine truth and reality and what we may imagine as believable through its virtual representation and distortion of religious conceptions of truth and reality. But to read *The Lion King* as distorting religious conceptions of truth in its attempt to present a pluralistic vision of reality is not the only way of reading it. We can also read it sacramentally as invoking a Christian capaciousness or fullness of truth.

The second way of reading *The Lion King* is to read it as evoking the notion of Christian fullness or capacity. Christian capaciousness opens *The Lion King* to an inclusive Christian reading of how religious traditions culminate through *The Lion King* in the Christian notions of messianism, righteousness, and restoration. Christian capaciousness can refer to the fullness of truth, where religious ideas that are resourced in *The Lion King* point to Christian theological themes and truths. That is, the fullness of truth is the idea that inter-religious resourcement accepts truths from other traditions but sees these truths as pointing to a Christian inclusivism that encompasses, draws in, and redeems the truths of other traditions through the Christian narrative. This is done not to draw out the incommensurability between religious traditions, but to show how non-Christian religious truths point to Christian conceptions of truth.

Between these two ways of reading *The Lion King*—as Christian capaciousness or as a pluralistic simulation—what we find are contested ways of reading religion in popular culture. In one sense, it is to read *The Lion King* as provoking how Christian conceptions of truth may include truths of other traditions. This involves an appreciation of other religious traditions' conceptions of truth and reality through the lens of Christian ideas of truth and reality. But when Christians read *The Lion King* inter-religiously, they may see it not as invoking Christian themes but rather as simulating a virtual conception of truth that distorts Christian conceptions of truth. Whichever way we read it, the point is to realize that Christian capaciousness and pluralistic simulations of truth and reality are two sides of the same coin. It is not so simple that Christians can either read *The Lion King* redemptively or that they can simply condemn it. I think Christians must read it from both perspectives because it helps them to understand how truth may be imagined and contested in a post-Christian culture.

AN INTER-RELIGIOUS RESOURCEMENT OF RIGHTEOUSNESS

If *The Lion King* envisions an inter-religious resourcement of the concept of righteousness, it does so by drawing upon multiple religious ideas found throughout world religions. From a medieval view of the cosmos, the priestly role of Rafiki offers a traditional medieval vision of an inherent social and moral order to the cosmos, where society is imagined as a cohesive whole, and hierarchically ordered by a religious world. From the Daoist perspective, *The Lion King* envisions righteousness as a cosmonomic ecological vision—where harmony with nature governs social, cosmic, and moral orders. Furthermore, the Hindu notions of *ṛta*, *dharma*, and *adharma* offer an analogy with *The Lion King* of a cosmic notion of righteousness that morally orders a social hierarchy and the duties of Kingship. Within Jewish and Christian traditions, *The Lion King* analogously reimagines the messianic notions of righteousness and renewal in Israel's exile and the *metanoia* of the Christian disciple as highlighted in the character and life of Simba. The following sections analyze each of these notions, drawing out how *The Lion King* inter-religiously resources and imagines the concept of "righteousness."

Medieval Analogies in *The Lion King*

At the beginning of *The Lion King*, Rafiki is called to Pride Rock to present to the subjects of the Kingdom the promised Son of King Mufasa. Simba is marked by Rafiki on the forehead and lifted high above Pride Rock, publicly presenting Mufasa's righteous successor to the subjects of the Pride Lands. Symbolically representing a public, ritual baptism and the presentation to the people of the righteous successor of Mufasa, Simba is acknowledged as the rightful heir of Pride Rock. Rafiki plays the priestly role of an intermediary between the king and the people, which symbolically reflects the role the medieval priest played in mediating the people to God and God to the people. Underlying this medieval mediation of the church is the reality of the church's spiritual power in conjunction with its ability to wield and influence temporal power. This medieval mediation through the church is analogously imitated within Rafiki's presentation of Simba as the representative of order and righteousness in the Pride Lands.

Underlying this typology are the pre-modern notions of saeculum and heteronomy. Heteronomy entails the hierarchical order of society represented symbolically by the king and mediated to the people through the priestly role of church clergy. In the Middle Ages, the priest and church mediated the spiritual reality to the saeculum—the temporal world of ordinary life.[2] The king symbolically represented a vision of society ordered through hierarchy. This medieval social imaginary was marked by the concept of a great chain of being, where all aspects of society are divinely ordered by the moral, cosmic, political, and social vision of reality.[3] Kingship, as mandated by divine rule and symbolically mediated by the church, represented an inherent divine order to the social, moral, and cosmic chain of being reflected in the hierarchical structures of society. Kings in the Middle Ages were symbolic representatives of a cosmic, social, and moral imaginary displayed through a heteronomic hierarchy that symbolically presents the order of the saeculum to God.[4]

Furthermore, in the fourteenth century, the idea developed of an ordered cosmos where the individual microcosmically reflected the whole macrocosmic order of creation. Within this framework, individuals symbolically reflected within themselves and in society a macrocosmic order that they participated in, sustaining and embedding their identity within a divinely ordered cosmic, social, political, and moral hierarchy. But instead of developing this theme in merely Christian terms, this chapter juxtaposes this medieval idea of divine hierarchy and a medieval social imaginary in *The Lion King* with natural and primordial religious ideas found in Asian and African religions.

The Circle of Life: African, Chinese, and Hindu Perspectives

The Lion King presents a non-Western religious resourcement of the nature of righteousness through its emphasis on time, kingship, and ecology. It draws out the African emphasis on the past, Chinese perspectives on nature, and the Hindu notions of natural cosmic order and its opposite disorder through notions of *ṛta*, *dharma*, and *adharma*. The following analyzes each of these notions as they are found within *The Lion King*.

At the beginning of the film, Simba is instructed about the natural, cyclical order of the cosmos, the emphasis on the past, and the presence of the ancestors.[5] The African emphasis on the past is characterized by Raimon Panikkar as a pre-historical religious consciousness.[6] For Panikkar, this pre-historical consciousness is past-oriented, where the past is perfection and is sought to be emulated in the present time.[7] In African traditions, the past is remembered in such a way that its presence is found in an experience of "now-ness" that draws attention to the idea that memory of the past becomes a storehouse of past narration that is embodied and remembered in present experience.[8] Mufasa's heavenly call for Simba to remember his past highlights the primal continuity not only of the past in the present but also of the remembrance of the ancestors in the present experience.[9] Gerard Hall draws out the cosmocentric implications of a pre-historical religious consciousness (alternatively called the non-historical consciousness.[10] Hall states:

> To live is to be in communion with nature in a hierarchical universe prior to the separation of gods, mortals, and nature; memory of the past through knowledge of tradition and veneration of the ancestors is sacred; harmony is the supreme principle.[11]

As Mufasa instructs Simba about the cosmocentric balance between all creatures and nature, at the heart of this cyclical order is the notion of balance and harmony. Embodying the African respect for the spiritual nature of the natural world with a Chinese emphasis on cosmic, natural harmony—a cosmonomy—Simba learns that there is a natural balance to the cosmos. The Daoist idea of cosmonomy entails not only harmony within the natural world, but also harmony between nature and the individual, within the individual, and in an individual's social relations. Within the Daoist notion of cosmonomy, it is believed that morality is both intrinsic to the way of the cosmos and implies a normative way in which individuals are to act according to the Dao of nature. Within a Daoist vision of a normative framework of a moral cosmos, individuals are to live according to nature and are to be responsible agents concerning the environment.[12] Within the fourfold conception of the inter-relationships between and within nature, society, and individuals, moral harmony in the cosmos is maintained through *The Lion King's* conception of the circle of life.

In the circle of life, life ends in death, and death gives life: just as the lion eats the antelope, all animals die and provide the nutrients for the grass to grow, thus furthering the natural cycle of the cosmos.[13] The natural reality of life is not only that it ends in death but also that death becomes a means for life in the nourishment of the plants and animals on the earth. The Daoist idea of cosmonomy governs the circle of life—there is a cosmic law of balance and harmony to be maintained to support and sustain life. With the extremes of natural deficiency and useless death under Scar's heinous rule, life cannot be sustained in the circle of life.

Not only is this cyclical order cosmonomic, but it is also intrinsically and morally constituted. The Pride Lands under Mufasa not only represent the Chinese notion of a moral cosmonomy of balance and harmony, but also the Hindu ideas of *ṛta*, *dharma*, and *adharma*. Hindu traditions believe that the cosmos is intrinsically divine and inherently ordered by a moral law that governs not only the cosmic natural order (the Hindu notion of *ṛta*), but also implies an inherent moral order of law, duty, and righteousness that undergirds and sustains the cosmic, divine, and social worlds. This is the Hindu understanding of *dharma*. In Hinduism, *dharma* is a polysemic word and can signify law, righteousness, duty, order, and so on, and has a connotation of an inherent or intrinsic morality governing, maintaining, and sustaining the social, moral, and natural world.[14]

The classical Hindu notion of *dharma* includes the meaning implied by the Vedic Hindu idea of *ṛta*—an inherent cosmic order that governs the movements of the stars, sun, moon, day, and night through the maintaining, sustaining performance of sacrifice.[15] The Hindu notions of *dharma* and *ṛta* imply that there is an inherent *moral* order to the cosmos and society. But the opposite of *dharma* is *adharma*—moral disorder and cosmic chaos. When the moral, righteous order of the Pride Lands is disrupted by murder, violence, and ecological abuse, not only does tyranny reign under the *adharma* of Scar and the hyenas, but the Pride Lands fall into a stark, deathly desolation where neither *dharma* is upheld nor the circle of life maintained or sustained. But this is not the end!

Restoration of the Righteous King and the Renewal of the Circle of Life

Before Simba can rise to reign, tragedy befalls him and his father, King Mufasa. Mufasa's younger brother Scar deviously plans a revolt and premeditates the murder of the rightful king and his successor, Simba. Mufasa is tragically betrayed and killed, and Simba is naively convinced of his sinless guilt in his [false] role in killing his father. Scar's heinous yet incompetent henchmen then fail to kill Simba, and Simba enters his exile from the Pride Lands. With no hope and despair over life itself, Simba is picked up by Timon and Pumbaa and is taught to live by the motto of Hakuna Matata. This singsong lifestyle is oddly representative of forgetting and burying the past, living as if nothing is wrong, and denying one's nature to live in an idealized utopia of peace and harmony.

Before all of this, Simba reflects a certain childish arrogance in the idea that he will one day be king. Simba's excitement urges him into rash decisions to travel to the elephant graveyard beyond the reign and rule of the king, which results in his rescue and instruction by his father Mufasa on what it means to be king. Within these lessons, Simba is reminded of the love and mercy of his father, just as he is reprimanded by him. Truly, to be king is not just to be brave, but also to be just and merciful—to be king is to be an agent of restoration.[16] When Simba enters his exile, we find resonances between Simba and the Jewish people during the Babylonian Exile.

The Jewish Babylonian Exile not only broke the Jews but called them to reinterpret their identity. The Babylonian Exile transformed the identity of the Jewish people in such a way that their previous identity as God's chosen people would mean something new. Before the exile, to be God's chosen people meant that they would be protected and that God would fight for Israel. With the exile and after, Israel became a people who understood themselves as the suffering servant of God—suffering became the calling card of righteousness, and the Jewish people saw themselves as righteous precisely through the formative powers of their suffering and oppression because of their chosenness as the people YHWH entered into a covenantal relationship with.

Likewise, suffering is essential to the character formation of a mature Christian. Jesus's beatitudes are a lesson not of the transactional nature of God's blessing to his people, but rather of the character formation of a believer who suffers for righteousness' sake while holding in tension the fallenness of this world with the hope for its restoration. Jonathan Pennington argues that the beatitudes are focused on "true human flourishing [as] found in the midst of (and even in a mysterious way because of) persecution and suffering," because suffering produces the virtuous character of a disciple.[17] The orientation of righteousness in the Gospel of Matthew is transformative of the believer into a particular character that hopes in the restoration to come while yet cultivating a character of righteousness precisely through maintaining one's faith, trust, dependence, and obedience to the law of grace through faith and the promise of restoration through Christ.[18]

The story of Simba's exile is analogous to the restoration and transformative foci of both the Jewish Babylonian Exile and the suffering of a Christian for righteousness' sake. However, while Simba's exile humbled and transformed him, it did so through the denial and forgetting of his representative role as rightful king. He denies and buries his guilt in a false identity, with no cares and no worries, allowing himself to try to live freely and unchained from his past. When Simba adopts Hakuna Matata as his way of life, he denies his lion-ness, his past, and his rightful place as king and representative of a divine order in the Pride Lands. Here, the Hindu notion of *dharma* as the responsibility to maintain moral, social, and cosmic harmony by doing the social duties one was born to do takes a central role in Simba's (un)righteousness. Simba's exile not only analogously reflects Jewish and Christian notions of identity transformation and restoration through suffering, but also non-Western notions of his social and moral duties that he is born to do as the rightful king. Not only must Simba take his rightful throne, but his actions must also represent and reflect the righteousness of his position as king within a heteronomic social and cosmic hierarchy. When Nala challenges Simba to return to Pride Rock, and when Simba is confronted by the remembrance of his past and the starry ghost of his father, he sets out to return and finds the Pride Lands in desolation.

When Simba and Nala return to the Pride Lands, Simba sees the devastation and *adharma* inflicted upon the land by Scar's unrighteous rule and Simba's failure to uphold his *dharma* as the rightful King of Pride Rock. Taking it upon himself to fulfill his *dharma* and restore righteous rulership in the Pride Lands, Simba challenges Scar and the hyenas in a clashing, violent battle upon Pride Rock. Through fire and storm, Simba and Scar battle, and at last Simba emerges victorious. When Simba roars at the head of Pride Rock as the restored righteous king, not only is the waste of *adharma* and fallen cosmonomy washed away by the storm, but the balance of righteous rule is restored, and the Pride Lands are renewed with the circle of life.

In the Christian tradition, building on the Old Testament and Second Temple Jewish hope for the restoration of the Kingdom of God and Israel, there is the hope and expectation for a messiah who will restore God's Kingdom on earth. Underlying the Jewish and early Christian emphasis on the Kingdom of God is the expectation for the restoration of creation and the Kingdom through the coming king. This king will rule over his Kingdom and restore Israel to its righteous place among the nations. But this restoration, while mediated through the Messianic King, will not end with the mere restoration of Israel and humanity, but also the renewal of creation.[19] The Christian tradition expects the second coming of Christ when he will fully consummate the Kingdom of God on earth and renew the cosmos. Within this framework, the notions of restoration and renewal entail the spiritual transformation of created, material existence. In the renewal and restoration of the cosmos with the coming of the righteous king, Simba reflects the righteous, messianic king who restores creation and rules the Kingdom in righteousness.

CAPACIOUSNESS AND SIMULATION RECONSIDERED

The account above demonstrates how *The Lion King* analyzes, through an inter-religious resourcement, the concept of righteousness. In doing so, it offers important interpretative understandings of what we can imagine as "truth" in our contemporary world. The pluralistic and Christian imaginary displayed in the film's inter-religious resourcement shows us something of how Disney envisions our world. Exclusive questions of religious truth remain unasked. Rather, the film seeks to envision a world that not merely tolerates the pluralism of truth within its synthesis of religious ideas but also simulates a pluralistic message in the creation of an image that ideally becomes our reality—or rather, a pluralistic simulacrum of truth and reality that not only distorts and makes irrelevant religious difference, but one in which they all coalesce in a religious imagination that defers whether religious difference even matters.[20]

This pluralistic simulation of reality includes an ability to distort Christian views of truth. The virtual reality implied in *The Lion King* invokes religious truths from many religious traditions. So, Christians may wonder, why should we watch the film if it is referring to non-Christian views of truth and reality? Does it not distort the so-called "purity" of Christian truth as found in the gospel of Jesus Christ? Why would we need to wrestle with non-Christian views of truth if all they do is distort the gospel message? The analysis of this chapter subtlety deconstructs the Christian message of an "us versus them" mentality where Christian Truth is seen as the only Truth over against the falsity of non-Christian religions. Rather, this chapter presents not only how *The Lion King* simulates religious truths and realities but also suggests how non-Christian religious ideas and truths can be read alongside Christian theological themes and truths.

The Lion King envisions a Christian inclusive capaciousness and fullness of truth that can include non-Christian views of truth. Through inter-religious resourcement, the film can open us to a Christian capaciousness to include and encompass several religious conceptions of truth and reality that find their end and goal in Christian imagery. This Christian imagery includes the truths of participating in and cultivating creation and of inherent righteousness and order to reality and nature that culminates in righteous kingship. By reading *The Lion King* through the lens of Christian capaciousness to include and redeem the truths of non-Christian traditions, what we find is a potential reversal of the pluralistic simulation of a virtual reality that points back to a capacious Christian representation and sacramentality of truth. If inter-religious resourcement invokes a pluralistic simulacrum that invokes non-Christian religious truths that distort Christian views of truth, it may also invoke the ability to re-read Christian themes and truths *in* non-Christian ideas via the Christian capacity to include and re-narrate truths of non-Christian traditions *through* the Christian lens of redemption and restoration.

THE DEFERRAL AND DECONSTRUCTION OF A MORAL DILEMMA

The questions of how we ought to imagine our world, and of how we actually conceive our world to be, are central questions of moral theology. Within the realms of popular culture, how we imagine our world is always contested by various contending creations and simulations of reality. The simulacra we imagine and believe is indeed pluralistic, whether we see it or not. The world of popular culture vies for our attention. Our interests and tastes reflect not only the appeal of consumerism in a market economy but, even more subtly, the consumerism of a spiritual marketplace.[21]

The possibility of the re-enchantment of religious belief is not only about religious resourcement—tapping into religion or religious ideas as alternate ways of imagining and conceiving our world. It is equally about what vision we want and whether the simulacra it creates is *moving* and *makes sense*. *The Lion King* highlights an apt example of the consumerism of our spiritual marketplace. Its vision of a pluralistic imaginary by re-enchanting our world with African, Chinese, Hindu, and Abrahamic forms of righteousness shows us not only that this spiritual marketplace syncretizes and synthesizes religious ideas into an imaginary world, but also that it reflects a deep desire for the enchantment of a grand order in touch with contemporary sensibilities of religious pluralism and re-enchantment.

But when we use "re-enchantment" we must make a distinction between what we mean. If we mean the renewed possibilities of belief, then clearly *The Lion King* is re-enchanting. But if we are asking whether Christendom should or can return after the processes of modernity, we must answer no. Charles Taylor and his commentators are adamant not only that this *should* not happen but that it *cannot* happen.[22] Taylor's account in *A Secular Age* and Hans Joas's accounts demonstrate how the complexity of historical processes in Western history since the fifteenth century will not allow a mere return to Christendom.[23] Furthermore, Raimon Panikkar argues that three types of Christian perspectives are correlated to three rivers, three different moments in the history of Christianity, and three Christian viewpoints of truth.[24] If Christendom is correlated with the Tiber River and Rome, it implies the inclusiveness of the Roman Church as it spread across the Western world into the Middle Ages. If Christianity is correlated with the Jordan River and its Jewish roots, it implies the exclusivity of its God and the holiness of the Christian community. However, Panikkar advocates for "Christianness" as correlated with the Ganges River and the lived faith of Christian believers in a pluralistic world. Between these accounts, the future of Christianity must grapple with its position in a pluralistic world where its faith is contested and must be lived in tension with a world no longer dominated by the Christian worldview.

Moreover, the question of how we imagine religion in a secular society remains a central question of contemporary contexts.[25] Disney's portrayal of a pluralistic imaginary shows us not only the possibility of re-imagining righteousness via inter-religious resourcement but also that the simulacra it creates through its simulation of a virtual world do not merely tolerate religion but rather subtly and imaginatively synthesize religious ideas. *The Lion King's* vision of inter-religious resourcement and a pluralistic imaginary imagines our world in ways that implicitly shape what we may believe in ways that may be against Christianity. Moreover, it transforms contemporary sensibilities on the relationship between religion and secular society. If Christianity is to survive, it must not only prove itself and its religious ideas as cohesive, sufficient, and relevant to contemporary society, but it must do so in ways that move us to imagine an alternative that will inevitably challenge the contemporary world's emphasis on relativism, pluralism, and the polysemic identities we adopt.

Christianity must also navigate the consumerism of the contemporary world not only in terms of appropriation or rejection of a pluralistic culture, but also in terms of truth in a spiritual marketplace marked by religious preference, consumerism, and imagination. *The Lion King* displays how the contemporary religious imagination implies a pluralistic message that utilizes inter-religious resourcement to articulate an alternative to the Christian message. But *The Lion King* also invokes an underlying Christian capaciousness to include compatible truths of non-Christian traditions through the narrative of the story. The question remaining is not whether this imaginary is believable—it is already implicitly so—but rather whether it is *true*. But the judgment of its commendation or condemnation is not as simple as adamant rejection or full-scale appropriation.[26] The moral judgments concerning how we imagine our world are also grounded in our aesthetic appreciation of what *moves* us in the virtual presentation, resourcement, and rescription of belief and reality.

The nuance in our religious imagination must not only be grounded within a religious perspective (and the more traditional that perspective is, the more challenging that perspective becomes to appropriating a pluralistic imaginary). It must also be grounded in its believability and its ability to imagine our world in alternative ways that mark it as *better*. For it to be better means it must challenge and imagine anew how we live in the world. By being grounded within a religious perspective, Christians must discern the moral dilemma of the appropriation of a pluralistic imaginary and must be able to imagine alternate ways of living in contemporary society. By doing so, Christians can not only begin to nuance and imagine in new ways how they can understand their society and culture based on their religious perspective, but they may also begin to come to grips with the moral dynamics of truth in non-Christian religious representations found in popular culture. Here they must sit between and learn to listen graciously to the contestation between Christian capaciousness and pluralistic simulations of how truth and reality can be imagined in a post-Christian culture and society.

NOTES

1. C.f. Jean Baudrillard, *Simulations*, trans. Paul Foss, Paul Patton, and Philip Beitchman (USA: Semiotext[e], 1983), 11–12; Graham Ward, *Cities of God* (London and New York: Routledge, 2000), 60–62; Steven Shakespeare, *Radical Orthodoxy: A Critical Introduction* (London: SPCK, 2007), 135–136.

2. José Casanova, *Public Religions in the Modern World* (Chicago: The University of Chicago Press, 1994), 13–16.

3. Taylor, *Modern Social Imaginaries*, 49–68; Charles Taylor, *A Secular Age* (Cambridge, MA: The Belknap Press of Harvard University Press, 2007), 146–158; Arthur Lovejoy, *The Great Chain of Being: A Study in the History of an Idea* (Cambridge, MA: Harvard University Press, 1961).

4. Ernst Kantorowicz, *The King's Two Bodies* (Princeton, NJ: Princeton University Press, 1957).

5. John S. Mbiti, *African Religions and Philosophy* (Garden City, NY: Anchor Books, 1970), 19–36.

6. Raimon Panikkar, *The Cosmotheandric Experience: Emerging Religious Consciousness*, ed. Scott Eastham (Maryknoll: Orbis Books, 1993).

7. Francis X. D'Sa, "Time, History, and Christophany," in *Raimon Panikkar: A Companion to His Life and Thought*, ed. Peter Phan and Young-Chan Ro (Cambridge: James Clarke and Co., 2018), 171–193, 181; Panikkar, *The Cosmotheandric Experience*, 80.

8. Mbiti, *African Religions and Philosophy*, 28–29.

9. *The Lion King*, DVD (Walt Disney Pictures, 1994), 24:50ff.

10. Panikkar, *The Cosmotheandric Experience*, 93–99.

11. Gerard Hall, "Anthropology: Being Human," in *Raimon Panikkar: A Companion to His Life and Thought*, ed. Peter Phan and Young-Chan Ro (Cambridge: James Clarke and Co., 2018), 194–216, 209.

12. Livia Kohn, *Cosmos and Community* (Cambridge: Three Pines Press, 2004), 13.

13. *The Lion King*, 9:40ff.

14. Joseph Prabhu, "Dharma as an Alternative to Human Rights," in *Studies in Orientology: Essays in Memory of Prof. AL Basham*, ed. S. K. Maity, Upendra Thakur, and A. K. Narain (Agra: YL Publishers, 1988), 174–179, 178.

15. Barbara Holdrege, "Dharma," in *The Hindu World*, ed. Sushil Mittal and Gene Thursby (New York: Routledge, 2004), 213–248, 215.

16. *The Lion King*, 23:55ff.

17. Jonathan Pennington, *The Sermon on the Mount and Human Flourishing: A Theological Commentary* (Grand Rapids, MI: Baker Academic, 2018), 159.

18. Pennington, *The Sermon on the Mount and Human Flourishing*, 87–91.

19. N. T. Wright, *Paul and the Faithfulness of God*, vol. 1, 2 vols. (Minneapolis: Fortress Press, 2013), 75–196.

20. Jean Baudrillard, *Simulacra and Simulation*, trans. Sheila Faria Glaser, 14th Printing Edition (Ann Arbor, MI: University of Michigan Press, 1994).

21. David Bentley Hart, *The Beauty of the Infinite* (Grand Rapids, MI: Eerdmans, 2003), 431–439; Leslie Newbigin, "Religion for the Marketplace," in *Christian Uniqueness Reconsidered: The Myth of a Pluralistic Theology of Religions*, ed. Gavin D'Costa (Maryknoll, NY: Orbis Books, 1992), 135–148.

22. Ruth Abbey, *Philosophy Now: Charles Taylor* (Princeton: Princeton University Press, 2000), 199.

23. Taylor, *A Secular Age*; Charles Taylor, *A Catholic Modernity?*, ed. James L. Heft (Oxford: Oxford University Press, 1999); Charles Taylor, *Dilemmas and Connections* (Cambridge: Harvard University Press, 2011); Hans Joas, *The Power of the Sacred: An Alternative to the Narrative of Disenchantment* (Oxford: Oxford University Press, 2021); Hans Joas, *Faith as an Option: Possible Futures for Christianity* (Stanford, CA: Stanford University Press, 2014).

24. Raimon Panikkar, "Trisangam: The Jordan, The Tiber, and the Ganges—The Three Kairological Moments of Christic Self-Consciousness," in *Christianity: A Christophany*, ed. Milena Carrara Pavan, vol. III.2, XII vols., Opera Omnia (Maryknoll, NY: Orbis Books, 2016), 3–25.

25. C.f. José Casanova, "Exploring the Post-Secular: Three Meanings of 'the Secular' and Their Possible Transcendence," in *Habermas and Religion*, ed. Craig Calhoun, Eduardo Mendieta, and Jonathan VanAntwerpen (Malden, MA: Polity Press, 2013), 27–48; Craig Calhoun, Eduardo Mendieta, and Jonathan VanAntwerpen, "Editor's Introduction," in *Habermas and Religion* (Malden, MA: Polity Press, 2013), 1–23.

26. D. A. Carson, *Christ and Culture Revisited* (Grand Rapids, MI: Eerdmans, 2012); H. Richard Niebuhr, *Christ and Culture* (New York: Harper and Row, 2001).

Chapter 5

Rescripting Theology in *Lucifer*

The previous two chapters introduced and offered analyses of two of the three methodological frameworks that shape the approach in the analysis of this book between post-Christian religion and popular culture. Chapter 3 analyzed the problem of "re-enchantment" in the Marvel Cinematic Universe. Chapter 4 addressed the idea of "resourcement" through a deconstructive analysis of how *The Lion King* may be read through the lens of both Christian capaciousness for including truths of non-Christian religions and an inter-religious, pluralistic simulation of truth.

This chapter addresses the third methodological theme that governs the analysis of this volume: "rescription." Rescription is an idea utilized in practical theology to reflect on how theological ideas are rescripted through the languages and practices of ordinary people. As such, rescription is especially concerned with how beliefs are articulated through the practices of lived religion. For example, Mark Cartledge argues that how Pentecostals articulate theological ideas in ordinary life implies a rescription of Christian theology in ways that may produce unorthodox theological ideas.[1] But rescription is also a tool that may be used when we are trying to articulate post-Christian theological doctrine (as content of belief) as a contrast to orthodox Christian theology.

This chapter investigates what may be deemed a popular cultural rescription of Christian theology by arguing how the television show *Lucifer* rescripts Christian theological ideas of the Devil in ways that move beyond traditional Christianity. This chapter works with Christian theology as a point of departure. But this point of departure is also something *imagined*. Arguably, *Lucifer's* rescription of Christian theology exemplifies an example of an imagined theology that can characterize and intimate potential ways of articulating post-Christian theological doctrines. As a post-Christian theology, *Lucifer's* imagined theology is less concerned with whether it is real or true. Rather, its imagined theology represents a concern with whether people find it believable when it offers alternative theological doctrines of belief that may be more desirable than traditional theological accounts.

This chapter articulates this post-Christian rescription of Christian theology by paying attention to several theological alterations found within the television show *Lucifer*: the extent to which *Lucifer* reflects and moves beyond traditional Christian theology by articulating both a celestial hierarchy and its rescription of angelology and demonology; the complex interplay between free will and determinism and the implications of divine fallibility; and finally, the question of "calling" through an examination of two character arcs to explore angelic self-actualization in Amenadiel and the question of how the Devil and the damned are redeemable. Through these analyses, we not only find un-orthodox rescriptions of Christian theology, but arguably some possible contours of a post-Christian theology that may be believable and desirable to a post-Christian culture that wrestles with desire, love, and forgiveness in light of existential questions of free will, determinism, and divine fallibility.

Thus, this chapter explores how *Lucifer* offers a post-Christian theological alternative to Christian theology. But before turning to the analysis of *Lucifer*, it is worth articulating a contrast to the theological rescriptions in *Lucifer* because it will more vividly display the departures between orthodox Christian theology and Lucifer's theological rescription of it. This contrast will be done through contemporary evangelical scholarship on what the Christian tradition understands about sin and the Devil. It is to this that we first turn.

"HE'S THE DEVIL!": LUCIFER IN CHRISTIAN TRADITION

Before diving into the irreverence of *Lucifer*, it is proper to frame the analysis of *Lucifer* in light of traditional theology to demonstrate a reference point to refer back to throughout this chapter. The enframing power of Christian tradition will serve as an orientation that will situate the analyses below of free will and determination, divine fallibility, and angelic self-actualization in subtle ways that we will come back to throughout the rest of this chapter. When it comes to Christian tradition, the relevant points of contact with angels, demons, and Satan come from a few key places in the biblical account, but moreover throughout medieval Christian theological tradition. It is to these that we turn via the evangelical theologies of Graham A. Cole and Thomas H. McCall.

Thomas H. McCall summarizes what scholars have concluded about Satan in the biblical accounts. First, Satan is the tempter who leads people away from Christ (who will crush Satan). "Second, Satan was part of the heavenly court—he was an angel," who, in contrast with God, is malevolent, deceitful, and distortive of God's purposes to create and sustain creation.[2] Furthermore, Satan knows about divine matters and precedes Adam and Eve. Third, because "Satan is—or was—an angel, then Satan is a creature" created by God.[3] But because all things are created by God and because God does not create evil, Satan must have been good but rebelled against God between creation and the Garden of Eden.[4] McCall's commentary on Isaiah 14:12–19 reveals that "Satan wanted to be like God, as God, even above God. But he was cast down. . . . He is a defeated foe, and his future is grim" while remaining "both fascinating and frightening in his evil power."[5] Likewise, McCall's commentary on Ezekiel 28 is telling: that Satan as "King of Tyre" is "a being radiant in beauty and splendor," "full of wisdom and perfect in beauty" (Ezek. 28:12).[6] But once "filled with violence" (Ezek. 28:16), he is cast down and destroyed because his "heart was proud because of [his] beauty; you corrupted your wisdom for the sake of your splendor" (Ezek. 28:17).[7]

While Protestant biblical accounts of Satan are limited, there is nonetheless a wealth of material on Satan from throughout the Medieval Christian tradition. John of Damascus offers a succinct summary of a standard position. He states that Satan

> was not made wicked in nature but was good, and made for good ends and received from his creator no trace whatsoever of evil in himself. But he did not sustain the brightness and honor that the Creator had bestowed on him, and of his free choice he was changed from what was in harmony to what was at variance with his nature, and became roused against God who created him and determined to rise in rebellion against him, and he was the first to depart from good and became evil.[8]

Furthermore, when it comes to determinations of what angels and demons are, Augustine notes that good or evil angels have the same nature, but that their differences lie "in their wills and desires."[9] Furthermore, even Aquinas "denies that the devils are evil by nature."[10] Furthermore, building on the *Wisdom of Solomon*, Irenaeus of Lyons views the sin of the Devil to be the envy of humanity. As a hostile apostate, he is against and tries to rob God of humanity's elevation to God's glory above the status of angels.[11] When it comes to the nature of demons, Graham Cole states that they are "fallen angels who are now malicious spiritual beings," but who still have attributes of unfallen angels—as communicative agents, with intelligence, but limited in relation to God's purposes.[12] They express emotions like fear, can possess humans, and can affect the physical form of humans.[13] And yet, Karl Barth articulates a striking limitation to the nature of angels and their differentiation from God as creatures:

> Angels cannot . . . speak words which as their own are the words of God. They cannot do works which as their own are divine works. They cannot save, redeem, or liberate the earthly creature. They cannot forgive even the smallest sin, or remove even the slightest pain. They can do nothing to bring about the reconciliation of the world with God. Nor are they judges of the world. They did not create it. They can neither be wrathful nor gracious toward it. They did not establish the covenant between God and Man, and they cannot fulfill, maintain, renew, or confirm it. They do not overcome death. They do not rule the history of salvation, or universal history, or any history. Otherwise, they would not be angels of God.[14]

This striking statement reflects not only a high view of the glory of God but also important differences between God and created things, particularly that of angels. Barth basically says, "Angels are not, and cannot fulfill the function or role of, God." And yet, Graham Cole states that angels do play a mediatorial role between God and creation, as mediating communicators of God's will to creation.[15] This is seen throughout the biblical text and in *Lucifer*—for example, through the agencies of unfallen angels like (the fictional) Amenadiel and (the rescripted) Gabriel.

Moving into Latin scholasticism proper, the reflections on Satan are traced by McCall, for our purposes, primarily through the intellectual developments that start with Anselm and end with John Duns Scotus. According to McCall, Anselm of Canterbury's arguments show how Satan fell because he exercised the freedom of his will to reject what God had offered him.[16] Because free will is something given to creatures and because of Satan's pride over his exaltation and beauty, he rejected God's sovereignty—Satan could sin because, as the Medievalists say, it matters what creatures *do with their will* that determines good and evil.[17]

As an important point in the medieval debates, McCall situates John Duns Scotus's work as an important development in the discourse on Satan. McCall shows how, for Duns Scotus, divine freedom is subtly combined with divine love in ways that demonstrate how there is a radical contingency in giving creatures the freedom of the will to love God. But what goes wrong for Lucifer is that his freedom to will was disordered to love and elevate himself as God. Duns Scotus makes a distinction between "affection for justice" and "affection for advantage," where the former refers to the normative and functional desire to order creation properly toward God, and the latter refers to ordering our wills according to our own desires. For Duns Scotus, Lucifer's desire was for himself, a disordered desire. But God created our desires to will to God in terms of an affection of justice—that our desires should be ordered properly to God, not to ourselves, as the end/goal (*telos*) of created existence.[18]

What is important from the account above are several threads for our analysis below. First is the nature of angels and demons. Second is the nature of desire and its implications for evil tied to the nature of Satan. But more important is how the show *Lucifer* rescripts several of these orthodox Christian doctrines from biblical sources and Christian tradition in non-orthodox ways—pointing us to not only the absence of Christ in *Lucifer* but also to ways of rescripting theology in post-Christian popular culture. With this orthodox theological backdrop in place, we can now turn to how the show *Lucifer* rescripts in its development of a post-Christian theology.

"MY FATHER . . . ": CELESTIAL HIERARCHY IN *LUCIFER*

In *Lucifer*, there are not only your typical angels and archangels found across the biblical, Rabbinic, and Quranic traditions like Michael, Gabriel, and Uriel. There are also Neil Gaiman's reimaginings of Lucifer as Samael and the creation of non-biblical angels and demons like Amenadiel and Mazekeen. The power of the literary imagination is that it is not limited to traditional interpretations and accounts of what angels or demons are understood to be within orthodox theological traditions. Another side of this is the celestial hierarchy as imagined within *Lucifer*.

In *Lucifer*, Michael and Samael (Lucifer) are competitive twins who hate one another. Uriel is the younger, weaker brother who plays to his strengths by effectively understanding and applying patterns to fulfill God's commands. Gabriel is a messenger angel who can communicate and cross between universes. Amenadiel is "God's favorite Son," "God's mightiest warrior." But what underlies each of these angels is that they are *children* of God. Each of these angels sees God the Father as *their* Father in ways reminiscent of a filial relationship as God's sons and daughters—not as creatures, but rather in ways that reflect both how human siblings quarrel with one another for their father's favor and how human daughters and sons rebel against, are disgraced, and redeemed by their father.

Another thread to this celestial hierarchy lies in the rescription of the medieval and Rabbinic accounts of Lilith, who is thought in some traditions to be Adam's first wife. While that is still true within *Lucifer*, what differentiates Lilith in *Lucifer* from the medieval tradition is that Lilith becomes the immortal mother of demons. As such, the demons in *Lucifer* are not fallen angels, are not children of God, but are the soulless offspring of a rebellious wife and cold-hearted mother who abandons her children. Mazekeen's unredeemed story of seeking reconciliation with her mother and her successful desire for, and growth of, a soul so that she may receive love are both illustrative depictions of the theological rescription of demons in *Lucifer*.

The third and final element of *Lucifer*'s celestial hierarchy lies in the centrality that God the Father is married to the Goddess of creation. Not only does this play with and rescript traditional Abrahamic theological tradition by transposing from pagan tradition the idea of a Mother Goddess, rescripted to give birth to the angels, but also suggests that she becomes the disgruntled and neglected wife of a Divine husband who is too concerned with ruling and caring for his creation to properly love her. In the show, Lucifer's solution to give his Mother her own universe and to send his Father to be her spouse in *her* universe illustrates a theological rescription that is so heterodox in its imaginings that it leaves behind the Abrahamic emphasis on monotheism in its appeal to divine marriage.

"WHAT DO YOU DESIRE?": RESCRIPTING ANGELOLOGY AND DEMONOLOGY

One of the mainstays throughout the show *Lucifer* is the powers of angels. Each angel is created for a specific purpose by their Father, God. But they are each given certain powers inherent to their nature, similar to the idea that they become the "angels of . . . " in similar terms to that they become "gods of . . . " Michael is given the power to draw out people's fears. Gabriel is given the power to cross the boundaries of universes as the messenger angel of God. Amenadiel is given not only super strength but faith that, even when fallen, it is part of God's plan. And of course, Lucifer's gift is to draw out people's *desires*.

It is fitting that Lucifer is given this gift. Satan is not only the tempter but plays on our desires, gifting humans the seductive power and spiral of/to sin. But how Lucifer in the show uses his gift to draw out human desires is striking. Lucifer utilizes this power for the purpose not only to gift humans what they sexually want in his libertine and licentiously open sex life but also for two other things. First, the favors he grants to humans requesting his influence create a debt they then owe to the devil. These favors may be called in at any time that he asks, and his gift is therefore is often used for a third important purpose: to catch criminals, draw out true confessions, and save his friends in the Los Angeles Police Department.

But underlying the gift of drawing out human desires is not only that Lucifer uses it to obtain his desires. The power of desire plays an important role throughout the series in illustrating the nature of sin and how the character rescripts the picture of the Devil. Throughout the series, we see the character of Lucifer as a witty, irreverent, charmingly handsome, self-absorbed player with daddy issues. If we pay attention to his character arc, there is hardly the impression that Lucifer is evil. Consistent with Abrahamic traditions, the show correctly portrays Lucifer as indeed having rebelled against God and being banished from heaven for his rebellion. But two things are added to *Lucifer*'s rescription of Abrahamic theology. First, he is *given* by his Father, God, the *reign* of, *and banishment to*, hell as a punishment for his rebellion. Second, most irreverent is the depiction of the fall not only of Satan tempting Eve in the Garden but also of her sexual infidelity with Lucifer as his first love.

Building on this interpretation rescripted in *Lucifer*, Father Kinley's obsession with a vague prophecy about Lucifer's first love is actually shown to mean his sexual relationship with Eve. The prophecy states that when "the devil walks on earth and falls for his first love, evil shall be released."[19] Season four's main thread is not only Father Kinley trying to kill Lucifer through Chloe because Kinley thinks Chloe is his first love, but also that with the descent of Eve to earth, it is revealed that Lucifer's inflamed passion with Eve results in the physical transformation of Lucifer's appearance into having horns, red skin, and bat wings. It is only through Lucifer's desire to forgive himself and recant his self-hatred for being held responsible for humanity's sins that the world is saved from the evil in him being released.[20] At the heart of this is not only the question of who is to blame for sin, but also the redemption of the Devil that we will pick up below.

"NOT TO WORRY, IT'S ALL UNDER CONTROL!": DIVINE FALLIBILITY, FREE WILL, AND DETERMINISM

Throughout *Lucifer*, there is a seeming contradiction between whether humans have free will or whether they are determined by God to be destined for heaven or hell. As Lucifer often says with witty sarcasm, "It's all part of the plan." But it is precisely in doubting the power of the Father that this may be questioned. *Lucifer* asks important questions about free will, determinism, and divine fallibility in generative ways that reflect not only a post-Christian culture's questioning of traditional theological to pat answers about free will and determinism, but they also reflect, somewhat surprisingly, *popular* conceptions of free will and determinism and, in their simplicity, how these shed light on the *inadequacy* of those answers.

Often throughout *Lucifer*, humans are depicted as both determined by God for heaven or hell and having their actions be the cause of their destiny because of their free will. In popular parlance, this is a contradiction. It is not only the question of *who* determines whether we go to heaven or hell, God's will or a human's free will, but also whether that determination is made by an omniscient God to condemn some and not others whom he predetermines to have faith in him or not. Furthermore, it is marked by whether humans are determined for heaven or hell by the human exercise of using their free will to intentionally sin. And yet, surprisingly, what *Lucifer* rescripts as a solution to this problem is the role of *guilt*. In *Lucifer*, what determines whether someone goes to heaven or hell is whether they hold or have guilt over something they had done (or not done!) during their life on earth. Those who go to hell are trapped in never-ending "hell-loops" of the repeated tortures of reexperiencing those events in their lives they feel most guilty about.

Not only does this defer the question of free will and determinism, but it also orients a shift in a post-Christian theology that holds a latent Christian emphasis on guilt. Often guilt is invoked in harmful and abusive ways by both Christians and non-Christians alike. Certainly, Western culture does not like being told that we humans are guilty. Nor do individuals like to be told of their guilt when they have transgressed against others. But the nature of guilt in *Lucifer* is specifically tailored not only to every individual's guilt-loop in hell but, more importantly, to their choices in life that perpetuate the eternal effects of guilt behind their individuated doors in hell. So, what does this mean when it comes to divine culpability? Is God responsible for the guilt humans hold for their actions on earth? Paraphrasing Lucifer, "Don't blame me! You put yourself here. I had nothing to do with it!" This reflects not only Lucifer's deferral of the blame attributed to him by the quippant remark, "The Devil made me do it!" It also reflects something important in the Christian tradition about sin: humans are held responsible for their sin and guilt.

But *Lucifer* offers another set of questions about divine fallibility. If humans are created, and God is fallible, does this not mean that humans were imperfectly created by an imperfect God and that God is held accountable for a flawed creation? The Christian tradition holds to the idea of a perfect God, who created creation to reflect his perfection. Indeed, throughout the story of scripture, we not only find a perfect creation where Adam and Eve were both able to sin and to not sin, but that by sinning, humans will from then on no longer have the ability to not sin—humans will inevitably commit acts of sin because of the systemic pattern of and bondage to sin. As Wesley develops: "The universal misery of humanity is both the source and the result of the sin that plagues humanity."[21] And yet, God also offers an answer to the problem of sin through the atoning work of Christ on the Cross and through the resurrection, ascension, and second coming.

The problem of sin has been given an answer in and through the work of Christ in the Christian tradition, and through faith in the work of Christ, the power of sin no longer has the power to enslave humans to sin. And yet, sin still abounds, but, as Paul says, "grace abounds all the more" (Romans 5:20). Furthermore, the Book of Revelation reveals how the apostle John understands God as the continual coming of Christ through his reference as the alpha and omega of all history, who brings creation to completion through the Spirit in the destruction and renewal of the heavens and the earth through Christ's second coming by giving justice for the oppressed and restoration of a new innocence that has known sin—yet one that chooses (the) righteousness (of God through Christ). The story above presents a story of not only good news, but of God's perfect plan to dispense justice and righteousness on sin for the righteous oppressed. But *Lucifer* rescripts Christian theology in an important way—*by not referring to Christ or what was just presented.* The implications of this for a post-Christian theology imply vivid possibilities of thinking of a post-Christian theology *without* the center of what makes Christian theology so distinctively Christian: *Christ.*

Lucifer also rescripts theology in another important and challenging way. What *Lucifer* presents of God the Father, however, is not only of a wrathful judge and loving Father to his angelic sons and daughters, *but of a God who is fallible—imperfect.* In *Lucifer*, God is asked by Lucifer to tell him he loves his sons, and God tells Lucifer, "If I had to tell you that, I would have failed."[22] And yet, after God retires, he not only tells his sons that they would figure out who would succeed him, but before he enters into his wife's universe, he tells Lucifer with great emotion, "I love you, son."[23] Tied to his retirement into his wife's universe, throughout season five, we not only see God losing control of his faculties as God with many episodes of singing and dancing—and of exploding Dan for sleeping with his wife—but we see through this the idea that *God is not perfect.* In *Lucifer*, God is fallible, and therefore, as Dan reflects, God's reign is under question because God is imperfect.[24] The fallibility of God in *Lucifer* not only raises important existential and theological questions in Dan but, more pertinent to the story of *Lucifer*, of who is to reign as God once God retires. The question of Amenadiel and Lucifer's "calling" is now brought into center stage.

"IT'S MY CALLING": SELF-ACTUALIZATION AND REDEMPTION

The quote above from Karl Barth on what angels are not capable of lies in direct contrast to what *Lucifer* imagines of angels. In *Lucifer*, angels are capable of self-actualization. A central part of angelic self-actualization in *Lucifer* comes from their lives on earth and interactions with humans. Through this intermingling in the storylines of Amenadiel and Lucifer, we find by the end of the series a sense of their callings. Often a calling is used by Christians in terms of a determinative decision of what God wants a particular person to do. Sadly, this is often abused by pastors and many Christians, particularly when it comes to relationships between young Christians in the church.

But another way to understand a "calling" is that there is a sense of fittingness in what is presented before us throughout our lives regarding what we want to pursue and what God intends for us. This sense of fittingness lies at the intersection of what we love and what brings God glory. It is not only the idea that when our loves and desires are in sync with what God loves or desires—that is, God's righteousness and the flourishing of what is not God—but also that our loves and what we intentionally pursue are intended by us to bring God glory; it is based on the notion that I intentionally act and pursue things for God because I hold God as worthy of glory in and through my actions and intentions. But a calling also gives the sense of pursuing what we love for God's glory, even if we do not know what that looks like in the face of the unknown. There is a level of discernment in calling, of reflection on our lives, their patterns, our gifts, the opportunities presented and available to us, and their intersections with what brings God glory. With this in mind, we can look at this sense of calling in the character arcs of Amenadiel and Lucifer throughout the show.

Amenadiel: Becoming God through Becoming Human

Throughout the series, the character arc of Amenadiel offers a vivid example of angelic self-actualization. After Lucifer abandons Hell and comes to Earth to enjoy its pleasures, Amenadiel is ordered to rule Hell in Lucifer's absence. In an attempt to get Lucifer to return to his task, Amenadiel allows a damned soul to return to Earth, who then tries to kill Lucifer after unsatiated consumption leads him to madness and evil. Not only this, but Amenadiel begins sexual relations with Lucifer's sidekick demon, Mazikeen. For both of these, Amenadiel's angel wings begin to decay and fall off, and he loses his power to slow and pause time. Amenadiel's actions have led him to a fall from grace in his father's eyes. And yet, he does not lose faith.

Throughout several seasons, Amenadiel, though having lost his celestial powers, does not lose faith in his father's tests and plans. Amenadiel's faith is striking. It is not only that he blindly trusts in his father's punishment as part of his plan, but also that everything becomes a test to determine whether he is worthy of receiving back his celestial powers. What Amenadiel's story reveals in the formative power of these tests is not only the sustaining power of his faith but also the formation of dependency and trust as hallmarks of his character. The process of Amenadiel's spiritual and character formation runs through despair but fortitude to set things right, through faith in his father's plan, but also to a mature faith and trust that his father's punishment ought to transform a fundamental disposition in his character.

It is by being dispossessed of his angelic powers that he learns to become human, to live among them, and to appreciate them—to the point of procreating with them. Amenadiel's sympathies with humanity only come when his angelic pride is broken, and when he learns to live among humans as one of them. Here we see glimpses of Christ in significant ways, but, while for Christ it was a willing setting aside of his divinity for his Father's glory, for Amenadiel the dispossession of his celestial powers was a punishment for his transgressions. But throughout both Amenadiel's dispossession of his angelic powers and Christ's humility and kenosis, there lies a common thread: both maintained trust in God's intentions and plans.

For Christ, it was to die a horrific death for the salvation of many. For Amenadiel, it was to form a character worthy of becoming God. Amenadiel's exposure to humanity, contrasted with his many brothers and sisters, reveals an understanding of humanity that his siblings lacked. They began answering prayers unbeknownst to their apocalyptic effects on Earth. Among the Angels, it is only Amenadiel and Lucifer (and to a lesser extent Azrael), who understand and have lived among humanity, that have a proper understanding of what prayers to answer, and therefore, they have the wisdom to answer prayers in ways that lead to flourishing and justice rather than destruction. But if we turn to Lucifer, we see another instance of calling, but this one offers two striking questions: Are the damned—and the Devil—redeemable?

Lucifer: Redemption through Therapy

There are two ways in which the character arc of Lucifer redeems the damned. But they are also intricately interwoven throughout the seasons of *Lucifer*. The first and last of the thread lie in, well, therapy. Throughout *Lucifer*, we do not only see the devil consulting with the LAPD to get close to the Detective until he learns she is part of his father's designs. But we also see Lucifer's self-absorption throughout the entire series—characterized by his self-centeredness, selfishness, depravity, sexual licentiousness, deflecting of blame, and reading his own (daddy) issues into his cases with the detective—being given counsel by his therapist, Dr. Linda Martin. The entirety of the show is not just individual cases of solving crime with the detective. It is not only a police drama but also a sustained therapy session where Lucifer comes to terms with those who blame him for evil, his daddy and mommy issues, his self-blame, self-hatred, and unforgiveness of himself.

The character development of Lucifer strikingly asks the question of whether the Devil is redeemable. And tied to this is also whether the damned are redeemable. While Lucifer diffuses his responsibility for the guilt of those in hell, it is only near the end of the series that we see him coming to terms with his calling. He had wasted thousands of millennia ruling hell, only to learn in his ascension to earth and years of therapy, that his role as ruler of hell was to help the damned deal with their guilt. The first instance of this comes with the hell-loop of the bank robber at the beginning of season five, who by the end of the season ends up in heaven after he confronts the heart of his hell-loop—he confronts his deepest guilt, and this saves him from an eternity of replaying his hell-loop.[25] But we see in season six a continuation of Lucifer's own therapy for the damned—intended for the preparation that he be able to love humans if he were to become God. Throughout season six, Lucifer helps those in hell he hates most and those on Earth he doesn't care about and finds himself, at the end of the series, leading a therapy session in hell with several characters we were introduced to throughout the series—*with the intent to help them confront their guilt so that they can go to heaven.*[26]

Lucifer learns through therapy how to be a therapist. Throughout the series, we see him coming to terms with his identity as the devil, his mommy and daddy issues, being a father, his love for Chloe, and the ability to love himself. Love comes into center stage throughout the series, but not primarily to illustrate sexual depravity and licentiousness. Rather, at the center of the stage is the ability to (accept and receive) love and forgive ourselves of our guilt in light of reconciled relationships with parents, lovers, and children. The redemptive power of love lies in forgiveness, and mere forgiveness for sin by God through Christ is not enough to assuage the consciousness of guilt for some. The story arc of Lucifer demonstrates how the path to forgiveness, whether of those who have mistreated us or of ourselves and the weights we carry, takes time and intentional commitment to the healing process through the messy rhythms of therapy and daily life with those we love and trust most.

CONCLUSION

Lucifer paints a picture of post-Christian theology in significant ways. It rescripts traditional Christian and Abrahamic theology in ways that not only question the evil of Satan but also rescript celestial hierarchies and the nature of angels and demons. But *Lucifer* also rescripts theology in ways that generate elements of post-Christian theology—those latent hopes for redemption, love, and forgiveness in light of existential questions of divine fallibility, free will, and determinism that serve as hang-ups for many people today. What *Lucifer* offers is a post-Christian theological rescription in ways that generate new ways of thinking theologically in light of popular culture. But what happens when popular culture not only deconstructs, resources, or rescripts theology and religion? What happens when we begin to come to terms with another side of post-Christian religion—the problems and promises of modernity and modern structures that have led to dehumanizing effects across time and history? It is in part III that we turn to ask these questions through an analysis of *Cloud Atlas* (both film and book) and imaginaries of Black humanity via *Black Panther* and *Wakanda Forever*.

NOTES

1. Mark Cartledge, *Testimony in the Spirit* (Burlington, VT: Ashgate Publishing Company, 2010).
2. Thomas H. McCall, *Against God and Nature: The Doctrine of Sin* (Wheaton, IL: Crossway, 2019), 137.
3. McCall, *Against God and Nature*, 137.
4. McCall, *Against God and Nature*, 138.
5. McCall, *Against God and Nature*, 138.
6. McCall, *Against God and Nature*, 138.
7. McCall, *Against God and Nature*, 138–139.
8. John of Damascus, *De Fide Orthodoxa,* II.IV (2.4); Opt. cit. in McCall, *Against God and Nature*, 140.
9. Augustine, *De Civitas Dei*, XII.1; Opt. cit. in McCall, *Against God and Nature*, 140.
10. McCall, *Against God and Nature*, 144.
11. Graham A. Cole, *Against the Darkness: The Doctrine of Angels, Satan, and Demons* (Wheaton, IL: Crossway, 2019), 93–94.
12. Cole, *Against the Darkness*, 112.
13. Cole, *Against the Darkness*, 112.
14. Karl Barth, *Church Dogmatics*, III/3 (460); Opt. Cit. in Cole, *Against the Darkness*, 51–52.
15. Cole, *Against the Darkness*, 52.
16. McCall, *Against God and Nature*, 141.
17. McCall, *Against God and Nature*, 141–144.
18. McCall, *Against God and Nature*, 144–147.
19. "O, Ye of Little Faith, Father," Streaming, *Lucifer* (Burbank, CA: Netflix, May 8, 2019).
20. "Save Lucifer," Streaming, *Lucifer* (Burbank, CA: Netflix, May 8, 2019).
21. McCall, *Against God and Nature*, 26.
22. "Family Dinner," Streaming, *Lucifer* (Burbank, CA: Netflix, May 28, 2021).
23. "Nothing Lasts Forever," Streaming, *Lucifer* (Burbank, CA: Netflix, May 28, 2021).
24. "Daniel Espinoza: Naked and Afraid," Streaming, *Lucifer* (Burbank, CA: Netflix, May 28, 2021).

25. "Really Sad Devil Guy," Streaming, *Lucifer* (Burbank, CA: Netflix, May 28, 2021); "A Chance at a Happy Ending," Streaming, *Lucifer* (Burbank, CA: Netflix, May 28, 2021).

26. "Buckets of Baggage," Streaming, *Lucifer* (Burbank, CA: Netflix, September 10, 2021); "Yabba Dabba Do Me," Streaming, *Lucifer* (Burbank, CA: Netflix, September 10, 2021); "Partners Til the End," Streaming, *Lucifer* (Burbank, CA: Netflix, September 10, 2021).

Part III

PROBLEMS AND PROPHECIES OF MODERNITY

Chapter 6

The Tragedy and Trajectory of Modernity in *Cloud Atlas*

Throughout parts I and II, the focus of the analysis was to lay out a theoretical framework for this book and begin to put into practice three methodological approaches by which we can articulate and begin to think theologically about how twenty-first-century popular culture presents messages of post-Christian theology and religion. The focus in part III, however, is to interpret two types of biblical literary genres in a post-Christian context. While this chapter develops an example of post-Christian apocalyptic "literature" through an analysis of the book-adapted-to-film *Cloud Atlas*, the next chapter will analyze an example of prophetic "literature" through philosophical analyses of the films *Black Panther* and *Wakanda Forever*. What unites both of these chapters in part III are their analyses of the problems and promises of modernity. As such, modernity is under examination in part III, particularly its religious latencies and critiques in terms of the horrors modernity can (or has) generate(d). The point of part III is not only to pause to sit in the effects of modernity but also to prophesy against the horrors (that can be) generated out of it. While this chapter illustrates a fictional modern apocalypse in *Cloud Atlas*, the following chapter will analyze through philosophical analyses the modern formation of Black humanity to call us to grieve the possibilities and realities modernity has generated.

The heart of this chapter is to argue how *Cloud Atlas'* critique of modernity represents a counter-movement to modernity that prophesies its totalization and collapse, its subversions, and its tragedy and trajectory. This chapter argues how *Cloud Atlas* presents an example of secularized apocalyptic literature through its analyses of both the strategies of modernity and the tactics of love and humanization in the dystopian trajectory of modernity's dehumanizing will to power. This chapter develops how *Cloud Atlas* prophesies a trajectory of modern utopia as leading to a strategic dystopian future, marked by universal Unanimity and conformity to homogeneity, which eventually leads to tragedy: the collapse of human society and an ecological holocaust.

This chapter adopts the methodological frameworks of Michel de Certeau, narrates a karmic teleology of modernity that charts the trajectory of modernity as it is imagined by *Cloud Atlas*, and draws us into a postmodern critique of modernity that points out how love tactically demonstrates what it means to be human in the interconnectedness of life and relationships across time. If the will to power, control, and domination are the governing beliefs of modernity, then the promise and trajectory of modern utopia do not lie in its ability to humanize us. Rather, the promise and trajectory of modern utopia lie in the tragedy of dystopian dehumanization—which can only be countered by tactics of love. Thus, this chapter analyzes the apocalyptic prophecies of what the driving forces of modernity will generate—at least fictionally through the eyes of David Mitchell's *Cloud Atlas* and the Wachowski Sisters' film adaptation of it. While what *Cloud Atlas* imagines is fictional, it should cause us to pause in its prescience to anticipate what the trajectories of modern ideologies may produce in the destruction of both humanity and the earth.

METHODOLOGICAL CONSIDERATIONS: CERTEAU'S TACTICS AND STRATEGIES

The introduction of this chapter alluded to several words that are the calling cards of Michel de Certeau: *strategies* and *tactics*. This chapter utilizes these terms and de Certeau's understanding of them to analyze the narratives found within *Cloud Atlas*. This chapter argues that in *Cloud Atlas*, the *strategic* imaginings of the trajectory of modern utopia are subverted through the *tactics* of love. De Certeau defines these terms in specific ways. He argues that tactics

> are not any more localizable than the technocratic (and scriptural) strategies that seek to create places in conformity with abstract models. But what distinguishes them at the same time concerns the types of operations and the role of spaces: *strategies can produce, tabulate, and impose these spaces, when those operations take place, whereas tactics can only use, manipulate, and divert these spaces.*[1]

That is, tactics are counter-movements alongside the strategies of modernity.[2] They work to subvert strategies and further manipulate them to produce alternate visions of reality. Michael Gardiner, reflecting on de Certeau, states that strategies attempt to negate time and memory, by reducing them to elements within an observable and readable system. Tactics, by contrast, are dispersed, hidden and ephemeral, and improvised in response to the concrete demands of the situation at hand. They are also temporal in nature, and reliant on the art of collective memory, on a tradition of popular resistance and subversion passed on from generation to generation.[3]

Tactics move in subtle, striking, and alternate ways against the grain of modernity, while yet encompassed within the historical trajectory of modern strategies. Most strikingly, in *Cloud Atlas*, if modern *strategies* seek to control and conform all of human life to a universal ideal through the will to power, it results in the dehumanization of humanity, technology, and creation via the conformity to homogeneity that the dominating structures of modern strategies produce. By contrast, *Cloud Atlas' tactics* of subversion are most strikingly the counter-movements of love and humanization. These ideas are central to the methodological approach of this chapter, and the following section argues that the strategies of modernity are defined by a certain totalizing vision of reality that projects itself and onto the future in *Cloud Atlas*.

CLOUD ATLAS' POSTMODERN CRITIQUE OF MODERNITY

Often, we think of modernity as a good thing. Both the promises of technological and medicinal advancement and the betterment of the conditions of human life point to something worthy of the progress and promises of modernity. And yet, we also find dangerous ideas underlying those promises. One of the promises of modernity is utopia. But in *Cloud Atlas*, the modern promise of utopia points us in the direction of a universal homogeneous order, where all things are ordered and controlled by a universal societal order. But, as postmodern thought has pointed out, universalization and homogeneity neglect the variability and complexity of human life. They do injustice to love and lead to oppression and the silencing of the other. It leads to (the potential of) rebellion and nuclear holocaust. The trajectory of modern utopia is toward an ordered system that does not tolerate disharmony or dissension. The tragedy of the promises of modern utopia is its dystopian future: the collapse of society and order in an ecological holocaust. And the preceding thoughts are all found within the novel and film, *Cloud Atlas*.[4]

Modernity is marked by the promise of reason and the progressive betterment of humanity. Underlying modernity's promise of reason is the ability to control, organize, and understand reality through instrumental reasoning. Instrumental reasoning is the idea that reason is marked by means aimed at a certain end—it implies that reasoning is aimed towards a certain *telos* (end-goal) whose means are justified by its ends. As Unanimity in *Cloud Atlas* might say, "If I want to create a society that is marked by order and conformity, then I must control the dissemination of ideas so that the homogenized consumer can be created, controlled, and maintained."

Tied to this instrumental way of viewing the world are the modern promises of the progressive betterment of humanity. Ruth Abbey defines this as a commitment to practical universal benevolence. She argues that "this refers to a belief that society should do as much as it can to minimize unnecessary human suffering."[5] Reason in modernity is understood as instrumental, calling humans to be responsible agents who understand and control the world for the progressive betterment of humanity. Modern instrumental reason is where human rationality abandons the teleological nature of the cosmos and finds in the ends of production the efficient means that eventually eclipse the possibility of their ends in the gradual production of a technocratic, consumer society.[6]

While medicine and technology have certainly created better conditions for human life, underlying modern progress is the promise of an unrealized and unrealizable utopia.[7] Modern progress is supported by a philosophical worldview—the classical liberal—that advocates human rights, equality, freedom, and the pursuit of happiness.[8] This worldview is supported by the promise that reason will bring about a utopian society through its vision of the progressive betterment of society. And yet this vision of history has not (yet) produced the utopia it has promised. It is always deferred. Instead, several of its byproducts are the production of further oppression and totalization through political regimes (such as Nazi Germany, Stalin's Soviet Union, the Khmer Rouge in Cambodia, Communist China, and the discrimination and oppression of African Americans in the United States). The promise of utopia by the power of instrumental reasoning does not lead to freedom. It leads to the totalization and domination of power.

Throughout the book, *Cloud Atlas* paints several pictures that represent the controlling, domineering, and totalizing powers of modernity. In "The Half-lives of Luisa Rey," we see an instance of this domineering power. The owner of the nuclear power plant surveys the room and thinks to himself several principles of the modern tendencies toward human domination. He can ruin everyone in the room through his mastery over others because of his charisma, his ability to cultivate and use it, and finally his will to power and domination.[9] In the 1930s, Robert Frobisher has a conversation with a diamond trader who reflects this sentiment just before World War II:

> What sparks wars? The will to power is the backbone of human nature. The threat of violence, the fear of violence, or actual violence is the instrument of

this dreadful will. You can see the will to power in bedrooms, kitchens, factories, unions, and the borders of states. Listen to this and remember it. The nation-state is merely human nature inflated to monstrous proportions.[10]

In *Cloud Atlas*, this will to power results several centuries later in the bureaucratic corpocracy of Unanimity with genomic recycling, racism, slavery, dehumanization, and an infinite gap between those with monetary means that separates the elite and consumers from the poor and oppressed in a world controlled by those with the will to power. This world is ironically both communist and capitalist. Those in power use communist corpocracy to control and maintain capitalistic structures that reduce humanity to mere consumer. In advance of a post-nuclear apocalypse on the big island of Hawaii, we learn from Meronym that the fall was caused by humanity's hungering for more despite their knowledge. This hungering is for power, and that hunger could never be satiated as they ruined the earth with their will to power, leading to an ecological and nuclear holocaust.[11] The human hunger that birthed civilization also killed humanity.[12] Meronym tells Zachry later that the distinction between savagery and civilized living is not just the difference between their beliefs; it is also whether one acts on hunger or pauses with patience to plan for the long term. She tells Zachry that the Old Humanity had the smarts of gods but the savagery of jackals, and that is what tripped the fall of humanity.[13]

At the heart of this totalizing control over humanity is the role not only of technology but also of the Enlightenment vision of humanity. Theodor Adorno and Max Horkheimer famously state that the "Enlightenment . . . has always aimed at liberating human beings from fear and installing them as masters" through knowledge.[14] Adorno and Horkheimer state that the essence of knowledge is to dominate, understand, and control nature through technology which "aims to produce" a method that exploits "the labor of others, capital."[15] Humans "learn from nature . . . how to use it to dominate . . . both [nature] and human beings."[16] Adorno and Horkheimer state that

> reason serves as a universal tool for the fabrication of all other tools, rigidly purpose-directed and as calamitous as the precisely calculated operations of material production the results of which for human beings escape all calculation. Reason's old ambition to be purely an instrument of purposes has finally been fulfilled.[17]

There is an exclusivity to this logic between the "adherence to function" and "the compulsive character of self-preservation" where the dialectic between survival and doom is magnified with a fortuitous efficiency that reifies and dehumanizes human beings.[18] The role of technique, according to Jacques Ellul, is the systematization of efficiency—of producing a technological society that represents a monistic universalism with a differentiation of methods and functions effected through "having [the] absolute [efficiency]" to determine results "in every field of human activity."[19]

This efficiency is displayed across the histories throughout the book through the idea of human hunger for knowledge and power. This hunger results in the totalization and domination of a corpocratic Unanimity through the will to power throughout the book in ways that reflect the obverse side of the modern vision of progress. In the 1840s, on a voyage across the South Pacific, Adam Ewing listens to a conversation about the white man's hunger for power and domination as the reason why the white man is superior and other races are not only lesser but to be subjugated.[20] The progressive betterment of humanity cannot dispel the reality of its dystopia. In *Cloud Atlas*, the totalizing power of a hungering humanity for more leads to a world marked by the will to power in ways that lead to the destruction of humanity and the poisoning of the earth into deadlands, pestilence, and nuclear apocalypse.[21]

Totalization is marked by the universalizing power of reason to determine, control, and create a society blinded and silenced by dependence on the rule of conformity. That is, totalization creates a utopia through societal dependence upon the state for order and sustenance. The societal dependence upon the state implicates a utopian trade-off: I depend on the state to survive, and the state determines that dependence by conforming me to what it envisions me to be. The state's power lies in what the state determines me to be and know. Knowledge becomes censored and controlled in its dissemination. We see this most clearly in *Cloud Atlas* when Unanimity banned Solzhenitsyn.[22]

Furthermore, Emmanuel Levinas's negative reflections on freedom and otherness identify the implications of a modernity that denies otherness and freedom in its totalizing strategies. Levinas argues that freedom is contingent on openness to otherness without collapsing it into the same. Levinas states that "the presence of the Other, a privileged heteronomy, does not clash with freedom but invests it."[23] Levinas argues that

> freedom is not maintained but reduced to being the reflection of a universal order which maintains itself and justifies itself all by itself. . . . This privilege of the universal order, that it sustains itself and justifies itself . . . constitutes the divine dignity of this order. Knowing would be the way by which freedom would denounce its own contingency, by which it would vanish into totality.[24]

That is, in the drive to universalization, the same subverts the other into the same in ways that negate freedom. As such, when modernity affirms "the supremacy of the same [it] reduces itself to an impersonal relation within a universal order."[25] Levinas argues that in the reduction into the same, we negate the other into a neuter that has no freedom of self-determination. The homogenization of society we find in *Cloud Atlas'* Unanimity is one that tellingly describes and prophesies the negation of both otherness and freedom.

If the trajectory of modernity lies in its utopian promise of a dystopian order, we also find its cultural and historical roots within the transitions between a medieval West and that of modernity. José Casanova argues that there were several transitions between a medieval social imaginary, characterized by an enchanted and spiritualized worldview and a teleologically ordered cosmos, and a modern social imaginary, which Charles Taylor describes as having come about through the collapse of transcendence into a horizontal, direct access society and the creation of the public sphere, nation-state, and the market economy.[26] According to Casanova, this transition came about in three stages. First, the cosmic order was replaced by science and technology. Second, the institutional social order of the state, market, and public sphere replaced the church. And third, the moral order shifted from communal, group identity to individual human rights.[27] Charles Taylor argues that the shift to a modern cosmology is a shift between a reality based on Ideas to a universe ruled by understandable mechanisms. And yet, this cosmological vision is one grounded in a disengaged idea of freedom: "the ability to act on one's own, without outside interference or subordination to outside authority. It defines its own peculiar notion of human dignity, closely connected to freedom. And these in turn are linked to ideals of efficacy, power, and unperturbability."[28] These shifts to modernity implicate the strategies of modernization through an imaginary that provokes the totalizing power of human freedom—ideally grounded in human benevolence.

And yet, the progressive trajectory of modernity according to *Cloud Atlas* lies in a political, social, and economic utopia that produces a dystopia. It is a utopian strategy of universalization that produces dystopian tactics of rebellion and its subversion to the consumptive tendencies of modernity. We see in *Cloud Atlas* how the rebellion tactically subverts the promises of Unanimity through the transmission of knowledge, acts of rebellion, and the exposure of technological dehumanization. The dystopian tactics of modernity run *against* the *telos* of utopia. The promise of modern utopia produces the dystopian tactics that subvert it. As such, the trajectory of modernity is not only its utopian promises but also the production of its dystopian subversions. But it also points to the teleological tragedy of modernity in its potential for destruction and collapse. To illustrate this, the next section argues that it can be demonstrated through an imagined, karmic teleology of history that we can find in the film *Cloud Atlas* and it is here that we can begin to see the tragedy and trajectory of modernity.

CLOUD ATLAS' KARMIC TELEOLOGY OF MODERNITY

Let me tell you a story. This is a story that jumps between and across times and places. But it is a story that tells us of the tragedy and trajectory of modernity. The film imagines what I call a karmic teleology of modernity. It starts with modern slavery in the 1840s. It ends in life on Mars. Between it lies the beauty of the *Cloud Atlas Sextet* at the beginning of World War II, the exploitation and crisis of nuclear energy in the 1970s, the comedic affair of the publisher Timothy Cavendish in 2012, the revolutionary tale and import of Sonmi 451 and her challenges to Unanimity in the twenty-second century, and the struggles of survival in a post-nuclear holocaust rustic society on Hawaii in the twenty-fourth century. Between it all are threads of love that tie lives together into an intricate tapestry of love and karma. *Cloud Atlas* displays a teleology of history that demonstrates not only the tragedy and trajectory of modernity but also the religious significance of love and karma across lives.

Cloud Atlas paints a vivid picture of modernity. From the selling of slaves and the propaganda for slavery under the auspices of a natural order in the cosmos according to the laws of reason and domination, to owing of a life to a self-freed slave, the first narrative paints a picture of white modernity's racial greed, pride, and superiority over the rest of humanity. But it also subverts this story through the friendship, trust, and faithfulness between Autua and Adam Ewing toward one another—leading to both Autua saving Ewing from the mischievous attempt by Doctor Henry Goose to poison, kill, and steal Ewing's gold and Ewing joining the abolitionists to fight against slavery. Ewing's father-in-law challenges Ewing's decision with a revealing dialogue:

> *Moore:* "There is a natural order to this world, and those who try to upend it do not fare well. This movement will never survive; if you join them, you and your entire family will be shunned. At best, you will exist as a pariah to be spat on and beaten—at worst, to be lynched or crucified. And for what? For what? No matter what you do it will never amount to anything more than a single drop in a limitless ocean."
>
> *Ewing:* "What is an ocean but a multitude of drops?"[29]

Underlying this dialogue is both an Eastern wisdom applied as a subversion to modern universalizing strategies. The strategy of modernity is the creation of order and superiority. To go against the grain of this trend means to be persecuted and oppressed—to suffer. And yet, even if it amounts to nothing, the subversion of an ocean made of a multitude of drops makes ripples across time and eternity. A most insightful and aesthetic composition of these ripples was Robert Frobisher's *Cloud Atlas Sextet*.

Frobisher's life was a mess. And yet, it highlights the beauty of love and the revelation of the interconnectedness of all things. Similar to the Vedic seers (ṛśi) of old, Frobisher was attuned to the musical patterns that governed reality. Trained as an amanuensis who sells his services to the famous composer Vivian Ayrs, Frobisher finds a connection with Ayrs at the meeting across lives. Frobisher states that he could not have produced the *Cloud Atlas Sextet* if he had never met Ayrs. Frobisher states, "There are whole movements imagining us meeting again and again in different lives, different ages."[30] It is at this intersection across lives that Luisa Rey makes a connection to Frobisher through Frobisher's lover, Rufus Sixsmith, and her listening to the *Cloud Atlas Sextet*.

If Frobisher's life ended in the early 1930s, then the story of Luisa Rey picks up on the crisis and exploitation of energy in the 1970s. Rey, a journalist, meets Sixsmith, a nuclear physicist, who gives her a tip about a conspiracy at a nuclear power plant. Lloyd Hooks, the person in charge of the nuclear power plant, purposefully smudges and tries to erase the potential failure of the nuclear power plant because of his conflicting interests in the capitalization of oil. Rey finds out that Hooks wants the reactor to fail so that he can make money off of the return to oil as an energy source. A hit is put out on Rey and others, and her soulmate is killed in a plane bombing.

Across lives again, in the early twenty-first century, we find Dermot Hoggins at a literary reception where he murders the literary critic who humiliated him and his book. We pick up here with his publisher, Timothy Cavendish, the story of Cavendish's flight from Hoggins's gangster friends and family who are after money, and the trick of Cavendish's brother to get Timothy to self-commit to a retirement home where he would be locked up until his death. Upon his escape, Cavendish created a movie script of his trials and ghastly affair, to be watched many years later by Sonmi-451.

Sonmi 451 was a fabricant, a genetically engineered—and recycled—human. Sonmi lives in the age of Unanimity, a unified humanity that controls the dissemination of knowledge. Unanimity governed humanity as a totalitarian technocratic bureaucracy and was challenged by the rebellion, most notably embodied by Sonmi's lover Hae-Joo Chang. Sonmi's role in the rebellion was to shed light on the dehumanizing strategies of Unanimity. In her broadcasted speech before her capture, and again in her recounting to the archivist of what she had learned, she cast doubts on the totalizing powers of modernity by pointing to the interconnectedness of life.

Later, after the fall and a nuclear holocaust, Zachry and his tribe reverted to a primal way of life in Hawaii and lived in fear of the cannibals that lived inland. Zachry's tribe worshiped Sonmi as a God, and Zachry only came to know the true story of Sonmi through Meronym and her attempt to save her people by calling out to the off-world colonies for help. Meronym states that Sonmi's life was a sad story and that she was human just as they were. But Sonmi's message held power—the power to enchant because of its truth. Zachry's tribe in Hawaii believed in Sonmi and were guided by her message as a way of life.

Sonmi states: "Our lives are not our own. From womb to tomb, we are bound to others, past and present, and by each crime and every kindness, we birth our future."[31] Sonmi articulates the karmic link across time and life. Karma is not just about the vague retribution of getting due rewards and punishments for our actions. It connotates an intrinsic moral law of justice across lifetimes.[32] Arvind Sharma states that

> the idea of Karma is especially seen as implying rebirth. If something good or bad happens to us for which no obvious cause is traceable in this life, then in Hinduism, it is explained in terms of an *effect* of some *action* performed by us in a past life.[33]

That is, karma births the possibilities of our next lives—it determines the conditions of life in our next rebirth. Raimon Panikkar expands upon this definition of karma and also highlights how it connects us to all other beings and reality. Raimon Panikkar states that karma is:

> The link that connects us to every particle of reality and restores our sense of unity with the whole universe, for all beings are, without exception, governed (and nurtured by the same cosmic law). This law is not a mere causal chain, for there are forms of dependence that belong to karman and are not necessarily causal, unless we expand the concept of cause to any process of interdependence. Essential in this view is the universality of such a law. All that is, precisely because it is, has an [intrinsic] relatedness to everything else.[34]

Karma is displayed throughout the film *Cloud Atlas* most notably in the characters played by Tom Hanks. From Henry Goose to the hotel manager in Frobisher's life; to Luisa Rey's soulmate, Isaac Sachs; to Dermot Hoggins; and, finally, to Zachry, we find the karmic effects of retribution across lifetimes. The evil and sleazy actions of Dr. Goose and the hotel manager result in the karmic death of the morally conscious Isaac Sachs in a plane bombing. Further retribution is applied to Hoggins' imprisonment and in his next rebirth as Zachry. Between each of the characters played throughout the film by Tom Hanks, we see both reincarnation and karma. Across history, the actions of human life ripple across time. These ripples make waves through the course of history. And these waves are tensed, patterned, and musical. Frobisher's composition heard this rhythm of being and subverted its tendencies with his suicide. The beauty of *Cloud Atlas* lies in its ability to tap into the rhythms of life and time across history through the subverting power of love.

STRATEGIES AND TACTICS IN *CLOUD ATLAS*

The section above articulated the karmic teleology of modernity as imagined by *Cloud Atlas*. It argued that this teleology is marked by a strategic movement towards universalization, totalization, and conformity—and leads to its collapse. But it is also marked by the karmic subversions of this story through the tactics of love. This section develops the strategies and tactics of modernity as found within *Cloud Atlas* to articulate the dehumanizing strategies of totalization and the karmic tactics that re-humanize through love.

Strategies of Totalization in *Cloud Atlas*

Cloud Atlas depicts, in the story of Sonmi 451, a totalized society ruled by Unanimity. This world is the embodiment of an actualized modern (dystopian) utopia. Everything is controlled by technology and the corpocratic bureaucracy. Everyone has a place in society that they are not to transgress against. The technologically ordered control of society by Unanimity entails the totality of a technocratic society. Technocracy here is a world not only governed by technology and its possibilities, but rather it is a world controlled by the political, social, and economic wielding of technology for the totalizing and universalizing control of human life.

If Jeremy Bentham and Michel Foucault describe the modern panopticon, and Zygmunt Bauman describes the postmodern synopticon, then what each implies are visions of control over society.[35] Panopticon entails the ordered control of society, most notably in a prison system, where everything is observed at all times in hopes of conforming society to happiness. The synopticon is technological surveillance, most notably through the internet, where everything about us can be known by the state in hopes of conforming society to obedience through the manipulation to and of its desires.[36] The technological surveillance and control of society embodied by Unanimity implies in *Cloud Atlas* the teleological production of a homogeneous society towards which modern totalizing powers are aimed.

Hence, *Cloud Atlas* depicts the strategic trajectory of modernity as one marked by technological, totalizing control over society, and especially of knowledge, to guard against dissension from conformity. The control of society is a modern strategy geared towards universalization and conformity in the totalization of mass society into the image of submission and obedience to the state. Furthermore, the technocratic society is one marked by dehumanization because it aims to conform humanity into a single image. Modern strategies seek to conform to a universal ideal to the exclusion, repression, and oppression of the Other. The homogeneous trends of modernity into a single, univocal image implicate its equivocal dissension and the oppression of difference. It does so in a dialectical tension between the dehumanizing conformity to an image of a unanimous humanity and the tactical variability, pluriformity, and complexity of human life. It is to explore these humanizing tactics that we now turn to.

Tactics of Humanization in *Cloud Atlas*

Cloud Atlas offers a tactical subversion of the totalizing and dehumanizing strategies of modernity through its emphasis on love. Love is a powerful tactic. It diffuses the offense, subverts manipulation, and humanizes truth. Love is the embodiment of what it means to be human. It speaks of the interconnections between humans, the bonds that tie us together, across time and place. It intimates knowledge in ways that can only be partially understood. Love reveals the truth. In the story of Sonmi 451, we find in *Cloud Atlas* a tactical revelation of love and truth that humanizes us against the conforming, universalizing, and totalizing forces of modernity.

When Sonmi is interviewed by the Archivist before her execution—or recycling—she speaks of truth as singular and of its versions as mistruths.[37] Truth is singular because it speaks of the interconnectedness of all partial truths reflected in the whole truth. Its versions are mistruths because we can only grasp parts or glimpses of its truth. This is what Raimon Panikkar identifies as the idea of the *pars pro toto* effect. The *pars pro toto* effect demonstrates how the part always reflects the whole, and yet does not grasp the whole in its totality. Panikkar states that the part

> is limited, and yet it re-presents the Whole [as] the *pars pro toto* effect (part for the whole).... We see the whole through our window; we see, and even are, the *totum in parte* (whole in the part). The concrete is the *pars pro toto*. The particular is the *pars pro toto*. We may 'sacrifice' the particular for the sake of the whole [but] we cannot do that without the concrete.[38]

The *pars pro toto* effect implies how the part is a concrete particular that reveals the whole. Or rather, it taps into an insight into truth as a whole and that its parts reveal in their partial knowledge of truth their mistruths about the whole nature of reality.

When we try to conform humanity to our own will, we abuse humanity when we totalize it and control it, subverting humanity to something less than human. Love is the tactical interplay of what makes us human. The tactical subversion of love humanizes us in ways that produce faith, hope, and love as the truth of reality. Sonmi's revelation of the interconnectedness of love is striking:

> *Archivist:* "In your Revelation, you spoke of the consequences of an individual's life rippling through eternity. Does this mean that you believe in an afterlife? In a heaven or a hell?"
>
> *Sonmi-451:* "I believe death is only a door. When it closes, another opens. If I cared to imagine a heaven, I would imagine a door opening, and behind it, I would find him there."[39]

The religious imaginary found in love tactically subverts the totalizing powers of modernity. We find towards the end of Sonmi's interview with the archivist the intuitive questioning and recovery of humanity. The archivist asks her why she would do such a thing if no one were to believe it. In the very asking of that question, Sonmi points out that someone—the archivist—already does believe it.[40] The tactical subversions of love speak to the truth of being human. Love rehumanizes us against totalizing forces. It is a truth that opens us to connection, relationship, vulnerability, and intimacy with others. The redeeming narrative of love in *Cloud Atlas* tactically subverts the trajectory of modernity back into what it means to be human.

MEDITATIONS ON THE FALL IN *CLOUD ATLAS*

If *Cloud Atlas* paints a picture of the trajectory of modernity, it also paints its tragedy. The tragedy of modernity lies in the potential for destruction—ecological and human—through the misuse and abuse of technology. *Cloud Atlas* paints a picture of an ecological, technological, and eschatological fall. In the storyline of Zachry Bailey, we see the big island of Hawaii a hundred or so years after the fall. This fall is not the fall of Adam and Eve from Eden, though it does rescript this fall in a post-apocalyptic future. The fall in *Cloud Atlas* is from a nuclear holocaust. If the Fall of Adam and Eve is a fall from innocence, the post-apocalyptic fall is a fall from the hubris of humanity in their hunger for more via their systemic abuse of technology.

If from Adam and Eve you have the beginnings of a fallen humanity, then the fall of *Cloud Atlas* is a result of the hubris of the Old Ones who grasped at the stars and led to the collapse and destruction of humanity on a poisoned earth. The ecological holocaust, caused by technological abuse and human will to power, results in an earth that only leads to death. The radiation poisoning affects the Prescients, who are gradually dying from radiation exposure. The Prescients are the remnant of a technological age, utilizing fusion engines and ships that glide on water. In the film, Meronym sets out to find a guide and finds it in Zachry, to Mona Sol, where she reaches out through satellites to the off-world colonies for rescue.

The post-apocalyptic fall in *Cloud Atlas* depicts an eschatological fall, yet not one not redeemed through the promise and agency of God. This eschatological fall does not display the sovereignty of God. Rather, it depicts a human eschatology that is marked by a buffered hope in technology. Technology divorced from the concern for human flourishing marks its abuse.[41] It is from this that humans have a buffered hope in technology. It is a hope in technology that serves human flourishing and survival. For Meronym, the survival of humanity is characterized by the hope for salvation and rescue from the off-world colonies. She puts her hope and faith in something unseen and unknown to save her and her people from the nuclear radiation of her world and the human incapacity to dwell and flourish in the midst of it.

The post-apocalyptic fall in *Cloud Atlas* follows the pattern of a fallen humanity. Its tragedy is the continuation of human pride and domination—which lasts even beyond the fall in murder, rape, slavery, pedophilia, and cannibalism. And yet, humans still have hope, and faith remains. The characteristics of faith, hope, and love amid brokenness—the fallenness of humanity and the poisoning of the earth—are central marks of the human condition in this dystopian prophecy of the tragedy and trajectory of modernity. But here we also see intimacies of redemption even amid fallenness. These intimacies of redemption are grounded in the tactics of faith, hope, and love amid tragedy.

Throughout *Cloud Atlas*, we see the prophetic tragedy of humanity in strategies of domination, control, and the totalization of reality through technological advancement and abuse. But we also see the tactics of its redemption in faith, hope, and love. The faith in things not yet seen is found in Meronym's plea for help from the off-world colonies, of which she is not even sure if they are out there. But there is hope in that, even when there is no reason to hope. It is in hope, even when there is no reason to hope, that we find the tactical humanization of the world. And love is what binds it all together. Love is the thread that connects the ligaments of stories throughout *Cloud Atlas*—it is the tactical, redemptive arc that exists between human lives through time and history. Love is the redemptive tactic that subverts the abuses of the human will to power. Love is the humanizing tactic that allows us to recover what it means to be human and shapes the purposes for the use of technology. The tactical redemption of love throughout *Cloud Atlas* reveals pathways for being human that make us more so against the strategies of modernity dominated by the will to power.

NOTES

1. Michel De Certeau, *The Practice of Everyday Life*, trans. Steven Randall (Berkeley, CA: University of California Press, 1984), 29–30. My emphasis.
2. Certeau, *The Practice of Everyday Life*, 29–42.
3. Michael E. Gardiner, *Critiques of Everyday Life* (London and New York: Routledge, 2000), 172.
4. *Cloud Atlas*, DVD (Warner Bros. Pictures, 2012).
5. Ruth Abbey, *Philosophy Now: Charles Taylor* (Princeton, NJ: Princeton University Press, 2000), 91.
6. Jean Baudrillard, *The Consumer Society: Myths and Structures*, rev. ed. (London: Sage Publications, 2017); Zygmunt Bauman, *Globalization: The Human Consequences* (New York: Columbia University Press, 1998), 77–89.
7. Karl Mannheim, *Ideology and Utopia* (London: Routledge, 1960).
8. Abbey, *Charles Taylor*, 81–84.
9. David Mitchell, *Cloud Atlas* (New York: Random House, 2004), 129.
10. Mitchell, *Cloud Atlas*, 444.
11. Mitchell, *Cloud Atlas*, 272.
12. Mitchell, *Cloud Atlas*, 273.
13. Mitchell, *Cloud Atlas*, 303, 445.
14. Max Horkheimer and Theodor W. Adorno, *Dialectic of Enlightenment: Philosophical Fragments*, ed. Gunzelin Schmid Noerr, trans. Edmund Jephcott (Stanford, CA: Stanford University Press, 2002), 1.
15. Horkheimer and Adorno, *Dialectic of Enlightenment*, 2.
16. Horkheimer and Adorno, *Dialectic of Enlightenment*, 2.
17. Horkheimer and Adorno, *Dialectic of Enlightenment*, 23.
18. Horkheimer and Adorno, *Dialectic of Enlightenment*, 23.
19. Jacques Ellul, *The Technological Society*, trans. John Wilkinson (New York: Vintage Books, 1964), xxv.
20. C.f. Mitchell, *Cloud Atlas*, 487–489.
21. C.f. Mitchell, *Cloud Atlas*, 325.
22. *Cloud Atlas* (1:09:40).
23. Emmanuel Levinas, *Totality and Infinity: An Essay on Exteriority*, trans. Alphonso Lingis (Pittsburgh, PA: Duquesne University Press, 1969), 88.
24. Levinas, *Totality and Infinity*, 87.
25. Levinas, *Totality and Infinity*, 87–88.
26. C.f. Charles Taylor, "Modes of Secularism," in *Secularism and Its Critics*, ed. Rajeev Bhargava (Delhi: Oxford University Press, 1998), 31–53.
27. C.f. José Casanova, "A Secular Age: Dawn or Twilight?," in *Varieties of Secularism in a Secular Age*, ed. Michael Warner, Jonathan VanAntwerpen, and Craig Calhoun (Cambridge, MA: Harvard University Press, 2010), 265–281, 277.
28. Charles Taylor, *Human Agency and Language*, Philosophical Papers 1 (Cambridge: Cambridge University Press, 1985), 4–5.
29. *Cloud Atlas* (2:39:33-2:40:32).

30. *Cloud Atlas* (1:29:44-1:29:53).

31. *Cloud Atlas* (2:33:43-2:34:10).

32. Arvind Sharma, *Classical Hindu Thought: An Introduction* (Oxford: Oxford University Press, 2000), 10.

33. Sharma, *Classical Hindu Thought*, 11.

34. Raimon Panikkar, *Mysticism and Spirituality: Mysticism, The Fullness of Life*, ed. Milena Carrara Pavan, vol. I.1, XII vols., Opera Omnia (Maryknoll, NY: Orbis Books, 2014), 56.

35. C.f. Miran Božovič, ed., *Jeremy Bentham: The Panopticon Writings* (London: Verso, 1995), 29–95; Michel Foucault, *Discipline and Punish: The Birth of the Prison* (New York: Pantheon Books, 1977); Zygmunt Bauman, *Liquid Modernity* (Cambridge, MA: Polity Press, 2000), 85; Bauman, *Globalization*, 52.

36. C.f. on Consumerism and the manipulation of desire: Zygmunt Bauman, *Work Consumerism and the New Poor* (Buckingham: Open University Press, 1998); Bauman, *Globalization*, 85–86; Baudrillard, *The Consumer Society*; Theodor Adorno and Max Horkheimer, *The Culture Industry* (London: Routledge, 1991).

37. *Cloud Atlas* (04:30-04:38).

38. Raimon Panikkar, "Trisangam: The Jordan, The Tiber, and the Ganges—The Three Kairological Moments of Christic Self-Consciousness," in *Christianity: A Christophany*, ed. Milena Carrara Pavan, vol. III.2, XII vols., Opera Omnia (Maryknoll, NY: Orbis Books, 2016), 3–25, 20.

39. *Cloud Atlas* (2:34:38-2:35:20).

40. *Cloud Atlas* (2:36:20-2:36:28).

41. C.f. Heidegger's Critique of Technology: Martin Heidegger, "The Question Concerning Technology," in *Basic Writings*, ed. David Farrell Krell (New York: Harper Collins Publishers, 2008), 307–342, 312.

Chapter 7

Grieving in the Wake of Wakanda

Throughout the previous chapter, attention was paid to the apocalyptic rescriptions and the tragedy and trajectory of modernity. While the previous chapter offered a postmodern critique of modern dehumanization, domination, and the will to power in ways that imagine the potential of what these things may entail in the future, this chapter, by contrast offers a prophetic critique of modernity, particularly by paying attention to the historical structures, ideologies, and conditions that have shaped the Black experience. That is, while the previous chapter is apocalyptic in articulating what modernity *may* produce, this chapter is prophetic in calling us to account for what modernity *has* produced. The horrors of the Black experience and the conditions that shape Black humanity are intimately tied to the modern structures that have shaped a Black ontology. To analyze these conditions of what modernity has produced, a study of Blackness via *Wakanda Forever* can be a helpful prophetic witness to call us into account for the problems and promises of modernity.

My chapter in Travis Harris, Kimberly Hampton, and Matthew William Brake's forthcoming *Theology and Black Panther* on a "Wakandan Politics of Identity" argues that *Black Panther* envisions new possibilities of imagining Black humanity along the veins of Afro-futurism.[1] And yet, it approaches Black ontology not from philosophical discourses on Black (non-)being in the wake of Black experience. Instead, while still intuiting the struggle to sit with the tensions in the wake of the Black experience, it argues from an Afro-futurist approach of what *Black Panther* imagines of Black ontology. My "Wakandan Politics of Identity" argues that Black ontology must self-determine itself against a dialectical overcoming of Blackness by Whiteness. Black self-determination must generate out of itself the possibilities of its future. But what model of Black ontology allows this generative force? Arguably, *Black Panther* imagines Wakanda as a noble vision of Black humanity as a powerful nation, and indeed, it does provide resources for re-imagining Black identity surrounding contemporary discourses of Black ontology.

However, there are gaps in my original chapter: I was not aware of the dominant discourses in Black philosophy. It is with these in mind that this chapter offers a revisitation of my "Wakandan Politics of Identity" that addresses its silences and ignorance of Black philosophy. This chapter offers another side of meditations on Black ontology to demonstrate the formation of Black humanity in light of the Black experience of enslavement, emancipation, and anti-blackness through analyses and assistance from Zakkiyah Iman Jackson, Achille Mbembe, Calvin Warren, and Christina Sharpe. Throughout, it also addresses how the recent *Wakanda Forever* and episodes of *What If . . . ?* flesh out continuities and other sides of Black self-determination and grieving. It is within the reality of modernity that the formation of Black humanity should cause us to grieve—and *Black Panther* and *Wakanda Forever* can offer resources that can prophetically help us to grieve in the wake of modernity.

This chapter begins with a summary of the basic argument in my original "Wakandan Politics of Identity." Then it is followed first by an analysis of Jackson, Warren, and Mbembe on the formation of Blackness, second by an analysis of Warren's Afro-pessimistic vision of Black ontology and humanity, and third by revisiting how Sharpe and Warren generate the possibilities of generating the future of Black humanity. Closing out the chapter, it offers a sustained analysis of what Christina Sharpe's "Wake Work" looks like in the character arc of Shuri's grief in *Wakanda Forever*. Between each of these analyses is a sustained reflection on the prophetic exposure to the modern history of Black humanity in light of both what Wakanda imagines of Black identity *and* of contemporary discourses in Black philosophy that can potentially imagine a future of Black humanity that adequately pays attention to and gives account of the Black experience.

BLACK SELF-DETERMINATION: A SUMMARY

My "Wakandan Politics of Identity" argues that Black being must self-determine themselves over against the patterns and images of Whiteness. First, it addresses how Black self-determination must grapple with its African and African American heritage, not in an attempt for African Americans to become African, but rather to point out resources from African religiosity to spark and imagine the possibilities of how it shows up and is rescripted in *Black Panther*. Implicit in this, slavery and its afterlives are inescapable, and their effects on the Black experience become the background to any Black religiosity. The interplay between Black experience and Black religiosity is dynamic. The Black experience calls out for Black religiosity, and Black religiosity gives sense to the Black experience. The Black experience cries out to God in lament over the conditions of the Black experience, while Black religiosity grounds the Black response to the Black experience. Black self-determination must address this interplay between Black experience and Black religiosity in ways that generate the possibilities of its future.

That chapter also argues that a Wakandan politics of identity reimagines the possibilities of Black self-determination in ways that defy its overcoming *by* Whiteness. This overcoming by Whiteness has two possibilities. To resist the overcoming by Whiteness, Black resistance to it must wrestle with the reality that Blacks must not become White in their attempt to determine themselves. The first possibility is to become White and paradoxically deny Black self-determination. This is illustrated in how Killmonger envisions the overcoming by Whiteness as a Black revolution in *"What If . . . ?"* For Killmonger, the revolution of Blackness as the new oppressor over the White oppressed must "burn it down" rather than "work the system from within."[2] In this reading, Killmonger's vision implies that Blackness must become the new White. But this not only betrays the Black experience, it also denies Black identity any self-determination outside of what is already established by Whiteness. The original chapter was adamant that a mere reversal of the oppressor/oppressed dialectic is not authentic to Black identity: if Black humanity becomes the new oppressor, Black humanity will become White.

The second possibility guards against the overcoming by Whiteness. It is to sit in solidarity with and wrestle with the Black experience without negating it for White patterns of oppression. It is not only to acknowledge the Black experience, the afterlives, and the wake of slavery. It is also to be present to the suffering and injustice caused against Blacks by Whites. This overcoming *of* Whiteness—in the sense of living and sitting with and serving those affected by the oppressive wake of slavery—is generative of a Black ontology because it grounds their lives and experiences within a situated context that cannot be forgotten. To deny the Black experience is to deny something central to Black self-determination: learning to endure suffering, injustice, and enslavement and to *insist* on their existence.

The third point argued in the original chapter is that Wakandan technological superiority paints a picture that counters a Black ontology marked by an overcoming by Whiteness. A Wakandan technocracy, portrayed through the mastery of the fictional Vibranium, depicts a vision of Black humanity not geared towards dominating others, but by serving in solidarity with the oppressed. Wakandan technocracy not only imaginatively challenges the hegemony of Western technology and power, but it also opens up the door to serving the poor and oppressed by working towards a better future for them. The Womanist ethics of care embodied by Nakia open the door from isolationism, not to domination as Killmonger envisions it, but to international service in making a better world embodied by a Wakandan politics of identity.

While this is not realized in *Wakanda Forever* because of the death of T'Challa and the greed of Western White humanity, in the second film we see another side of a Wakandan Politics of Identity—one centrally revolving around the use and abuse of Vibranium. Though T'Challa had promised to share resources after his death, his mother Queen Ramonda listened to the whispers of White Western powers and denied them the ability to use the Vibranium for fear of them creating weapons of mass destruction. This illustrates an ethical problem of the potential use and abuse of technology—one that Wakanda was reticent to experience in the wake of modernity. As an often-quipped remark of Akoya toward Everett Ross as a "colonizer," there are tellingly subtle undertones of an awareness of White forms of power that seek to dominate and abuse power. Queen Ramonda denies the sharing of Vibranium because of the long history of White, Western humanity in its strategic drive to dominate and control the world.

On the other side, when Western powers discovered Vibranium in the ocean, little did the world know there was a hidden nation underwater led by Namor. A central tactic of Namor is to remain anonymous while yet forcefully defending the Vibranium of Talokan against incursions. But there is also another side to how Vibranium is wielded when we contrast the Wakandans to Namor and the Talokanians. While the Wakandans are reticent to share the Vibranium, they are not willing to be aggressors—they are merely concerned with defending their Vibranium so that it would not be used and abused as weapons of mass destruction. By contrast, Namor wished to use Vibranium to wage an anonymous war on the surface world as a way of protecting Talokanian Vibranium out of hatred for the abuses of colonizers. The use of Vibranium for both is united by their desire to protect the Vibranium from the use of the Western, White powers' intent to use it to control and dominate the world. And yet, the difference between Wakanda and Namor is their orientation towards violence. The Wakandans advocate restraint and warning against incursions, while Namor and Talokan advocate for aggression and war against the surface world because of the surface world's corrupted desire to wield Vibranium as a weapon of "colonizers."

The history of colonization, however, displays a particular difference between the Mesoamerican origins of Namor and Talokan and the African origins of Wakanda. The Spanish conquistadors were relentless in their colonizing abuses. Mesoamericans experienced their own horrors in light of colonization and modernity that cannot be equated to the horrors of enslaved Black humanity. Analogous to both the Mesoamerican and Black experiences, racism, and racial superiority were implicit in how they were treated.

Yet there are differences between the Mesoamerican and Black experiences. An aim of the Spanish colonizers was also religious—they wanted to convert a new humanity and had to wrestle with the theological problems of "discovering" the New World.[3] In turn, Black humanity was oppressed in ways that their identity was stripped from them by the colonizers and through enslavement. In the case of the fictional Wakanda, the MCU envisions a Black humanity that is not determined by modern, colonial, historical factors.

Arguably, Wakanda presents an imagined vision of a better humanity. "Black is better," I think, is what Wakanda imagines of a Black humanity and Black ontology. Because it is a fictional story of Blackness, a Wakandan politics of identity is imagined, but the power of imagination in shaping our world cannot be undone. *Black Panther* envisions a new future for Black humanity as noble, righteous, honorable, and good. But this is not the common discourse of Black ontology. What happens when Black ontology recognizes the wake and afterlives of slavery and when Black being is the terror of non-being? Where indeed did Blackness come from, and how does it differ from the qualifier "African"? It is to these discourses that this chapter now turns through an analysis of the contributions of Jackson, Mbembe, Warren, and Sharpe as a response and revisitation to the silences of my original chapter on Black ontology.

FORMATIONS OF BLACKNESS

Achille Mbembe argues that the trans-Atlantic slave trade generated a general fungibility between Blackness and its origins out of Africa.[4] However, he and Calvin Warren also emphasize the complex asymmetry between "Black" and "African."[5] Mbembe does so through an analysis of colonialization and its doubling effects on Black self-consciousness. Not only does colonialization carry the pain of Africans at being subjected to Western colonialism, but this doubles through their selling into the capitalization of Black humanity as a commodity. In selling fellow Africans into slavery, Africa holds in painful tension the selling out of their self-determination for Western colonialism and capitalism. The African sense of Blackness holds in painful tension their complicity in slavery with their buying into the temptation to become White by extracting and subjecting their fellows to slavery. Once in slavery, Blacks were left dispossessed of their own identity, alienated, and subjected to a state of being marked by the "disjuncture" between memory and remembrance of who they are and how it relates to their African origins.[6]

This disjuncture for enslaved Black humanity from the memory and remembrance of their African origins is characterized at one end by the Black diaspora living in the afterlives of slavery who are denied their African heritage through the breaking of both their kinship relations to family *and* of their belonging to the land due to the effects of their enslavement.[7] On the other end, you have the multiplicity of African identities, cultures, religions, and languages across the African continent that deny a universal definition of "Blackness." And yet the inextricable asymmetry between Blackness and African is always present. The modern formation of Blackness views them as the degraded human because s/he is the subhuman animal. The signification between Africa and Blackness intimately stigmatizes their inescapable asymmetry and the negative connotations of their abuse. Mbembe argues that Blackness and race are "open-ended signifiers" that posit an existential function to being Black.[8] Even more so, the asymmetrical tension between Blackness and Africa signifies a racialization that denies a common humanity marked by proximity and resemblance.[9]

In the diasporic movement of Black beings, what we find are the institutions and solubility of what Mbembe calls the "becoming Black of the world."[10] This becoming Black of the world is intimately linked to the modern processes of slavery and its cultural, social, and economic productions of a racialized Blackness. Mbembe states:

> The term "black" was the product of a social and technological machine tightly linked to the emergence and globalization of capitalism. It was invented to signify exclusion, brutalization, and degradation, to point to a limit constantly conjured and abhorred. The Black Man, despised and profoundly dishonored, is the only human in the modern order whose skin has been transformed into the form and spirit of merchandise.[11]

Zakiyyah Iman Jackson agrees with Mbembe:

> Slavery and colonialism not only catalyzed the conscription of black people into hegemonically imperialist and racialized conceptions of "modernity" and "universal humanity" but also inaugurated Western modernity's condition of possibility, initiating a chain of events that have given rise to a transnational capitalistic order.[12]

The link between slavery and modern capitalism initiates the possibility of racism as a modern structure that culturally produces the continued systemic degradation of Black being called antiblackness. Jackson argues that antiblackness is a cultural production that

> comprises the very notion of the African Diaspora and of Blackness. . . . Antiblackness's pliability is essential to the intransigent, complementary, and universalizing impetus of antiblack paradigms. Irrespective of the innumerable and ever-transient definitions of black identity across the diaspora, which by

definition are ephemerally produced, all black(ened) people must contend with the burden of the antiblack animalization of the global paradigm of blackness, which will infringe on all articulations and political maneuverings that seek redress for present and historical violence.[13]

The pliable nature of antiblackness generates the possibility of constitutive violence that shapes the Black experience as something subjected and abjected into what Western antiblackness envisions it to be as a cultural, social, economic, and political phenomenon. Mbembe argues that Blackness is constantly produced through "a social link of subjection" to "a *body of extraction*" marked and determined by "the will of the master . . . to extract maximum profit."[14] But this extraction of Black being for profit also implies the "tearing and separation of humans from their origins and birthplaces."[15] The separation of Black being from their origins through enslavement creates a break that tears apart their identity and rootedness of belonging, both filially and topologically. In this break and their displacement of identity, their being is exploited in the very extraction of their lives into slavery for profit.

Mbembe argues that because of slavery, colonialism, and apartheid, the Black Man is separated from himself, cut off from his belonging, and alienated and estranged from the determining factors that rooted his existence. Even more so, the Black Man is then disappropriated by his dispossession of himself, his origins, and his rootedness in the extraction and subjugation of his humanity through enslavement. Finally, the Black Man is then degraded through humiliation and abject servitude.[16] Each of these points not only to the dehumanization of Black humanity through the modern capitalistic reduction of their humanity as a commodity but also to the social death Orlando Patterson rightly points out as the breaking of social ties through power dynamics of enslavement that deny ownership over one's own life, identity, and self-determination.[17]

But the nature of enslaved life is also defined by the exploitation of social relations marked by "segmented forms of subjection, distrust, intrigue, rivalry, and jealousy."[18] Each of these enslaved ways of living produces "ambivalent tactics born out of complicity," where the degradation of Black being is not only reduced to capitalistic functions of production and commodity but also the distortions and degradation of a social life marked by the breakdown of trust and kinship, playing one off of another, in a continued afterlife of enslaved ways of coping with the breakdown of social ties.[19]

Mbembe makes a distinction between two types of Black reason. One is the "Western consciousness of Blackness," and the other is the "Black consciousness of Blackness."[20] The first refers to the Western academy making sense of the fragments of the Black experience, identity, and suffering in the wake of slavery, in light of the racialized instrumentalization of the

Black experience at the service of racial superiority.[21] The second refers to the Black community's attempt to create out of these fragments, stories, and experiences a community that can endure within the afterlives of slavery.[22] The debate or conflict of Black reason, Mbembe argues, refers to the struggle with modernity, its imagining of what it means to be human, and its tensions with its animality.[23]

This tension between Black humanity and its animality is tied to the development of Western discourses and visions of humanity. Sylvia Wynter argues that Blackness is produced by the transition in modern visions of humanity from the early modern colonial distinction between rational and civilized humans and the hope for educating and civilizing irrational humans to the eighteenth- and nineteenth-century racialized distinction between the Western human and the subhuman animality of Blackness.[24] The determination of Black humanity for Mbembe between these two Western visions of Black humanity lies in the tension between the potential *ratio* of humanity and the *animalitas* that possess his spirit.[25] Building on the *animalitas* of Black humanity, Zakkiyah Jackson argues that

> in the process of animalizing "the African," *blackness would be defined as the emblematic state of animal man, as the nadir of the human*. By virtue of racialization, the category of "the animal" could even potentially racialize animals in addition to animalizing blackness.[26]

Part of the modern vision of Blackness was the tension between the hope to civilize the Black Man to become like White humanity and to convert them to the White image of humanity, even when Whites still recognized Blacks as inferior to them.[27]

Challenging the Enlightenment views of universal, liberal humanism and its language of dehumanization, Jackson argues that to deny or exclude humanity is a bestialized dehumanization that does not deny Africans their humanity but rather appropriates, inverts, and plasticizes the abjection of their animality. Furthermore, she argues that "Blackness is not so much derived *from* a discourse on nonhuman animals—rather the discourse on 'the animal' is formed through enslavement and the colonial encounter encompassing *both human and nonhuman* forms of life."[28] Jackson argues that slavery's ability is not to dehumanize Black humanity as an animal but rather to abject their *human* animality.[29]

This abjection of human animality results in the plasticity between Black humanity and animality. This plasticity feeds into the antiblack discourse that bestializes Black humanity, abjecting their humanity from their animality through the "alienation, exploitation, subjection, and domestication" of slavery.[30] Indeed, the technologies of slavery do not deny humanity but make it plastic, malleable, and reusable through the degradation of their human animality.[31] Jackson argues that this plasticity produced by slavery's violence is grounded in a "matrix of subjecthood and subjectivity" where the Black being is "transmogrified" in its humanity to its biological animality, reducing its humanity to its animality.[32]

If Jackson articulates the Black being as the plasticity between its humanity and animality, Calvin Warren articulates the Black being in Heideggerian terms as "equipment." In the reduction of Black being to enslaved equipment, Warren argues that

> antiblack dealings with black bodies do not expose the essential unfolding, or essence, of the equipment; rather, the purpose of antiblack dealings is to systematically obliterate the flesh, and to impose nothing onto that obliterated space—care and value are obsolete in this encounter . . . we might say . . . that the essence of black equipment is nothing—being is not there.[33]

The Black human is "equipment in human form, embodied nothingness. Using black equipment reveals existence but not being."[34] While Warren remains a pessimist over the possibilities of the idea of a Black humanity because of the structured nothingness embedded within systemic antiblackness, in contrast, Zakkiyah Jackson contextualizes Black humanity in tension with this antiblackness, holding out hope for Black being while recognizing the limits of a universal humanity precisely because of the racialized dis-ease antiblackness inculcates.[35]

And yet, antiblackness perpetuates the conditions of Black being. While Black being may be emancipated, they can never be freed from the constraints and contours of antiblackness.[36] The emancipation of Black being entraps "black ~~being~~ in an abyss of shattered signification, terroristic operations, and irreparable violation. The ontological transformation that emancipation promises is deceptive; rather than transforming property (~~being~~ for another) into human (being for itself), it suspends becoming."[37] Metaphysically speaking, Warren argues that Black being can never escape the emancipation of its being by antiblack violence. The structures of antiblackness are inescapable and mark the weight of nothingness that eludes Black ~~being~~. For Warren, this metaphysical infrastructure of antiblackness inculcates the terror of Black ~~being~~ from being anything other than nothing.[38] It is to Warren's afro-pessimistic vision of Black ontology that we now turn to.

CALVIN WARREN'S AFRO-PESSIMISTIC ONTOLOGY

In contrast to my original arguments linking Black ontology to Afro-futurism in *Black Panther*, in Calvin Warren we find a negative account of Black ontology, one defined by both its alignment with Afro-pessimism and its definition of Black being as a functional nothingness—an "ontological terror." Warren sits within the tradition of Afro-pessimism albeit his approach is defined by a metaphysical account of a Black ontology in terms of non-being. Afro-pessimism is a tradition within Black discourse that challenges antiblackness and White visions of Black humanity with a radical confrontation of Black being to White ways of being in the world. And yet, Afro-pessimism for Warren is not really to confront White ways of being with Black ways of being. Rather, Warren confronts us with the ontological terror of Black (non-)being as nothing. Tied to this, Warren argues for a nihilistic rejection of the modern liberal humanistic hope of Black Lives Matter for the equality and freedom of Black humanity. But what he replaces it with should hold us in the wake of terror. He argues that Black being is in reality the terror of its nothingness.[39] His interpretation of Black being as the reduction to function in the antiblack afterlives of slavery leads him to argue that Black being is nothingness—and that is terrifying.

Following and making a spin on Heidegger's ontological indestructibility of the structures of Being, Warren argues that the reduction of Black being to pure function is one "which enables human beingness to engage in its projectionality into the world and to restore its forgotten relationship with Being." In a word, Black being helps the human being re-member its relation to Being through its lack of relationality."[40] Warren describes Blackness as "the abyss of ontology" to point out how Black being experiences the "tensions, contradictions, and impasses" of its intelligibility, where its nothingness is a "condition of [its] possibility" to include the exclusion of its being as nothingness.[41] The purpose of ontological terror is to open up the possibilities of understanding Black being in ways that meditate on the "(non) relation between blackness and Being." Ontological terror is to incarnate a

> metaphysical nothing . . . in an antiblack world. Blacks, then, have a function but not Being—the function of black(ness) is to give form to a terrifying formlessness (nothing). Being claims function as its property . . . , but the aim of black nihilism is to expose the unbridgeable rift between Being and function for blackness. The puzzle of blackness, then, is that it functions in an antiblack world without being—much like "nothing" functions philosophically without our metaphysical understanding of being. . . . Put differently, metaphysics is obsessed with both blackness and nothing, and the two become synonyms for that which ruptures metaphysical organization and form . . . [Black being] must assume the function of nothing in a metaphysical world.[42]

Warren, working in the tradition of Franz Fanon's colonial reflections on Black being's danger and retaliation against Whiteness,[43] argues that Black being, through the development of antiblackness and its racialized perpetuation of the afterlives of slavery, points out how terrorizing Black ~~being~~ is: it leaves in the wake of its recognition and realization of its negation the terror of (Black) ~~being~~ nothing. The negation of Black being is marked not by the denial of its humanity but rather by the negation of Black ~~being's~~ ability to determine itself outside the constructs of Western, White modernity. To be confronted with Blackness is to be confronted not only with the terror of Black being in the eyes of Whites. It is also to be confronted by the terrible nothingness determined by the abjection and dispossession of their Being as nothingness.[44] The abjection of Black ~~being~~ as nothingness is marked by the idea that their ~~Being~~ is expelled in order to be a subject marked by an ontological nothingness. In this abjection of Black being as nothingness, there is a "terror that ontological security is gone, the terror that ethical claims no longer have an anchor, and the terror of inhibiting existence outside the precincts of humanity and humanism."[45]

At the heart of Warren's ontological terror is an Afro-pessimistic vision of Black ontology that denies the possibilities of Black humanity—at least insofar as it is overcome by Whiteness. The racialized constructions of Western modernity intimate that the afterlives of slavery imply the abjection, subjection, and negation of Black humanity through the antiblack structures systemically embedded within the structures of Western modernity and liberalism. So, what are we to do with the reality of ontological terror? What does this generate regarding the possibilities of the future of Black humanity? Arguably, while Warren's pessimism confronts us with the reality that while there may be no redemptive future for the idea of Black humanism, there also remain intimations of its renewal within Warren for an appeal to the Black spirit. Here we find in Warren, alongside Christina Sharpe's advocacy for living in the *wake* of slavery, the possibilities of understanding the future of Black humanity through an account of *enduring* the afterlives of slavery and *insisting* on the existence of Black humanity.

RECONSIDERING AFRO-FUTURISM VIA THE SPIRIT OF ENDURANCE AND INSISTING ON EXISTENCE

In the terror of non-being, what then is Black humanity left with? Modernity produced through enslavement and colonialism the systemic structures of antiblackness, its violence, exploitation, and deferral of an unobtainable freedom. Based on these accounts, Killmonger's goal of burning the system to the ground through revolution and becoming the new oppressor certainly makes sense. And yet, my argument in "Wakandan Politics of Identity" remains: to upend antiblackness through violence to become the new oppressor by liberating the powerless is to be overcome by Whiteness.

And yet, this chapter adds a new spin that deepens my original account in "Wakandan Politics of Identity" of the future of Black humanity as marked by a Black self-determinism characterized by the *solidarity* with the Black experience of suffering, violence, and injustice in an antiblack world. Between emancipation's deferral of freedom and the nothingness of Black being, what image of Black humanity are we left with? I think Christina Sharpe's insistence on existing in the wake of slavery *and* Calvin Warren's ambiguous appeal to the Black spirit of endurance (as a spiritual practice) are both fruitful pathways to understanding the future of Black humanity.

Christina Sharpe argues that the wake of slavery generates the possibility of insisting on existence.[46] Her metaphors of "the wake" offer multiple senses of the pictures of mourning and grieving the loss of (Black) life according to the systemic structures of trans-Atlantic slavery and its afterlife in the emancipated structures of Black humanity amid continued antiblack sensibilities of oppression, inequality, and violence. Sharpe points us to the reality that the Black insistence on grieving in the wake opens us to the possibilities of discovering ways of being (a Black) human. Sharpe argues that her metaphors of the wake describe a consciousness of Black being that occupies and is "occupied by [the] continuous and changing present of slavery's as yet unresolved unfolding."[47] She states that

> living in the wake means living the history and present of terror, from slavery to the present, as the ground of our everyday black existence; living the historically and geographically dis/continuous but always present and endlessly reinvigorated brutality in, and on, our bodies while even as that terror is visited on our bodies the realities of that terror are erased. Put another way, living in the wake means living in and with terror in that in much of what passes for public discourse *about* terror we, Black people, become the *carriers* of terror, terror's embodiment, and not the primary objects of terror's multiple enactments; the ground of terror's possibility globally.[48]

Here we see Sharpe pointing to the reality of living *in the wake*. The insistence on existing in the wake is marked by fortitude and grieving amid the injustices, oppression, and sufferings marked by the afterlives of slavery. Notably, each of these is marked by *terror*. But this is not Calvin Warren's terror of Black humanity being nothing. Sharpe holds out hope for Black humanity to learn to *insist* on their existence in the wake of slavery. It is an opening to the possibility of *enduring* through the injustices, suffering, and oppression that mark the emancipation of Black being. "Wake work" for Sharpe is to work from within the wake of slavery and the death that marks Black social existence. To insist on wake work is to work amid the injustice, even, in an appeal to Warren, to endure through it.

This endurance for Warren is analogous to Sharpe's emphasis on the *praxis* of wake work. Warren seeks to redefine Black metaphysics not as humanism,[49] as Sharpe does in holding out for a generative Black human praxis, but rather as a spiritual praxis of enduring through the systemic structures of antiblackness.[50] To endure the nothingness of being does not necessarily intimate that nothing has no content. Warren ambiguously appeals to this content as the Black spirit.[51] Whether this Black spirit for Warren is linked to a Black culture embodied by the Black soul, psyche, and spirit, I do not know.[52] And yet, the idea of enduring as a spiritual praxis offers a reminiscence of the apostle Paul, who calls Christians to endure through persecution and suffering, where their faith grows through being tested in fidelity to the one who saves them from sin and death. The trials of one's faith produce the spirit of endurance through many sufferings. Indeed, like the Christian life depicted across the New Testament, the spirit of Blackness must endure through suffering "to imagine existence anew."[53]

GRIEVING AND REMEMBRANCE AS WAKE WORK IN *WAKANDA FOREVER*

If enduring through suffering is a central element of the Black spirit, then how does *Wakanda Forever* imagine grieving in the wake of suffering?[54] To illustrate this, one may discuss how *Wakanda Forever* imagines wake work in terms of Black religiosity. Throughout *Wakanda Forever*, not only does Shuri grieve her brother, but also throughout the film Shuri is consumed by her grief and channels it into her technological interests as a clutch for redeeming Wakanda in the loss of the Heart-Shaped Herb. Shuri blames herself for the death of her brother because technology and religiosity had failed her. She no longer believed in the myths of her ancestors, in Bast, or the power of Wakandan ritual and belief to help make sense of her loss and grief. After her mother's death, she turns to create a synthetic Heart-Shaped Herb and takes it. Though she does not believe in the ancestral realm, she comes to face not with her mother, but N'Jadaka. Throughout their dialogue, N'Jadaka challenges Shuri to "get things done" rather than be noble like her brother. Shuri is consumed by revenge against Namor for killing her mother. And yet, when she weighs whether to spare Namor's life, she remembers her mother, her brother, and the beauty of Talokan alongside the counsel of N'Jadaka.

Key to this narrative is not just forgiveness, but more centrally of *remembrance*. Key to Black religiosity is the power of remembrance to shape the present, to inform Shuri's actions in the present in light of the past. Here the past is a storehouse of memory: it is something to be remembered and is what shapes Shuri's actions in sparing Namor's life. She decides, like her brother, not to be consumed by hatred, but rather to remember her mother, her brother, the beauty of Talokan, and who she is in light of her experiences of suffering. Shuri's spirit to endure suffering becomes generative for a new way of imagining Black identity. By remembering her past, she eventually finds solace in the rituals of her Wakandan belief. She is allowed to grieve, or rather, allows herself to grieve rather than be consumed by the power of her grief as she sought answers in technology to create a new Black Panther.

The story of Shuri in *Wakanda Forever* is a dialectic between Wakandan technology and Wakandan religiosity. Shuri seeks answers in technology in such a way that her faith is in her ability to technologically recreate the powers of the Black Panther. Shuri trusts in technology and abandons the power of Wakandan ritual and belief. Moreover, like the relationship between magic and science in *Dr. Strange*, the power of technology in the Marvel Cinematic Universe has a relationship with the power of the divine. Technology becomes a human, this-worldly means to create what magic is already able to do. Shuri's ability to technologically re-create a synthetic heart-shaped herb is an advancement in technology that is compared to the miraculous events of Bast revealing the heart-shaped herb to the first Black Panther. Here, we see technology interpreted through the lens of enchantment—technological advancement is interpreted religiously in ways that imply the religious significance of Vibranium technology for the Wakandan people.

And yet, on the other side, Shuri's abandonment of Wakandan ritual and belief in the ancestors is a telling sign of her own wake work. The climax of her wake work comes at the point where she has to make a decision to be consumed by revenge or to show mercy to Namor. To make her decision, she remembers her history, her experience, her brother, and her mother. As Queen Ramonda says, "Show them who you are," echoes in Shuri as she remembers her experiences of suffering. She decides to allow herself to feel the power of her grief and to remember through her grief the power of memory and her experience. The power of her memories and experience offers a key point of connection to Black Religiosity: the remembrance of her past plays an important role in allowing her to determine who she is, and likewise is a telling element of the power of remembrance to shape Black self-determination.

CONCLUSION

This chapter has revisited arguments found within my original "Wakandan Politics of Identity" and has attempted to give an account of its silences. Those silences now speak. Through an analysis of the Black experience, its formation, nothingness, and its potential future, this chapter argued that even a negative Afro-pessimistic vision of Black ontology can generate pathways for understanding the future of Black humanity. However, what is clear is that Western, modern visions of humanity have not only abjected and subjected Black humanity to enslaved functionality and animality. We also see that these visions of Black humanity fail to give an adequate account of Black humanity. Though the formation of Blackness in tension between Africanness and antiblackness remains, what Black humanity must wrestle with is the possibility of imagining Black humanity and existence anew.

This is one of the beautiful things *Black Panther* and *Wakanda Forever* offer. They imagine Black humanity and existence anew in ways that generate not only the enduring future of Black humanity that is in touch with and solidarity with the Black experience of suffering, but also envisions a future of Black humanity that imagines it anew without denying its past. It is precisely in the wake work of the remembrance of the past for the present that Black identity is determined through the dialectical relation between Black experience and Black religiosity. While imagination is still imagination, and Wakanda and the Black Panther are fictional, their power to enchant the imagination renews how we may see and envision a Black ontology anew where the Black experience is not denied. It is one where the future of Black humanity can be given an alternate future to Western determinations of Blackness through the very remembrance of Black humanity's past as a way to determine Black formations of the future of Black humanity and identity.

NOTES

1. Andrew D. Thrasher, "Wakandan Imaginaries of Black Identity: Wakandan Politics of Identity," in *Theology and Black Panther*, ed. Travis Harris, Kimberly Hampton, and Matthew William Brake (Forthcoming).

2. C.f. "What If... Killmonger Rescued Tony Stark?," Streaming, *What If...?* (Burbank, CA: Disney+, August 11, 2021).

3. Willie James Jennings, *The Christian Imagination: Theology and the Origins of Race* (New Haven and London: Yale University Press, 2010).

4. For the reader's reference, this section presents exclusively Black voices in their articulations of the formation of Black humanity. To be clear, what is presented here is a terror and horror, both in its distortion of what it means to be (a Black) human and of what modern structures and Black philosophers present of what it means to be Black. Parts of this section stir in me great anger at the dehumanization of Black humanity, as well as immense grief. Having spent much time in Black thought and having grown up in Black culture, I have long since realized that to study Black theology and philosophy as a White male means to be confronted with the reality of racism. There is much to grieve in this.

5. Achille Mbembe, *Critique of Black Reason*, trans. Laurent Dubois (Durham and London: Duke University Press, 2017), 12–13; Calvin Warren, *Ontological*

Terror: Blackness, Nihilism, and Emancipation (Durham and London: Duke University Press, 2018), 39–40.

6. Mbembe, *Critique of Black Reason*, 119–122.

7. This is heartbreakingly illustrated in Saidiya Hartman's implicit search for her African heritage that she finds in the songs of the diaspora. C.f. Saidiya Hartman, *Lose Your Mother: A Journey Along the Atlantic Slave Route* (New York, NY: Farrar, Straus, and Giroux, 2007), 234–235.

8. Mbembe, *Critique of Black Reason*, 6.

9. Mbembe, *Critique of Black Reason*, 54.

10. Mbembe, *Critique of Black Reason*, 5–6.

11. Mbembe, *Critique of Black Reason*, 6.

12. Zakiyyah Iman Jackson, *Becoming Human: Matter and Meaning in an Antiblack World* (New York: New York University Press, 2020), 45.

13. Jackson, *Becoming Human*, 19.

14. Mbembe, *Critique of Black Reason*, 18.

15. Mbembe, *Critique of Black Reason*, 40.

16. Mbembe, *Critique of Black Reason*, 78.

17. Orlando Patterson, *Slavery and Social Death* (Cambridge, MA: Harvard University Press, 1982).

18. Mbembe, *Critique of Black Reason*, 18.

19. Mbembe, *Critique of Black Reason*, 18: "The social links defined by exploitation were never stable."

20. Mbembe, *Critique of Black Reason*, 28, 30.

21. Mbembe, *Critique of Black Reason*, 27–28.

22. Mbembe, *Critique of Black Reason*, 28–29.

23. Mbembe, *Critique of Black Reason*, 30–31.

24. Sylvia Wynter and David Scott, "The Re-Enchantment of Humanism: An Interview with Sylvia Wynter," *Small Axe* 8 (2000): 119–207, 174–177.

25. Mbembe, *Critique of Black Reason*, 31.

26. Jackson, *Becoming Human*, 22. Original Italics.

27. Mbembe, *Critique of Black Reason*, 75–76.

28. Jackson, *Becoming Human*, 23.

29. Jackson, *Becoming Human*, 46–47.

30. Jackson, *Becoming Human*, 59.

31. Jackson, *Becoming Human*, 71.

32. Jackson, *Becoming Human*, 81.

33. Warren, *Ontological Terror*, 46.

34. Warren, *Ontological Terror*, 46.

35. Jackson, *Becoming Human*, 20.

36. Warren, *Ontological Terror*, 51, 86, 87.

37. Warren, *Ontological Terror*, 88, 98.

38. Warren, *Ontological Terror*, 53.

39. Warren, *Ontological Terror*, 1–4.

40. Warren, *Ontological Terror*, 32.

41. Warren, *Ontological Terror*, 42.

42. Warren, *Ontological Terror*, 5–6.
43. Franz Fanon, *Black Skin, White Masks*, trans. R. Philcox (London: Grove Press, 2008).
44. Warren, *Ontological Terror*, 29.
45. Warren, *Ontological Terror*, 4.
46. Christina Sharpe, *In the Wake: On Blackness and Being* (Durham and London: Duke University Press, 2016), 11.
47. Sharpe, *In the Wake*, 13–14.
48. Sharpe, *In the Wake*, 15.
49. Warren, *Ontological Terror*, 170.
50. Warren, *Ontological Terror*, 172.
51. Warren, *Ontological Terror*, 171.
52. Warren, *Ontological Terror*, 169.
53. Warren, *Ontological Terror*, 172.
54. *Wakanda Forever*, Streaming (Walt Disney Pictures, 2022).

Part IV

RESCRIPTING SIN AS BROKENNESS

Chapter 8

Doxologies of Brokenness

At the heart of part III were analyses of how *Cloud Atlas* and *Black Panther/ Wakanda Forever* call us to account and wrestle with the dehumanizing effects of modernity. The previous two chapters shed light on the realities of Black suffering and the potential trajectory of modern ideologies that are influenced by the will to power, control, and domination. But what the previous two chapters also reveal are the latencies of sin and brokenness that are tempered by the power of love and the insistent cries for endurance in the face of suffering and dehumanization. Here, in part IV, we will turn to analyze the post-Christian human condition through analyses of sin as brokenness in contemporary secular doxologies that cry out for God and in depictions of urban poverty found in the show *Shameless*. Thus, the point of part IV is to analyze brokenness in ways that continue to cry out for God, and yet in ways that reflect on the human condition in the absence of God. Here I problematize whether sin is an adequate term to describe the post-Christian human condition. And yet, sin as brokenness also entails a theology grounded in the reverberating cries for an absent God.

Sin is hard to define in Western twenty-first-century culture. Indeed, it is something distasteful, hated, and borderline "canceled" in accepted parlance for understanding what it means to be human. But while sin is certainly abhorrent in contemporary Western culture, this does not mean that it is not present. Sin is hidden and manifests within the longings for love, the cries of our hearts, and the echoes of resignations to and of hopelessness that we find in contemporary twenty-first-century popular music. Arguably, it is in the doxological cries of our hearts against the absence and silence of a God we find dis-credited and incredulous that we can locate post-Christian echoes of sin as brokenness in the secular doxologies of Machine Gun Kelly, Halsey, and Linkin Park.

WHOSE SIN, WHICH BROKENNESS?

If one were to try to describe secular hamartiology (study of sin) in popular culture, a Christian might balk and charge that sin is the universal, inherited condition of all humanity born after the fall of Adam and Eve, that humans are utterly depraved (defined here as unable to be right with God by human works), and that sin is defined as rebellion against God. Each of these would imply that to study sin is something abhorrent, something not worthy of study; sin (and the study of sin) is something to be avoided. It leaves a taint on the purity of our souls, and the best way to avoid sin is to have faith in God through Christ to save us from its polluting effects that lead us to damnation. Each of these positions is a common way of thinking about sin among Christians. Despite this, even the great modern Christian apologist, C. S. Lewis, wrote diabolical literature.

Between his *Screwtape Letters* and his *Ransom/Space Trilogy*, Lewis sought to understand the nature and patterns of the demonic.[1] As a student once remarked to a class I taught on the religious dimensions of fantasy literature, the depictions of demonic logic in *Perelandra* are like demonic logic on steroids compared to those found in Lewis's *Screwtape Letters*. While the latter presents an inversion of Black and White, Good and Evil, and God and Demons from the perspective of the demonic, it remains quite simplistic and offers practical lessons for Christians to understand how the demonic can influence the ways and lives of Christians. Throughout both sets of literature, Lewis sought to understand how sin was patterned, originating in spiritual realities and their influences, and how sin is distortive of what it means to be human in light of the glory of God. C. S. Lewis, throughout his *Space Trilogy,* referred to two types of fallen spirituality: bentness and brokenness.

Bent spirituality for Lewis was marked by the openness and acceptance of the demonic into one's life in ways conscious of a greater vision than oneself.[2] Bent spirituality still believes in an ideal beyond ourselves by which we are driven to achieve greatness. This is particularly illustrated by the character Weston in the *Space Trilogy*. In *Out of the Silent Planet*, Weston is driven by the ideal of humanity as striving to survive beyond the scope of one world through the conquering and colonization of others. It presumes the superiority of (Western) humanity, modern science, progress, and human reason. However, by the time we encounter Weston in *Perelandra*, this ideal has been warped by demonic influence in ways that broke down the barriers of morality in the appeal to becoming One with a divine-cosmic reality that collapses Good and Evil as if there is no distinction between them in the true reality of things. This, in turn, created the possibility not only of demonic possession but one in which Weston was transformed into the Unman—which was created when Weston surrendered his will completely to demonic possession. Such *horrors* in a book so filled with the beauty of an unfallen world.

By contrast, Lewis argues that to have a broken spirituality is to be so selfish and greedy for self-advancement that one is merely a "talking animal."[3] Broken spirituality, according to the Oyarsa (planetary angel) of Malacandra (Mars), is something that ought to be destroyed because it is no longer a creature worth living, precisely because its love has become so distorted that it worships only itself at the expense of all else. This is particularly illustrated in the character of Devine, who in *That Hideous Strength* is known as Lord Feverstone. Throughout *Out of the Silent Planet*, we find Devine as ruthless and cruel, while also skittish when confronted with powers he does not understand. He is not motivated by any higher ideal other than the exploitation of Malacandra for his own benefit. We see this sentiment continue in *That Hideous Strength*, where he is willing to chase after his own benefit when things are both good and beginning to crumble. The internal monologue of Lord Feverstone is revealed as he slips out of the Banquet Hall before the curse of Babel and the violence ensue. He is already planning for new opportunities for his own self-advancement with no regard for others. What is true of brokenness is not only the irrelevance of belief but also the closure to any higher ideal to motivate our human actions.

But if we were to examine brokenness and bentness in the doxologies of Machine Gun Kelly, Halsey, and Linkin Park, what is telling is that these definitions of brokenness are inadequate when we analyze how their lyrics and doxologies cry out for love in the traces of an absent God. The problem of brokenness for these musical artists is not disbelief in God or any higher ideal but the consequential selfishness tied to it that we find in Lewis. But sin for these doxological artists of brokenness means to *recognize the absence* of what it means when we cry out in rebellion against, yet acknowledge the traces of an absent God. These are sentiments, I think, of the millennial experience of brokenness that Machine Gun Kelly, Halsey, and Linkin Park so eloquently cry out for in their doxologies of brokenness.

SIN, BROKENNESS, AND THE MILLENNIAL EXPERIENCE

When we examine the millennial experience in light of twenty-first-century music, this reveals an alternative vision of sin defined not as rebellion, but more astutely as brokenness. And yet, the idea of sin as brokenness in secular music does not truly reflect Lewis's idea of brokenness. Certainly, brokenness in the music of Machine Gun Kelly, Halsey, and Linkin Park may reflect a sense of selfishness. But more accurately, their doxologies of brokenness reflect a resigned crying out for love in the silent echoes left behind in the traces of an absence of God. Their doxologies of brokenness reveal something uniquely human that cannot be simply reduced to the "demonic" or rebellion against God (even while those may still be there). But we must also note that their doxologies point out that although they scream at the echoes and traces of God, there is a referential disconnect between God and their post-Christian reality. The millennial experience is marked by a level of brokenness that results not when we realize God does not exist, but rather with the reality of the schism or gap that is signified between who God is supposed to be and the disconnect of that image of God with and to the brokenness of life's experience.

Popular culture provides a useful resource for making sense of sin in ways that take us deeper into the heart of contemporary culture. If Paul Tillich was right that culture is the manifestation of ultimate concern, and that the ultimate concern of culture is the heart of religion,[4] then how popular culture reformulates sin displays a manifestation of contemporary religiosity. But the heart of contemporary culture as sinful cannot merely be condemned because it is "rebellious" against God. It may be understood as the echoes of longing against the silent glory of an absent God. Sin manifests in secular doxologies as a religious sentiment behind the echoes of nihilism that reverberate against the silences of an absent God. Machine Gun Kelly, Halsey, and Linkin Park demonstrate this echo of brokenness against the silence of God in the cries of a resigned heart of human longing for a redemptive nihilism that takes seriously the reality of brokenness.

The doxologies of brokenness in Machine Gun Kelly, Halsey, and Linkin Park require interpretation. The exegesis throughout this chapter offers a cultural rescription of sin (or even an apologetics for its cultural manifestation) in two ways: (1) it offers a post-Christian reading of how doxologies of brokenness rescript Christian notions of sin in contemporary culture; and (2) that basic Christian notions of sin as acts of rebellion do not adequately capture contemporary cultural manifestations of sin as brokenness. But it also challenges the Christian to appreciate (or at least consider) the worthiness of reflecting on the cultural manifestations of sin as brokenness in secular music. Furthermore, it challenges the Christian to speak redemptively into the cries of secular doxologies. In analyzing secular doxologies of brokenness, this chapter demonstrates how secular sentiments found in the music of Machine Gun Kelly, Halsey, and Linkin Park point to theological answers. But these theological answers must not only speak life into the brokenness of life's experience. They must also in some way contextualize their answers within the brokenness of this experience. This chapter does this by articulating intimations of the idea of a "redemptive nihilism" that seeks transcendence and redemption in the longing cries of brokenness.

Throughout the popular cultural exegesis and religious rescription of sin that follows, sin is examined through the lens of a redemptive nihilism found within the doxologies of Machine Gun Kelly, Halsey, and Linkin Park. Arguably, their music displays the religious heart of post-Christian religion—one defined by the resignation to/of brokenness, cries of hope against hopelessness, and a heart of longing for love. If the next section questions the relevance of traditional Christian notions of sin, then the section after offers three exegeses of each artist's flavor to their doxologies of brokenness. Each of these sections exegetes doxologies of brokenness as portraying the cries of secular hamartiology. Machine Gun Kelly offers an account of the resignation to brokenness and what is left behind in light of it. Halsey offers an account of how the brokenness of the heart of human longing reveals the ache for love. Finally, Linkin Park offers an account of the longing but empty cries for redemption against the nihilism of brokenness. What each of these demonstrates are cultural rescriptions of late modern sin as brokenness that will be examined in the conclusion: the paradoxical resignation and embrace of the nihilism of redemption and the contextualized promises for redemption from brokenness found in the idea of "redemptive nihilism."

THE INADEQUACY OF SIN?

Sin is a heavy and extremely disliked idea. Non-Christians tend to castigate its use because of its negative connotations of what it means to be human and/or because of the hurt they may have received from Christians who have abused their power or forced their religion on others. To be told that we are already condemned and sinful despite any good in us is off-putting, especially when we believe positively in what it means to be human (whether we are perfectible, innately good, or a good person, etc.). The Christian tradition is unique among world religions in its utter and equal condemnation of humans as unrighteous before a righteous God.[5] Nothing humans can do can set them right before God according to the notion of total depravity from the Reformed tradition of Christianity.[6]

However, while sin can be understood as total depravity, it also has a common, ordinary meaning among many Christians: to act in ways that are against God and his design for humans according to the law and gospel.[7] To define sin as an act of rebellion against what God has ordained for how humans are to live a righteous life before God is certainly a sin. However, this basic definition of sin does not capture the full scope of sin. Sin is not merely an *action* against God. For Christians, there is a deeper understanding of sin as a *condition of bondage* to sin and alienation from God.[8] We are "bound to sin" in two senses: we will inevitably sin (sin as action), and we are enslaved to sin (sin as condition). Bondage to sin includes both inevitable actions of sinning and a condition of enslavement to the power and patterns of sin. With this definition in mind, it is worth unpacking biblical and contemporary theological understandings of sin to offer a more substantial picture.

Thomas McCall offers a sustained word study into the Greek and Hebrew terms for sin in ways that illustrate a biblical account of what is understood as sin. In Hebrew, McCall reveals a conceptual understanding of sin as deviation, or volitionally missing the mark; twistedness and intentional perversion as a personal cause and effect of sin; as contrasted to something well-formed, straight, and healthy; as rebellion in terms of an intentional violation of trust; as committing acts of wickedness and being pronounced guilty because of those actions; and as evil, but where evil is understood as both natural evil and immoral affections and "actions—of sinful people."[9] Furthermore, McCall's study into the Greek New Testament words for sin offers a concept of sin that has connotations of sin as religious and moral deviation; as lawlessness understood as doing/transgressing God's law but also as a "'frame of mind' that [revels] in its rebellion";[10] as transgression—the "overstepping proper boundaries," especially concerning God's will and ways;[11] as a stronger, more willful, and habitual transgression against God; as unrighteousness to refer to both legal status *and* the behavior and character of the actor "who commits the acts of sin"[12]; and finally as impiety or theologically oriented godlessness—"the deliberate rejection of God and God's ways."[13] Furthermore, in a succinct statement, David H. Kelsey articulates five propositions about sin. He states:

> First, it is universal. All human creatures are born into it. Second, it is . . . not a change in what human creatures are. To use a classical distinction between essential and accidental properties of substance, the condition of original sin does not involve any change in the essence or nature of human creatures; it is an accidental property. Third, in it, death has a certain power it would not otherwise have. . . . Fourth, all persons born into the condition of original sin are born into guilt. . . . Fifth, in the condition of original sin, human creatures are in bondage.[14]

This implies that sin is both enacted and an inescapable condition that mars a fallen humanity. Humanity is understood to be in a condition of sin—which is defined as a patterned reality of failing to break our bonds of enslavement to our desires and ways of living. Enslavement to sin, according to Paul, implies that even though I may know what sin is according to the law, the "flesh" (or our earthly bodies and distorted desires) is bound to commit transgression and further bondage to the patterns of sin once we realize that the law points out our sin. For Paul, sin is universal and "disturbingly deep," affecting the mind, heart, and flesh.[15] It "includes ... our actions—*what we do* is impacted by sin. But it also infects our affections, so that what we *love and desire* is soiled by sin."[16] The solution, according to Paul, is faith in, and enslavement to, Jesus Christ.[17] The gospel displays a dependence and trust in the atoning work of Christ as that which justifies humans as righteous before God. Human works that try to justify humans before God cannot but be unrighteous—they cannot justify sinful humans before a holy God. But in a forensic theory of atonement, the work of Christ justifies humans as righteous before God because of Christ's propitiation for sin, which sets humans right before God through the imputation of the righteousness of God through Christ to the believer.[18]

Throughout the Christian tradition is the idea that sin and fallenness are worth redeeming based on the resurrection of Jesus Christ and the essential goodness of what it means to be created. If the resurrection of Christ recapitulates and redeems what it means to be human and created through the spiritual transformation of earthly bodies, this implies that though creation and humanity may be marred by sin, our physical embodiment is not condemned and tossed aside because it is irredeemable. Rather, Irenaeus of Lyon argues that it is precisely because of the resurrection of Christ that God affirms (and Christians are to find) the fallenness of humanity and creation as something inherently worth redeeming.[19] It is in this appeal that I urge us to see secular doxologies of sin as songs that hopelessly hope for redemption as they cry out in brokenness for redemption, even if they present non-Christian themes, lyrics, and ways of living.

But two other ways in which sin has been defined in recent years have been as disordered desire and distortion of what God intends for the flourishing of what is not God. James K. A. Smith's distinctly Augustinian reformation of sin as disordered desire challenges contemporary Western notions of human beings as believing beings or thinking things.[20] David H. Kelsey's Reformed reformulation of sin as a distortion of what God intends for the flourishing of what is not God implies how sin is lived in ways that fail to address ways of living that honor the triune God's glory and his intention for quotidian flourishing.[21] Both Smith and Kelsey offer Christian resourcements of sin in ways that provide helpful parameters for understanding sin as not merely an action or condition, but also as ways of understanding both how secular culture and liturgies may distort and reform human nature in ways that need to be reformed and as distortions of God's intention for the flourishing of human beings in quotidian life.[22]

Sin is not just personal. It is also systemic. Sin is personal because it deals with the distortion of who we are, what it means to be human, and how we are to live. It is also personal because the human heart desires after fallen realities that cannot or do not offer us lasting and trustworthy rest and redemption. Sin is personal when our human relationships display a lack as we long to be known and loved. The personal dynamics of sin indicate how humans are not merely sinful, but rather how we are in bondage to the effects of sin. Sin is also systemic because its disordering of our desires and our distortions of human flourishing produce effects that ripple across human civilization—ranging from politics, economics, society, and culture. Sin is systemic precisely in its orientation toward abuse and inequality in power structures, the degradation of human dignity, the oppression of human peoples, and the repressive conditions that fail to produce human flourishing and allow humans to re-order their desires to a lasting and fulfilling *telos* that reshapes what it means to be human creatures before God.

Are traditional and basic Christian notions of sin inadequate for understanding the heart of sin in contemporary popular culture? Yes and no. They are inadequate in the sense that simple definitions of sin do not easily capture how it manifests within contemporary culture. Sin in contemporary culture cannot *merely* be defined as rebellion against God, whether in action, condition, or the vocal condemnation of ourselves and God. And yet, Christian definitions of sin *are* adequate in the sense that sin remains the fundamental human problem because of how it permeates within culture both as something that distorts our sense of self with a sense of unease and as something that distorts, denies, and oppresses the possibilities of human flourishing. Traditional notions of sin are adequate, but how they manifest and are articulated in contemporary culture implies a disconnect when sin is defined as merely a condition of being in rebellion against God. This disconnect from God implies that sin can be defined as the failure to reference God or make sense of quotidian human life in light of who God is. Certainly, in the sense that secular life lives as if God does not exist, contemporary culture is largely sinful. This omission is a condition of rebellion, but a condition of rebellion that is often not self-consciously aware of it as rebellion. (But it can also be characterized as willfully and knowingly ignoring the possibility of God as worthy of determining how we ought to live.) Secular sin is defined primarily in terms of its assumed and unquestioned lack of reference to God in daily life.

If sin is to be an adequate concept to describe the religious sentiment of secular hamartiology, we must also address how it manifests in late modern culture. Arguably, we can examine secular sin through an analysis of secular or non-religious "doxologies" that have taken the world by storm in their intuitive entwinement with the heart of millennial sensibilities. To address contemporary doxologies of brokenness, the following section offers popular cultural exegeses of sin as brokenness in Machine Gun Kelly, Halsey, and Linkin Park. In doing so, it rescripts sin in terms of brokenness where its echoes reverberate against a God who remains silent and absent. In doing so, the following section exegetes what sin and brokenness look like in the absence of God. Or rather, it offers an implicit rescription of sin as brokenness and how it manifests as a post-Christian popular cultural reflection of secular hamartiology.

DOXOLOGIES OF BROKENNESS

A secular hamartiology can be exegeted and rescripted in terms of the doxologies of brokenness found in the music of Machine Gun Kelly, Halsey, and Linkin Park. This section starts with an exegesis of the doxologies of brokenness found in Machine Gun Kelly, describing his spin on brokenness as resignation to separation from God and its dysfunctional effects that play out in broken relationships. Second, it offers an exegesis of the doxologies of brokenness in Halsey as describing the heart and hope of human longing for love in dysfunctional relationships. Third, it offers an exegesis of the doxologies of brokenness in Linkin Park as crying out to a silent God against the nihilism of brokenness.

The Resignation to Brokenness in Machine Gun Kelly

Strikingly, Halsey and Machine Gun Kelly provide an agonizing image of disordered love through their evocations of human longing for love in brokenness and dysfunctional relationships.[23] If Machine Gun Kelly represents something like the millennial coming of age of sensibilities found in Blink-182, then Halsey represents the cries for longing for love amid broken relationships. Both Halsey and Machine Gun Kelly reflect something of the millennial experience: broken relationships, relational dysfunction, longing for love, all the while crying out in longing for lost loves and resigning to a generative *ressentiment* for the brokenness that generates the acceptance of fallenness and dysfunctional love.

Machine Gun Kelly's recent turn to Pop Punk reflects a legacy of Blink-182—one indeed where Blink-182's drummer Travis Barker produced and played drums on Machine Gun Kelly's pop punk albums *Mainstream Sellout* and *Tickets to My Downfall*. These two albums record a shift in Machine Gun Kelly's musical career from rap to pop punk. This shift also reflects a millennial sensibility of coming of age: of coming to terms with the brokenness of a life that leaves us to pick up the pieces of our lives in the aftermath of abuse, violence, drug addiction, self-harm, and broken relationships. Machine Gun Kelly's turn to pop punk reveals a reality of *ressentiment*—the idea that resignation to brokenness generates new possibilities for reconstructing our lives. But this reconstruction of our lives is something that carries our brokenness, owns it, and tries to live in light of its weight, carrying a heaviness to our lives that is sought to be overcome by leaving a legacy that speaks of enduring through brokenness.[24] This is an endurance through brokenness that is given voice in Machine Gun Kelly's music. It echoes the cries of how terrible the experience of a dysfunctional world is.

Not only does Machine Gun Kelly's music reflect the brokenness of the millennial experience, but it does so in ways that reflect a millennial flavor of post-Christianity. This is something that does not seek transcendence or God in brokenness. Rather, it embraces a resignation to brokenness as the reality of human experience. The nature of millennial post-Christian religion is marked by the absence of God—not only God's silence or our disbelief in God's love for us, but more strikingly a lack of reference to God as something that can adequately speak hope into our lives.

The brokenness of the millennial experience, as observed by Machine Gun Kelly, reveals how post-Christian religion cries out to an absent God. Truly, this is what atheism is in the millennial experience: it is not necessarily the disbelief in God, but rather is encapsulated by a way of life that has no reference to or from God because we believe God to be ineffective, imperfect, silent, and absent from the contingent conditions of the horrors found within our ordinary lives. Here, atheism is a conceptual lack in popular millennial experience: we know that Christians believe in God, and yet there is little in the Christian message or of its people that can connect to the millennial experience of brokenness. There is a conceptual lack of connection between a supposedly loving God and the millennial experience of agonizing, dysfunctional brokenness. As Illenium and Call Me Karizma state in their song "God Damnit": it is hard to believe in a perfect God who would create and love someone as broken and flawed as I am.[25]

But Machine Gun Kelly's music does not only reflect an experience of brokenness in the absence or silence of God. It also reflects the reality of dysfunctional relationships and the making-do in a relationship that is marked by resignation to dysfunction. His "Bloody Valentine" simulates the reality of dysfunctional love—of attaching to a significant other in unhealthy ways.[26] His "Forget Me Too" (with Halsey) reveals how much men can resent relationships with women and work towards the destruction of the relationship through drunkenness and avoidance. On the flip side, Halsey's lyrics in the song reveal how much we can be simultaneously resigned and committed to a relationship with someone who resents us as we try to make the relationship work.[27]

In the album *Mainstream Sellout* and Machine Gun Kelly's collaborations with Glaive and Bring Me the Horizon, the songs "Maybe," "God Save Me," and "More Than Life" reflect not only the idea of seeing ourselves as being beyond redemption in the eyes of God, but even more so the dysfunctional nature of relational attachment and dependency on, and the doubting of/in, others to give us meaning and identity.[28] There is an agonism, an ache in this hope for meaning through the dysfunctional relationship that doubts whether it is real. Machine Gun Kelly's pop-punk turn reveals not only the brokenness of a relationship with an absent God but how that relational schism that separates God from the brokenness of the millennial experience plays out in our dysfunctional relationships with a significant other. And this can be illustrated more vocally in the cries for love in the doxologies of Halsey.

The Heart of Brokenness in Halsey

In contrast to Machine Gun Kelly's harsh descriptions of brokenness, Halsey's music displays a perspective on what it means to experience a longing for love in broken and lost relationships. "Without Me," "Forget Me Too" (with Machine Gun Kelly), and "You Should Be Sad" are songs that reflect the longing for love and what it means to be hurt by men she has rebuilt.[29] The panging ache of her "So Good" reveals what it means to come to terms with realizing her love for the one that got away.[30] Her music displays the shallowness of men in their brokenness and the inability to love deeply what is beautiful in imperfection. Her music demonstrates a concern for care and the need and longing for love.[31] Halsey is heartbreakingly beautiful. She taps into our human longing for love in the midst of brokenness with agonizing beauty. Halsey demonstrates the heart of human longing for love in ways that evoke within us our longing for something more. This longing for more for Halsey is found primarily in (failed, broken) relationships. However, this longing for more in failed relationships is also found in being trapped within the inescapable love *for* broken relationships.[32] The personal patterns of sin affect human relationships in ways that our human self-centeredness hopes for the possibility of love and care for another to the detriment and destruction of ourselves in the midst of brokenness.

Halsey displays the heart of human longing precisely in her musical expression of the human longing for love—even failed love. Her lyrics tell us that human loves are broken and fallen. And yet, they also tell us of an ethics of care that points to the hope for the redemption of broken relationships and fallen loves. Halsey rescripts sin in ways that evoke the beauty of secular hamartiology. The beauty of Halsey demonstrates how human love has fallen and is crying out for redemption. But her music also points toward a redemptive nihilism of human love in the hope for love despite brokenness. But before we turn to redemptive nihilism, the next section interprets the cries of brokenness found in the doxologies of Linkin Park.

The Cries of Brokenness in Linkin Park

Linkin Park is renowned for music expressing the anguish and paradox of a society hoping for hope, trying to make a better world, and giving comfort to those who keenly feel how messed up this world is. Some of my friends receive great comfort from Linkin Park because they express something we feel: lost and searching for a way out; a better life; the weight of marginalization and abuse at the hands of a society so terribly messed up; and yet hoping for hope for a better world so paradoxically bound to these conditions.

Linkin Park set the stage for alternative music in the twenty-first century. From top hits such as "In the End" and "Crawling" from their first album *Hybrid Theory*,[33] to the heartbreaking brokenness of "Numb" and the longing for belonging in the pain and brokenness of "Somewhere I Belong" in their second album *Meterora*,[34] Linkin Park's first two albums display the brokenness of humanity. Furthermore, from the this-worldly nihilistic hope for redemption in "What I've Done" from *Minutes to Midnight*,[35] to the songs of suicide in *One More Light*, there remains a tragic and logical thread of the nihilism of brokenness that ended in the suicide of Chester Bennington on July 20, 2017. Linkin Park's music recorded the experience of two generations that spanned the last few decades of the twentieth century and the first two decades of the twenty-first. One could say that Linkin Park captured the millennial experience of both Generation X and Millennials: the vocalized experience of the heaviness of anger, anguish, abuse, and suicide via the crying out in the midst of mental darkness, brokenness, nihilism, hopelessness, and despair.

The complex emotions found within the discography of Linkin Park shed light on the experience of longing central to secular hamartiology. The music of Linkin Park evokes a sense of unobtainable longing paired with hopeful despair. From the lyrics of "Numb," "In the End," and "What I've Done," a message may be found in the first few albums of Linkin Park that encompasses what may be called the search for authenticity and the paradox of hope. The chorus of "In the End" speaks to an emptiness, one I think that strikingly points to what comes after the disbelief in the belief in God. Its vocalizations and repetitions of trying to trust and believe, only to realize it doesn't matter, offer an evocative sense of what it means to give up belief in God.[36] Even more so, "Numb" reflects the brokenness of crying out against dysfunction in ways that try to articulate authentically who we are apart from what others want or determine us to be.[37] "Crawling" expresses the reality of brokenness and the wounds that have been inflicted upon us so heavily that not only have they *not* healed, but we doubt that those wounds will *ever* heal.[38] These wounds are not just physical but also mental and social. This especially echoes in the newly released song "Lost," which dates to the *Meteora* era (and foreshadows the end of Chester Bennington's life).[39] Linkin Park reveals in "Somewhere I Belong" how the fragmentation of our belonging to others is because of numbness that results from the abuse we receive and the wounds that we carry.[40]

I do not think that Linkin Park leaves us merely with an emptiness. I think in the song "Numb" we do see the sense of absence of the relevancy of God to our everyday concerns. I am always moved by the lyrics in the first and second verses. Linkin Park articulates the anguish of our everyday life. How could God relate to our lives in such a way that these verses reflect?! But Linkin Park does not just point out the condition of the emptiness in the absence of God but tries to express an answer beyond it. In "What I've Done" we see hope beyond the aftermath of the drudges of everyday life without God. Between the first verse and the last, we see hope for redemption out of the emptiness apparent in the loss of God in secular belief. We see hope for redemption where we can forgive ourselves for everything we have done. Like Shai Linne's "Were You There?" on his first album *The Atonement*, we cannot truly resonate with Linkin Park's "What I've Done" unless we see ourselves as transgressors in a world so messed up.[41] Not only must we admit that we contribute to the horrors of this world, but so also must we struggle to forgive ourselves for what we have done in this world.

These complex emotions evoke the longings of the human heart and the brokenness of human experience. While some songs, such as "In the End," could be interpreted as evoking faithlessness in and of God, others, such as "One More Light" and "What I've Done," evoke an empty hope amid brokenness based on self-forgiveness and starting again.[42] They also evoke the longing for significance found in the loss of friendship through suicide.[43] Linkin Park casts hope into the netherworld of self-actualization and yet paradoxically and tragically affirms its grief through suicide.

Linkin Park reflects the millennial experience of brokenness and abuse, the emptiness, anguish, demands of living up to another's standards, and the failure to heal even as we scream for it. And all of this ends in the nihilism of suicide. It stretches both the limits of the human (in)capacity to wrestle with the demands of life and the effects of brokenness upon our experience in the world. Linkin Park evokes an image of redemptive nihilism that ends in suicide because of the failure of secular hopes to redeem, restore, and heal us of brokenness. It is in the longing for restoration that we find hope. The question is whether the conditions of secular experience can truly save us, even in their negation. As Linkin Park evokes, secular hamartiology is marked by the negation of life amid the hopeless hope for its redemption.

But this self-consciousness of the need for forgiveness and redemption adds a weight to our lives that I do not think can be lifted by us. We are bound to brokenness: God supposedly has nothing to do with us. We live in a world defined by the absence of God and Linkin Park sings of a post-Christian a-theology (absence theology). The absence of God in our daily lives results in an emptiness that we seek to fill with everything we can grasp. This can be drugs, sex, alcohol, relationships, or even self-harm. But yet nothing in our everyday lives can truly fulfill and redeem us. We even think that God cannot redeem us because of what we have done.

Machine Gun Kelly, Halsey, and Linkin Park doxologically reflect on the beautiful cries of secular hamartiology. The beautiful cries of secular hamartiology display the longing for love and the broken resignation of human experience by evoking its affirmation and embrace. It is in the emptiness of what is, that all that can be affirmed and imagined are the patterns of dysfunction and/or self-destruction. But the resignation of the heart of human longing that cries out against the nihilism of brokenness displays a redemptive nihilism wherein secular hamartiology manifests the affirmation and embrace of a hopeless hope in a longing that is never truly satisfied because of brokenness. At its heart, a secular hamartiology evokes both the embrace of and resignation to brokenness as a way of living where nothingness and emptiness become the reality of the human condition. What this exegesis of these three doxologies of brokenness shows is the longing cry for redemption amid brokenness even in the nihilation of life and love. Tied to this is the paradox of redemptive nihilism. Redemptive nihilism is *both* the hopeless longing for redemption in the midst of brokenness and nihilism *and* the resignation to hopelessness for the possibility of redemption. Redemptive nihilism holds both of these in tension. Secular hamartiology longs and hopes hopelessly for love and redemption, and yet remains resigned to its impossibility in light of the separation from, absence, and silence of God.

WHITHER SALVATION? REVERBERATING LOVE IN THE ABSENCE OF GOD

To conclude, McCall states succinctly the doctrine of sin as it was illustrated throughout the current chapter:

> Sin is whatever is opposed to God's will, as that will reflect God's holy character and as that will is expressed by God's commands. Sin is fundamentally opposed to nature and reason, and it is ultimately opposed to God. The results of sin are truly catastrophic—*sin wreaks havoc on our relationships with God, one another, and the rest of creation.* It is universal in human history *and manifests itself in various cultural expressions. It wrecks human lives, and it leaves us broken and vulnerable. It also leaves us needing grace and longing for redemption.*[44]

Throughout this chapter, we have examined some doxological expressions of brokenness, sin, and the longing for redemption that leave us vulnerable to the possibility of love, God, and death. This chapter has examined the popular cultural rescriptions of sin and has exegeted secular hamartiology through analyses of the beauty found in the doxologies of Machine Gun Kelly, Halsey, and Linkin Park. What underlies these twenty-first-century musical artists are theological sentiments of what it means to live in the perceived absence and silence of a God that seems both too incredible to be present and too incredulous to believe in. But what do these rescriptions and exegeses of secular sin have to do with post-Christian religiosity?

Each of these rescriptions of sin manifests in ways that point to post-Christian ideas of God and salvation. While each of these three doxologies articulates a secular rescription of hamartiology as post-Christian brokenness, arguably each of them also posits points of ache that point to God and salvation. The music of Halsey manifests a doxology that aches for love in ways that evoke emotional longings that ache for a *lost* love. While for Halsey, this may not include the feelings of what it means to long for the love of God, it remains a contact point that aches for the redemption of a fulfilling and satisfying love. The music of Linkin Park manifests most poignantly the cry against the nihilism of brokenness for a God that has failed them and remains silent and empty. And yet Linkin Park's music reveals the longing for hope for the redemption of nihilism through the redemptive nature of the cry against nothing. If Linkin Park was crying out against this nothingness, not only did Chester Bennington succumb to it, but so also does the music of Machine Gun Kelly work out the implications of Linkin Park's cry as a resignation to the brokenness. The theological implications of Machine Gun Kelly's resignation to brokenness are that he still tries to live life in the midst of dysfunction and create a lasting legacy of accomplishment that buffers the emptiness and brokenness of a life where reference to God is so lacking that there is no connection to or belief in what the Christian God is supposed to be.

The analyses above of secular hamartiology in popular culture have articulated how the resignation, longing, and cries of and against brokenness are sensibilities of the millennial experience. But these exegeses of several doxologies of brokenness also reveal how we may read them as reflecting a post-Christian religious reading of sin and salvation. This implies how a post-Christian exegesis of popular doxological expressions of the millennial experience can be read religiously in ways that shed light on contemporary forms of the human condition and post-Christian visions of salvation. This condition is marked by the desolation of brokenness in the absence of God. Post-Christian religion is marked by the perceived silence and absence of God in everyday life. Doxologies of sin and brokenness found in Machine Gun Kelly, Halsey, and Linkin Park evoke sentiments and sensibilities that capture a mood, a resonance, a reverberation of what it means to be if God is silent and absent. So how can we read doxologies of sin religiously? It lies precisely in their paradoxical embrace of redemptive nihilism.

Redemptive nihilism is marked by a paradox. It hopes for redemption in the hopelessness of despair. It embraces the resignation of becoming better even when we realize it is not actualizable or believable. It searches for meaning in the midst of meaninglessness. It seeks forgiveness when forgiveness is not enough. It embraces the emptiness of its own negation. Redemptive nihilism marks the (im-)possibility of belief in everyday life when the very possibilities of its transcendence are found in its resignation and negation. That is, redemptive nihilism is where hope and hopelessness, meaning and meaninglessness, despair and forgiveness, and brokenness and restoration are all tensely bound together in the paradox between resignation and love.

But even in redemptive nihilism, the tension between resignation and love produces the will to live. If Christianity is to present an alternative to this post-Christian vision of sin and salvation, then what needs to be done is to make a two-pronged case. It must not only make a case that God is not silent or absent but also *re*-present a case in which how Christians imagine God may become credible to the post-Christian through the Christian's lived witness and experience to the contextual conditions of post-Christian culture and experience. This requires that the re-enchantment of belief in God must present the credibility of what Christians believe of God as *desirable* through a credulous and sacrificial witness of love, grace, and forgiveness to the post-Christian experience. Through this, the paradoxical turn to hope despite doubts in the presence and reverberations of God to us can potentially meet the longings at the heart of the millennial experience.

Does the post-Christian condition require belief in God to be religious? No. The sentiments found throughout this chapter signify that in the recesses of our hearts and desires, there remain the echoes of religious sentiment that reverberate against the silence and absence of, and disbelief in, the possibility of God. But the cries of redemptive nihilism and the beauty of doxologies of brokenness cry out and echo against the silence—it echoes of God. In the reverberations and silences between our longings for love, the sound rebounds against something. What we must do is identify what these echoes are rebounding off of. It is at the points of reverberation that we must look and listen. We must examine ourselves at one point and identify what and where our screams are rebounding from. Brokenness points beyond itself in its lack to something not silent, but speaking. But it does not primarily speak condemnation; it aches of love. And Christians must make this love real in action, presence, and relationship, resounding with joy, grace, and forgiveness to those who cannot believe it is real. For God to become believable, credible, and desirable, Christians must speak love and live it as an enduring presence to the broken that will not abandon those who suffer.

NOTES

1. C. S. Lewis, *The Screwtape Letters* (New York: HarperOne, 2015); C. S. Lewis, *The Space Trilogy* (New York: Simon and Schuster, 2011).

2. This not only alludes to Weston's appeal to the idea of Humanity's continued existence in solar colonialism at the expense of human dignity but also Weston's belief in a spirituality beyond organized religion and the invitation of the demonic into him. C.f. C. S. Lewis, *Out of the Silent Planet* (New York: Scribner, 2003), 133–139; C. S. Lewis, *Perelandra* (New York: Scribner, 2003), 78–82.

3. This is Devine in *Out of the Silent Planet*, or, as he is also known in *That Hideous Strength* as Lord Feverstone.

4. Paul Tillich, *Theology of Culture* (New York: Oxford University Press, 1964), 42–43.

5. C.f. Romans 3:9-20; John 3:16-21. Also note that though all humans are already condemned, the means of redemption are universally applicable through faith in Christ: Romans 3:21–26; John 3:16–21.

6. C.f. John Calvin, *The Institutes of the Christian Religion*, Book II. 1–5.

7. Ernest Reisinger, *The Law and the Gospel*, Reprint ed. (Cape Coral, FL: Founders Press, 2019).

8. Anthony C. Thistleton, *The Living Paul* (Downers Grove, IL: IVP Academic, 2009), 77; David H. Kelsey, *Eccentric Existence: A Theological Anthropology* (Louisville, KY: Westminster John Knox Press, 2009), 422–423.

9. Thomas H. McCall, *Against God and Nature: The Doctrine of Sin* (Wheaton, IL: Crossway, 2019), 34–37, 37.

10. McCall, *Against God and Nature*, 38.

11. McCall, *Against God and Nature*, 38.

12. McCall, *Against God and Nature*, 39.

13. McCall, *Against God and Nature*, 39.

14. Kelsey, *Eccentric Existence*, 432–433.

15. McCall, *Against God and Nature*, 88.

16. McCall, *Against God and Nature*, 88.

17. Romans 6:15-7:23.

18. On 'Propitiation' and expiation, C.f. J. I. Packer, *Knowing God* (Downers Grove, IL: IVP Books, 1973), 180–184.

19. John Behr, *Irenaeus of Lyons: Identifying Christianity* (Oxford: Oxford University Press, 2013), 144–158, 180–189.

20. James K. A. Smith, *You Are What You Love: The Spiritual Power of Habit* (Grand Rapids, MI: Brazos Press, 2016), 1–25; James K. A. Smith, *Desiring the Kingdom: Worship, Worldview, and Cultural Formation*, vol. 1, 3 vols., Cultural Liturgies (Grand Rapids, MI: Baker Academic, 2009), 40–63.

21. C.f. Kelsey, *Eccentric Existence*, 402–438, 567–602, 847–889; Joy Ann McDougall, "A Trinitarian Grammar of Sin," in *The Theological Anthropology of David Kelsey: Responses to Eccentric Existence*, ed. Gene Outka (Grand Rapids, MI: Eerdmans Publishing, 2016), 107–126.

22. C.f. Kelsey, *Eccentric Existence*, 422–438; James K. A. Smith, "Secular Liturgies and the Prospects for a 'Post-Secular' Sociology of Religion," in *The Post-Secular in Question: Religion in Contemporary Society*, ed. Philip S. Gorski, David Kyumankim, John Torpey, and Jonathan Van Antwerpen (New York and London: New York University Press and Social Science Research Council, 2012), 159–184.

23. Machine Gun Kelly and Halsey, *Forget Me Too*, Tickets to My Downfall 5 (Santa Monica, CA: Bad Boy/Interscope Records, 2020).

24. Machine Gun Kelly, *27*, Bloom 13 (Santa Monica, CA: Bad Boy/Interscope Records, 2017).

25. Illenium and Call Me Karizma, *God Damnit*, Single (Santa Monica, CA: UMG Recordings, Inc., 2018).

26. Machine Gun Kelly, *Bloody Valentine*, Tickets to My Downfall 4 (Santa Monica, CA: Bad Boy/Interscope Records, 2020).

27. Machine Gun Kelly and Halsey, *Forget Me Too*.

28. Machine Gun Kelly and Bring Me the Horizon, *Maybe*, Mainstream Sellout 3 (Santa Monica, CA: Bad Boy/Interscope Records, 2022); Machine Gun Kelly, *God Save Me*, Mainstream Sellout 2 (Santa Monica, CA: Bad Boy/Interscope Records, 2022); Machine Gun Kelly and Glaive, *More Than Life*, Single (Santa Monica, CA: Bad Boy/Interscope Records, 2022).

29. C.f. Halsey, *You Should Be Sad*, Manic 4 (Los Angeles, CA: Capitol Records, 2020); Machine Gun Kelly and Halsey, *Forget Me Too*; Halsey, *Without Me*, Manic 9 (Los Angeles, CA: Capitol Records, 2020).

30. Halsey, *So Good*, Single (Los Angeles, CA: Capitol Records, 2022).

31. C.f. Halsey, *Without Me*.

32. Halsey, *More*, Manic 14 (Los Angeles, CA: Capitol Records, 2020).

33. Linkin Park, *In the End*, Hybrid Theory 8 (Los Angeles, CA: Warner Bros., 2000); Linkin Park, *Crawling*, Hybrid Theory 5 (Los Angeles, CA: Warner Bros., 2000).

34. Linkin Park, *Numb*, Meteora 13 (Los Angeles, CA: Warner Bros., 2003); Linkin Park, *Somewhere I Belong*, Meteora 3 (Los Angeles, CA: Warner Bros., 2003).

35. Linkin Park, *What I've Done*, Minutes to Midnight 6 (Los Angeles, CA: Warner Bros., 2007).

36. Linkin Park, *In The End*.

37. Linkin Park, *Numb*.

38. Linkin Park, *Crawling*.

39. Linkin Park, *Lost*, Single (Los Angeles, CA: Warner, 2023).

40. Linkin Park, *Somewhere I Belong*.

41. Shai Linne, *Were You There?*, The Atonement 6 (Philadelphia, PA: Lamp Mode Recordings, 2008).

42. Linkin Park, *What I've Done*.

43. Linkin Park, *One More Light*, One More Light 9 (Los Angeles, CA: Warner Bros., 2017).

44. McCall, *Against God and Nature*, 21. My italics.

Chapter 9

The Poverty of Sin in *Shameless*

Throughout the previous chapter and part IV, the focus of analysis is to understand the post-Christian human condition. This chapter continues part IV's analysis of sin and brokenness through a focused look at the logics of poverty and sin in the show *Shameless*. While the previous chapter addressed an absence theology by analyzing doxologies of brokenness, this chapter, by contrast analyzes systemic issues of sin as brokenness, with particular attention to what it looks like to live and love in the logics of the urban poor. What unites both of these chapters is that they reflect a certain wisdom and doxology of brokenness that wrestles not just with personal and systemic sin, but also with the absence of God. The reflections and analyses below on *Shameless* offer a certain "reflective wisdom" of what it means to live and love in the logics of poverty that reveal the intimate link between sociological conditions and theological reflections that stretch what it means to believe in a post-Christian context.

Shameless. Such an apt title. Running eleven seasons spanning over ten years, *Shameless* has aptly captured the *habitus* of American poverty. It is marked by systemic poverty and the struggle to survive. It is marked by the manipulation of the system, the brokenness of love, and the habitual dispositions of sin. *Shameless* captures the *habitus* of sin in enlightening ways. It highlights, through vulgar and cringe-worthy depictions, ways of living that strikingly reflect the shamefulness of sin by following the life of the Gallagher family. But it is precisely in the cringe that we see the shamefulness of shamelessness. It is in the cringe that we can observe how systemic sin functions in the *habituses* of fallen love and urban poverty.

And yet, we also see in this shame, sin, and brokenness the absence of representation. There is little to no visibility of what a Christian practice of faith offers as an alternative to the poverty of sin in *Shameless*. This leaves us with an important question: What can *Shameless* tell us about religion? Even in its silences, can it teach us something about the Christian faith without any real reference to God or a Christian praxis of faith? Arguably, it is in *Shameless's* absent portrayals of authentic Christian faith and practice that something important is revealed about post-Christian religion. Increasingly so, the visibility of the praxis of Christian faith in everyday life—the Christian counter-movement to post-Christian religion—is disappearing in a post-Christian world. Without this visible counter-movement, not only does Christianity become incredible, but we look upon it with incredulity because of its inability to be credibly lived.

This chapter explores what this post-Christian credulity towards religion looks like through a sociological, religious, and theological analysis of systemic sin that builds on the sociological contributions of Pierre Bourdieu and Michel de Certeau. With their theories in mind as a toolkit, the chapter then illustrates their sociological theories of practice through analyses of the field and tactics of poverty and the *habituses* of sin and brokenness by describing the notion of a fallen *habitus* of love in *Shameless*. It ends with reflections on what happens to Christianity in a post-Christian culture and world when the representation of authentic Christian faith and practice remains absent and invisible to the post-Christian experience in representations and simulations of popular culture.

A SOCIOLOGICAL TOOLKIT FOR ANALYSIS

Before we begin to analyze the poverty of sin within *Shameless*, we must turn to French sociological theory. French sociological theory offers important resources that shape the analyses below, particularly those theories offered by Pierre Bourdieu and Michel de Certeau. What Bourdieu and De Certeau offer are important sociological ideas that shape what scholars call a theory of practice. By first examining their theories of practice, the analysis below can be sustained by a sociological framework to understand the systemic structures of poverty and sin as they appear in *Shameless*.

Pierre Bourdieu was a French sociological theorist famous for his articulations of a theory of practice that paid attention to the patterns, rules, and habits of the organization of ordinary life, space, and the dynamics of fields of power that are enacted by individuals and shaped by their cultural, economic, and symbolic capital. Bourdieu's most well-known idea is the concept of *"habitus."* According to Bourdieu, a *habitus* does not just refer to habits, which conventionally refer to the rhythmic repetitious practices that govern daily life. Rather, for Bourdieu, *habitus* refers to a set of dispositions that shape and are shaped by assumptions on how life works.[1] These imply "dispositions," which express "first the *result of an organizing action*, with a meaning close to that of words such as structure; it also designates a *way of being, a habitual state* (especially of the body) and, in particular, a *predisposition, tendency, propensity or inclination*."[2]

Within these propensities or inclinations are the assumed and unquestioned rules of habitual states or ways of being. These "rules" are underlying, often unquestioned and assumed patterns of how one lives life and organizes the ordinary practices of human, social, cultural, symbolic, or even political life. As such, the rule and disposition of the *habitus* entail a plethora of ways in which people imagine and structure their reality. These structures are both structured and structuring. They are *structured* structures because they are already established, objective structures that shape and constitute the habits of human society and culture. These structured structures are established systems that shape the contours in which and by which human social, cultural, economic, and political life are organized and embedded within the rhythms of ordinary life. But they are also *structuring* structures because, though they always already shape and constitute the habits of human life, these structures are also ongoing, malleable, durable, and transposable. Structures are structuring when they allow mobility, such as when there is social, cultural, economic, or political mobility. They are also structuring because of the human's ability to adapt, adopt, and learn new ways of approaching and navigating the habits of the society, culture, economic, and/or political conditions in which we are placed. Bourdieu states

> the structure constitutive of a particular type of environment (e.g. the material conditions of existence characteristic of a class condition) produce *habitus*, systems of durable, transposable *dispositions*, structured structures, that is, as principles of the generation and structuring of practices and representations which can be objectively "regulated" and "regular" without in any way being the product of obedience to rules, objectively adapted to their goals without presupposing a conscious aiming intent or an express mastery of the operations necessary to attain them and, being all this, collectively orchestrated without being the product of the orchestrating action of a conductor.[3]

Central to Bourdieu's theory of practice is that the structures in which we are situated are called a "field"—a social space shaped by his idea of "capital".[4] This field is described by Patricia Thomson as something like a football field in which a game is played by players who follow a set of rules,[5] and is like a force field polarized between positive and negative forces of cultural and economic capital.[6] That is, there is a logic to this field of practice that situates us within boundaries and rules that determine the possibilities of economic, social, and cultural advancement in tension with the negative conditions and boundaries of capital that can inhibit and detrimentally determine where we dwell upon this field. Thomson states that "at stake in the field is the accumulation of capitals: they are both the process in, and product of, a field."[7] Thomson continues by listing Bourdieu's

> four forms of capital: economic (money and assets); cultural (e.g. forms of knowledge; taste, aesthetic and cultural preferences; language, narrative, and voice); social (e.g. affiliations and networks; family, religious, and cultural heritage); and symbolic (things which stand for all of the other forms of capital and can be "exchanged" in other fields, e.g. credentials).[8]

Rob Moore identifies two distinct but important ways in which symbolic capital is used by Bourdieu. Moore states:

> In the first, the values, tastes and life-styles of some social groups . . . are, in an arbitrary manner, elevated above those of others in a way that confers social advantage. . . . In a second way, forms of capital such as cultural capital can be understood in terms of the qualitative differences in *forms* of consciousness *within* different social groups . . . ; that is, in terms of *habitus* as a specialization . . . of consciousness and a recognized mastery of some technique(s). In other words, social membership in itself . . . does not automatically translate into a *habitus* that confers symbolic capital in a uniform way for all members.[9]

The notion of capital is not only something we inherit, but it is something that shapes how we live and who we are in significant ways. There is a *habitus* to the social capital we live in that is not only about the dispositions of our social circles but also of the social organizations in which we live and may have participated. In particular, Lip's connection to the people in the neighborhood he grew up in and his relationship with Brad and AA form an important social capital for Lip. The *habitus* of our economic capital is certainly something we inherit, and it is intimately tied to not just our parents but also to the economic conditions of our neighborhood, gender, race, and so on. In *Shameless*, the economic capital of the Gallagher family is largely non-existent as they are part of the urban poor. The *habitus* of our cultural capital lies not just in the symbolic power of the cultures in which we live or are attracted to, but also in the communities in which we work and belong. Again, in Lip's story, the cultural capital of the academy and university implies a certain language and etiquette that he both thrives in and feels the disconnect between the language and culture of his upbringing and that of the academy. The *habitus* of our symbolic capital is something that carries a weight of meaning and significance that sustains social, economic, and cultural status, even when its worthiness is devalued or simplified in its significance (i.e., a diploma). Bourdieu's theory of the *habitus* of capital offers important sociological, cultural, symbolic, and economic means to make sense of what it means to exist within the boundaries of a field.

A second French theorist of practice is Michel de Certeau. De Certeau is known for his work analyzing the obverse sides of everyday practice that shed light on things oppressed or suppressed in the practices of everyday life. His work on a theory of everyday practice noticeably pays attention to the incredulity of believing as a byproduct of popular culture in late modern society.[10] But it is de Certeau's ideas of strategies and tactics that are most well-known. De Certeau's idea of strategies implies the sense of intentionally organizing forces that dominate, control, and explicitly shape the structures of ordinary life. Tactics, by contrast are those counter-movements, subversions, and inversions of strategies that shape the obverse side of strategic structures. Tactics work alongside and against strategies in manipulative ways that weaken the powers of strategies to determine our reality. Clare Colebrook states that for de Certeau, "a tactic works metaphorically: rather than returning the logic to some ground, it thinks the logic from a different point of view."[11] Like Bourdieu, Michael Gardiner argues that for de Certeau, "the investigation of any social-cultural field requires understanding the complex of *practices* that constitute that field. A practice conforms to a particular logic, a characteristic way of thinking and acting."[12]

For example, one way in which strategies and tactics are displayed in *Shameless* is through Lip's relationship with the academy, as he comes from the urban poor. While there are certain strategies of the academic elite to set codes of honor against violence on campus, which Lip transgresses, there are also tactical subversions of Lip's academic expulsion via the efforts of Professor Youens to help Lip succeed in life through his connections to and favors from former students. In the academy, there is a general rule to "pay it forward" to the next generation of academics, which means supporting the efforts of one's students in their endeavors throughout life. This is not a dominating rule about controlling our student's future. Rather, it is an assumed obligation to fulfill the requests of one's students when they ask for references for their first jobs, as well as for college and graduate studies. But Lip also follows the *habituses* of his upbringing. While it takes him time to learn the processes of financial aid and life in the academy, these are always shadowed by the tactics of his impoverishment—how to take advantage of a system and manipulate it for his benefit. While Lip ultimately fails to integrate into the academy, he does grow out of some of his more dysfunctional patterns of ripping off others—unless they deserve it (such as the rich kids Brad sold his business to).

This means that the logic of practice can be either strategic or tactical. These logics also reveal certain *habituses* and fields that can help us make sense of what this chapter addresses as the "poverty of sin." To examine this idea, it is important to break down both the structures of poverty and the *habituses* of sin. The next section begins to explore these structures of the field of poverty and the *habituses* of sin through a series of analyses illustrated in *Shameless*. But it is important to keep these sociological theories of Pierre Bourdieu and Michel de Certeau in mind as they will remain with us as the toolkit by which we can examine the poverty of sin in *Shameless*.

A SOCIOLOGICAL EXEGESIS OF THE POVERTY OF SIN IN *SHAMELESS*

This section begins our analysis of the poverty of sin in *Shameless* by first addressing two dimensions involved in the field of poverty as illustrated through an analysis of Lip's field of capital and Frank's tactical manipulation of the system of poverty. Then it turns to analyze two dimensions of the *habitus* of sin within *Shameless*: first, the *habitus* of Lip and Fiona's love life, and second, through a Christian analysis of the *habitus* of sin as it is illustrated in *Shameless*.

The Gallaghers' Field of Capital

One of the most noticeable aspects of *Shameless* is not only the amount of cringe that shapes the show's allure, but also the Gallagher family's field of capital. The field of social space where the Gallaghers live and function is South Side Chicago urban white trash. The Gallaghers represent a certain economic capital and social field that shape the conditions of their lives. Their lives are marked by systemic conditions geared towards their oppression. And yet those systemic conditions that shape their social field are also things certain members of the Gallagher family seek, or are given the opportunity, to rise above. The Gallaghers suffer from the field of poverty. They have little social capital with the rich moving in to gentrify the neighborhood. The cultural and symbolic capital they carry and wield is not only that of an impoverished working class but one marked by loyalty to one's own—to family and those who have stuck by them through thick and thin like Kev and V. Certainly, the economic capital of the Gallagher family is slight, and yet Fiona strives to own property and assets that will increase her cultural and economic capital until it is taken away from her through the ruthlessness of commercial real estate.

As a case study of the Gallagher's capital, we can look at the character of Lip and his arc as an impoverished genius, his rise in educational status and its symbolic capital, the collapse and alienation he faced when that opportunity crashed down on him, and his relationships with Brad and Tami who stuck by him through the end of the show. In the early seasons, Lip is portrayed as the smartest kid in his school, and this wins him a full-ride scholarship to a local prestigious university. For about a year and a half, Lip was elevated above his inherited cultural, economic, social, and symbolic capital. That said, Lip was at a disadvantage. His finances were a mess by the beginning of his second year. He was at a social disadvantage that was only elevated by those women he had intimate relations with because of the economic and cultural-symbolic capital they wielded. Amanda came from and carried economic capital that she used to advance Lip's own capital out of love—until Lip spurned that love to the detriment of his own symbolic and cultural capital by having an affair with his professor. Helene offered Lip a level of social, cultural, and symbolic capital that lifted him for a time from the impoverished capital in which he was raised.

Helene played an important and impactful role in Lip's rise in cultural and symbolic capital, though he was never quite comfortable with the social or symbolic capital that was carried with it. Culturally, Lip's capital was raised through his education and relationship with Helene to the language and cultural capital of the educated elite. Symbolically, Lip's capital was exchanged not only as his professor's lover (confused as a son) at a conference he attended with her to see her in her element (which was rudely shut down by the hubris of academic elitism and expertise). His symbolic capital was also exchanged by the advocacy of Professor Youens to find him a job after he was kicked out of school.

Socially, Lip never quite felt comfortable with the social capital he was given as a lover to Helene. When they went to a party at the house of one of her friends a few blocks from where he grew up in his increasingly gentrifying neighborhood, he almost immediately withdrew from the social, symbolic, and cultural posh of this rich elite. He instinctively withdrew because of the closeness to home and the alienation and disconnect between the social circles in which he ran at school and the social circles at home. Lip had a taste and rose in his field of capital, and yet it was something he not only took for granted while feeling out of place with it but also lost it and began to self-destruct because that was his way of coping with poverty.

And yet, the reciprocal advocation Lip received from Professor Youens, Brad, and Tami throughout the latter seasons of the show demonstrated not just loyalty to one's own, but this was primarily through their demonstrable commitment to Lip. Brad and Tami stood by Lip in ways that proved their loyalty and commitment to him as friends and partners, but this only came through his abstinence from alcohol and learning to differentiate his love and attachments. Through that, he began to learn new ways of coping with his loss of capital and what that meant for his life. As the show progresses, we do not see Lip regain the symbolic and cultural capital he once had through college, but he does gain the social capital of those loyal to him, even while he never quite rose above the economic capital that he inherited. But it is with Frank Gallagher that we can also turn, but this time to examine his tactics of systemic poverty.

Frank's Tactics of Systemic Poverty

Common sociological threads throughout *Shameless* are not merely the challenges of impoverished capital. Another sociological thread that characterizes the poverty of the Gallagher family also includes the tactics of both maintaining systemic poverty and subverting the rich. If the strategies of the rich are geared toward ripping off the poor, gentrification of neighborhoods, and building economic wealth, then the tactics of poverty seek to become like the rich. However, the tactics of poverty are both challenged by the systemic structures that keep them from becoming rich and are marked by a certain *dis*advantage. And it is in this *dis*advantage that they take advantage. They manipulate the system to their advantage in ways that benefit the impoverished.

Frank Gallagher is a notable example of this manipulation of the system. Frank is disgraceful. He is a drunkard who manipulates others, his family, and the system for his own benefit. He is a weasel and a rangy dog. His bark is wimpy, and yet he has a charisma that has a great ability to manipulate others. Take for instance his speaking up for the LGBTQ community and becoming a spokesman for them. Shortly after he is given great luxury, he plays both sides and falls back into poverty. But not before he alienates himself and invokes their hatred. In season seven, Frank manages to found a homeless shelter and takes an unfair cut of other residents' money to make a buck—taking advantage not only of the system and philanthropists but also of the other homeless in his house. When Debbie becomes pregnant, Frank takes her to fill out paperwork for money from the state. Knowing the system, Frank initiates each of his children into the ways of manipulating the system—the Gallagher way.

What is central to Frank's tactical methods is not only the reality that he is manipulative of people for his own benefit but also that he manipulates the system to maintain his poverty—*precisely because he does not want to work*. Frank illegally feeds off the money sent by the state to his dead aunt so that he can drink his liver to death. Throughout the show, he constantly faces the problem of not having a place to sleep, except for becoming a boy-toy to a nymphomaniac germ-freak until he blows up her house. At the heart of Frank's tactics is a manipulation of the system so that he will not have to work. He manipulates the system in ways that tactically maintain his systemic poverty. However, how Frank represents what it means to be a Gallagher is not illustrated in the same way as the other Gallaghers. It is with Fiona and

Lip that we can begin to see not the manipulation of the system, but examples of their *habituses* of love.

THE *HABITUSES* OF FALLEN LOVE

If we look at the love life of Fiona and Lip, we can find certain characteristics of the dispositions of fallen love. Fiona's long-standing love affair with Jimmy-Steve serves to highlight both the passion of love and lust and the recognition of the need for growth. Fiona's love life is marked by her belief that she is not worthy of a good man. It is in relationships with the broken and dishonest that Fiona finds more passionate love. In season four, Jimmy-Steve disappears and Fiona starts to date Mike. Upon meeting his brother, she quickly falls into her habitual patterns of danger and charged intimacy. While season four was a whirlwind of emotions, Fiona came out of it knowing more of herself—and yet her patterns and dispositions were still present. Shortly after marrying Gus, Jimmy-Steve returns, and their passion is quickly consummated. Taking it further, when Fiona ghosted Gus for Sean, we see patterns of fallen love. Fiona's pattern of fallen love is marked by passion, lust, and brokenness. And she is trapped within it. She believes she does not deserve better, and sure enough, her patterns lead her to destroy existing relationships. If the biblical image of restoration is marked by peace, self-sacrifice, reconciliation, and flourishing, we do see glimpses of this throughout the show. Most notably, we see this in Fiona's relationship with Ford, a seemingly honest and worthy man until his stain was revealed, and she spiraled out of control into alcohol and violence. In this, we also see the trap of bondage to her patterns of love tie her to—self-destructive passion. No matter how much Fiona tries to defy and stand above Frank and Monica, she is certainly a Gallagher.

Likewise, Lip's love life signifies *habituses* of fallen love but in different ways that also point to redemption. Lip is certainly a lady's man, and attracts women like flies to light. But his relationships are also damaged by his loves. Between the first season and the sixth season, Lip develops an intimate love for Karen and Helene. And both of these relationships are destroyed. Karen was a jealous psychopath and nymphomaniac. Helene was a professional academic who slept with her students, searching for the angst she desired in young men. Lip fell for both Karen and Helene in deep and damaging ways. Karen's brain damage and Helene's disgrace ended both relationships—both times by women who had fallen in love with Lip, whom Lip only saw as women to enjoy with no attachment. Lip's fallen *habitus* of love is marked by the dual poles of unattachment and overattachment. Whoever loves Lip, Lip does not love and merely desires the physical enjoyment of their bodies.

Whoever Lip loves is marred by fallen loves themselves. Both Karen and Helene are nymphomaniacs. One hated her father and the other hated her husband. Their loves are marked by broken relationships with men who ideally were supposed to love and support them. And yet, their sexual escapades with Lip highlight astutely what Lip falls for. Lip falls for, like his sister, brokenness.

The *habitus* of the Gallaghers' love is marked by a certain brokenness. They are attracted to danger and are ruled by their passions. There is little self-control, and there is the trap of desire for brokenness precisely because they believe they are unlovable, especially Fiona. If Lip's love for Helene and Karen broke his ability to love, it set a pattern and disposition to love broken women as we find in Sierra and Tami. And yet, we see that Lip's relationship with Tami points to the redemption of his love. Tami and Lip live life as partners through the end of the show, and through their relationship, Lip learns to love himself and receive love in healthy ways. The challenge of both Tami's strong will for a better man she sees in Lip and Lip's challenge to Tami for exclusivity strengthened their relationship in healthy ways. But the fallen *habitus* of love still marks Fiona before her exit from the show. If Fiona's loves are passionate, these passions often destroy relationships with good men and distort her ability to discern what a good man is. The Gallagher's dispositions of fallen love mark a certain element of sin, but to call it sin would seemingly be a misnomer. And yet it is still deeply marred by the *patterns* of sin.

THE BONDAGE OF SIN AND BROKENNESS IN *SHAMELESS*

Sin in Christianity is often seen as doing something that does not honor God. While this is accurate, *it is not the whole story*. Sin leads to death, brokenness, and further bondage to sin. Sin is intimately relational, and as we saw with the fallen *habitus* of love in Fiona's and Lip's love lives, it is marked by certain patterns that both trap and damage their ability to love in healthy ways. Sin is a condition of patterns and dispositions to and by which they are bound and trapped. Because of this bondage to sin, the stories of Fiona and Lip illustrate a continual pattern of sin that would fall deeper and deeper into the patterns and traps that break their ability to love. By season eight, Fiona forswears meaningless sex and love. Lip's broken patterns of love result in an overattachment to Sierra, but like Fiona, he grows in self-awareness and turns down her love after manipulating Sierra's situation for his benefit.

Sin is a mire that draws Lip and Fiona deeper and deeper into dysfunction because the more they continue unhealthy patterns of sin, the more they become entrenched within the dysfunction, unable to escape its altering patterns as they grow. The lasting patterns of their love life in the early seasons damaged their relationships and ability to love in later seasons, making it hard for them to love in healthy ways, warping their minds into believing they were doing something that would help them learn independence rather than codependence. Granted, Fiona giving up on relationships and meaningless sex and Lip trying to set boundaries for his relationships with Sierra and Tami are important steps to counter their fallen *habituses* of love. The patterns of sin become binding habits that bind further and further and damage further and further. Without offering healthy patterns of love that are consistently seen, imitated, and lived, sin can become an inescapable trap. But how can they escape these *habituses* of sin and brokenness? It is to a few intimations of redemption in their stories that we now turn.

INTIMATIONS OF REDEMPTION IN *SHAMELESS*

One of the most striking things within *Shameless* is Fiona's growing awareness of her own identity and purpose in life. For much of the early seasons, Fiona takes it upon herself to care of her siblings in the absence of a drunken father and the abandonment of a bipolar mother. Fiona's identity is that of a helper and caretaker, holding the family together against striking odds that seek to tear themapart. Even when she begins to let her siblings go their own ways, she works in the background to push them to be self-sufficient without her as she discovers a purpose and seeks to build wealth out of her poverty. Fiona's love life is also marked by growth. When Jimmy-Steve returns, she tells him that he is not conducive to her growth and future. To say no to her long-term fling and lover is a striking sign of true awareness and growth. Furthermore, after the sleazy actions of Frank on the day of Fiona's wedding to Sean, she decides not to marry a liar and drug addict. Likewise, when it turns out that Ford was married with a kid in season nine, she self-destructed and spiraled out of control. Her commitment to others had been torn apart too many times for her to trust and love in healthy ways.

Fiona's bondage to sin and *habituses* of fallen love are something that highlights the complexity of the human heart. The human heart desires intentional love, honesty, and commitment from those we bond with. But Fiona's heart has been broken so many times that her heart is marred by patterns of sin and brokenness. And yet, there are glimpses of what she does not want to be. She comes to these in her awareness of her failures, of who she is, and strives to grow from her experiences. But the patterns of sin still bind her. The human escape through sex, drugs, alcohol, and money are only fleeting gods. They do not sustain the human heart. Drugs and alcohol lead down a spiral of self-destruction. Sex with no emotional attachment or a two-timed intimacy can lead to a damaged heart and overattachment when there is intimacy. Money helps us survive and better our lives, but it does not sustain our hearts. Money does not change the patterns of sin. It only makes more things available for us to sin in new ways. These false gods promise release or at least an easing of the struggle from the poverty of sin. But what the heart longs for is a level of intentional commitment, honesty, and love that opens the broken heart to a level of vulnerability that, yes, risks the possibility of being hurt. And yet it is in that risk that the potential and intimations of redemption are located. Broken loves take a long time to heal, and that requires a level of trust and commitment that by the end of the show only Lip and Ian had experienced.

SHAMELESS AND SYSTEMIC SIN

Throughout this chapter, an underlying theme illustrated is the systemic nature of sin found within the poverty of the Gallagher family. The point of this section is to connect *Shameless* to contemporary theological discourses and to return us to the systemic nature of sin. One way in which sin can be linked to poverty lies in the theological notion of those "sins crying to heaven" or "crying sins" that refer to those sins of committing injustice and oppression to the vulnerable—especially the poor, foreigners, orphans, and widows—those strata of society most noticeably marked by poverty and need.[13] And yet, it lies within the ligaments of liberation theology that we find potential answers to the systemic and structural problems of the poverty of sin.

Following Latin American liberation theology, Thomas McCall understands the structural nature of sin as something sinning humans beget with sinful actions, but that "to fight sin is to fight political, social, and economic oppression, and salvation from sin is (or at least definitely includes) liberation from political and economic oppression."[14] This is illustrated throughout *Shameless* not only in the cut-throat oppression of the Gallaghers by those with wealth and power but also perpetuated by the Gallaghers themselves, particularly Frank. Frank not only becomes a campaign manager for a pedophilic congressman who wins an election, but in doing so, swindles money from the campaign fund and is in turn dismissed as an economic liability. The economic oppression of the Gallaghers is notable in how Fiona runs into a bind and is screwed over by her business partner who buys her out and turns for himself a profit from how Fiona was building her wealth.

McCall follows Stephen Ray and gives an account of how structural sin is normalized—when excluded communities are denied just access to goods, desperate people in those communities "commit acts of moral evil" and the process is both "normalized and acts as a further instrument of sinful oppression."[15] This is apparent in Fiona's spiraling out of control during season nine in her turn toward alcohol, violence, and drugs. Not only does she spiral deeper into addiction, but she sees nothing wrong with her actions because she sees her actions of moral evil as justified in the face of a systemically unjust and broken society (and from a broken heart).

But sin can also be "institutionalized as it perverts and warps social structures and institutions," thereby creating further institutionalizations for systemic acts, patterns, and structures of sin.[16] According to Reinhold Niebuhr, injustice against the poor, weak, and despised are the central orienting referents of systemic sin.[17] But it is also important to differentiate between the systemic effects of institutional sin upon the oppressed and the systemic acts of sin by the oppressed. Frank not only chafes at an unjust system throughout the series but perpetuates his own poverty by tactically subverting the system to his own benefit. Frank not only cries out against institutional sin, but he himself perpetuates the institutions of sin through his various manipulations of people and opportunities to make a buck so that he can drink.

And yet, this does not dismiss the tactical *habituses* of Frank's perpetuation of systemic sin. This must be maintained and held in tension as a dialectical by-product of the systemic sin that begets itself through the perpetuation of systemic acts of sin found in the fallen human *habituses* of institutional structures that are both structuring and structured by the patterns and dispositions that maintain the conditions of poverty. Taking incarceration as a case in point, McCall demonstrates not only how the system targets African Americans, the impoverished, and dysfunctional families, but that it generates a cycle and pattern of continuous effects that further the dysfunction and injustice by benefiting the oppressors and punishing the oppressed.[18] This is continuously illustrated throughout the series with the stigma of mental illness, poverty, and doing time in prison through various characters like the Milkovichs, Fiona, and Ian and how this inhibits them from becoming "contributing members of society."

Throughout *Shameless*, the systemic nature of sin is distinctly apparent. The Gallaghers, as Carl illustrates in his letter of application to West Point in season nine, are a family that has experienced severe hardships. Their parents divorced; their parents were either bipolar or alcoholic; one parent abandoned her children and the other was a parasite off of them. They grew up on the South Side of Chicago, with everything against them. The systemic and economic structures of society beat them down and gave them little opportunity to dig themselves out of the hole. And yet, they are loyal to a fault to their own. The Gallagher kids support one another, carry one another's burdens, and prove to one another they can only depend on each other and those who have passed the test of loyalty and commitment to them. This dependency and loyalty to one's own is what marks the oppressed, the poor, and the weak. They may tactically strive to gain wealth, and yet, as Fiona's story illustrates, she is burnt out and made destitute by the strategies of the rich. Truly, sin is not only characterized by personal acts of sin as we see in *Shameless*. It also includes the systemic structures of sin that bury the poor and oppressed into more and more destitution as they cry out for justice in the face of the system.

PORTRAYALS OF RELIGION IN *SHAMELESS*

The analyses above have primarily worked through sociological, theological, and religious illustrations in *Shameless* of the structures of poverty and the *habituses* of sin and brokenness. But if we ask how *Shameless* positively depicts religion, we would be disappointed. What we see of religion in *Shameless* is a crutch to help with grieving, the fallenness and hypocrisy of American Christianity, the sexual abuse of the Catholic Church, Christian conversion therapy as it is aimed towards the LGBTQ community, Ian's hearing the voice of "Shim" to create the Church of Gay Jesus, and authentic expressions of the irrelevance of religion to the contextual experience of everyday life. But it is precisely in the absence of God that we can see so clearly the problem of the human condition. Sin is apparent in *Shameless*, especially if you know what to look for. Paul's descriptions of a life characterized by the old self/Adam in Colossians and Ephesians, and that of a life lived by the flesh in Galatians, characterize a sinful life as ruled by the passions and lust, as immoral and impure, and as marked by drunkenness and anger. By contrast, Paul highlights how the way of love is marked by consideration and service for others, loving the unlovable, and is marked by moral uprightness and endurance through suffering. *Shameless* does not typify the latter often, while it does typify the former regularly, and where it does for both we see glimpses of good and bad in illuminating ways. I think a shocking case in point is the relationship between Ian and Mickey, who display a level of commitment, vulnerability, and commitment to one another that illustrates the reality of agapeic love. In season eleven, Ian helps Mickey with his father wounds, committing his love for his beloved, and strongly affirms his belief that Mickey would make a great dad. Mickey, in turn, sacrificed his desire to be "king of the southside" and moved into an apartment with Ian on the Westside. We can learn from *Shameless* what sin is, what it looks like, and its patterns and habitual dispositions while also recognizing the complex situation of what love looks like when it is marked by agape—trust, healthy dependency, vulnerability, and intentional commitment to, and sacrifice for, one another.

Shameless is an important educational resource, not only for understanding what everyday life is like for the urban poor but also teaches us about the dispositions and sensibilities of the *habitus* of the impoverished—their ways of functioning, surviving, and thinking. *Shameless* depicts the manipulation of the system and the taking advantage of others as something worthy. It is in these fallen logics and dispositions that we find something antithetical to the Christian life. Sin is often not taken seriously in contemporary culture because it is not seen as a problem to be overcome. *Shameless* depicts sin in ways that glorify it in its cringe-worthiness. But in our laughter at the cringe of *Shameless*, we can also implicitly see what is so shameful about it. We can recognize in *Shameless* what shame is. *Shameless* offers important lessons about the *habitus* of sin and points to ways of living that both glorify it as well as highlight its brokenness. This dual-pole between laughter and brokenness paints an important impression of how sin is imagined in pop-cultural imaginings of poverty and provides a glimpse into the impoverished logic of post-Christian culture and society.

In the absence of God, what we find is both the glorification of sin and shame and the aching pain and awareness of brokenness. If the embodied and enacted presence of God's love and grace is *absent* from the lived experience of practices of faith that may be imitated in the human *habituses* and structures of ordinary life, why would, or even should, non-Christians care about what Christians offer or have to say? How could non-Christians find it credible if there is no notice, demonstration, or illustration of it in everyday life? The practice of the Christian faith would be irrelevant if it is not visible throughout everyday life. Such are the presuppositions implicit in the silences and depictions of religion in the poverty of sin in *Shameless*.

NOTES

1. C.f. Pierre Bourdieu, *The Logic of Practice* (Stanford, CA: Stanford University Press, 1990); Pierre Bourdieu, *Outline of a Theory of Practice* (Cambridge: Cambridge University Press, 1977).
2. Bourdieu, *Outline of a Theory of Practice*, 214.
3. Bourdieu, *Outline of a Theory of Practice*, 72.
4. Patricia Thomson, "Field," in *Pierre Bourdieu: Key Concepts*, ed. Michael Grenfell, Second Edition (London and New York: Routledge, 2012), 65–80, 65.
5. Thomson, "Field," 66–69.
6. Thomson, "Field," 69–73, 69.
7. Thomson, "Field," 67.
8. Thomson, "Field," 67.
9. Rob Moore, "Capital," in *Pierre Bourdieu: Key Concepts*, ed. Michael Grenfell, Second Edition (London and New York: Routledge, 2012), 98–113, 99.

10. Michel de Certeau, *The Practice of Everyday Life*, trans. Steven Randall (Berkeley, CA: University of California Press, 1984), 177–189.

11. Claire Colebrook, "Certeau and Foucault: Tactics and Strategic Essentialism," *South Atlantic Quarterly* 100, no. 2 (2001): 543–574, 546–547.

12. Michael Gardiner, *Critiques of Everyday Life* (London and New York: Routledge, 2000), 168–169.

13. Thomas H. McCall, *Against God and Nature: The Doctrine of Sin* (Wheaton, IL: Crossway, 2019), 246.

14. McCall, *Against God and Nature*, 260.

15. McCall, *Against God and Nature*, 265.

16. McCall, *Against God and Nature*, 265.

17. Reinhold Niebuhr, *The Nature and Destiny of Man: A Christian Interpretation*, vol. 1: Human Nature, 2 vols. (Louisville, KY: Westminster John Knox Press, 2021), 179; McCall, *Against God and Nature*, 265–266.

18. McCall, *Against God and Nature*, 266–268.

Part V
CONSTRUCTIVE CONCLUSIONS

Chapter 10

Messages of Post-Christian Theology

This concluding chapter offers a constructive proposal that attempts to articulate messages of a post-Christian theology. It argues most fundamentally that a post-Christian theology is characterized by a post-disenchantment theology. A post-disenchantment theology wrestles with the reality that what it means to believe in late modernity must wrestle with the aftereffects of modern structures. These modern structures presuppose a closure to enchantment, and yet enchantment remains. The lingering questions and presence of enchantment and religious belief set a stage where a post-Christian theology must take into account how the aftereffects of modern structures reinforce disbelief and vie against the viability and optionality of believing in a world where believing is strange and defamiliarizing. What it means to believe in a post-Christian context, then, means that *to* believe and the *content of* belief must take into account the strangeness of believing in a world often *closed* to believing. Furthermore, it entails that post-Christian theology is expressed especially when theology is rescripted and resourced in ways that move beyond, while maintaining significance to, Christian theological paradigms.

To address how post-Christian theology is a post-disenchantment theology, this chapter begins with methodological revaluations found throughout the book. These methodological revaluations articulate the methodological relevance of the themes of reenchantment, resourcement, and rescription as they appear throughout the book. The second section follows with an analysis of what theological messages are presented throughout the analyses found in this book to illustrate the ambiguous realities that mark post-Christian messages of what it means to believe in late modernity. The third section then analyzes the problems of a post-Christian theology that links the loss and transformation of theological orthodoxy with the structural effects of modernity that lead to dehumanization and brokenness. This is not only to show

how the latency of Christianity marks post-Christian theology but also how the problems of modernity shed light on the potential and historical tragedies of modernity and what they reveal as the structures that shape the conditions for belief in late modernity. The fourth section offers a constructive rescription of the classical Christian theological virtues with a set of post-Christian theological virtues that pay attention to the contextual conditions of the post-Christian experience.

The final section returns to the focus of this chapter: to shed constructive light on how a post-Christian theology is, by and large a post-disenchantment theology that must wrestle with the possibilities of believing in a world where belief in God is contested, yet a strange and potentially viable option because of how it imagines a broken world in ways that hold out for hope in a better world without negating the very real horrors of this world. It grounds the possibilities of believing in how we imagine our world differently, and what we consume has the potential to rescript the possibilities of belief through its resourcement of traditional religion in ways that can re-enchant the imagination. To believe in a post-disenchanted world means to hold out hope for a better world—and popular culture plays a central role in its potential to imagine beliefs anew. The central claim of a post-Christian, or post-disenchantment, theology is that it holds in tension the contestability and irrelevancy of religion with the possibilities of popular culture to reframe how we imagine religion and belief through the emphasis on presence, longing, love, and human agency.

METHODOLOGICAL REVALUATIONS

Throughout this book, the methodological approaches of re-enchantment, resourcement, and rescription of post-Christian religion and theology display a plethora of constructive exegetical conclusions and themes. This section makes these explicit through a summative analysis of the contributions of each chapter of the volume.

Part I offered two theoretical chapters, and part II followed with three methodological chapters that addressed critical, deconstructive, and theological essays in an attempt to put into practice the methods of re-enchantment, resourcement, and rescription. Chapter 1 analyzed the connection between a post-Christian popular cultural canon and the problem of consumption, while chapter 2 offered an analysis of how the consumptive poetics of belief contributes to an account of imagined realism, where what it means to believe is constituted by the consumption of popular culture—which both produces and is produced by a virtual actuality that reflects the ambiguity of what we believe through the interplay between what we believe and the messages we consume via popular culture and the mythic imagination. By examining the theoretical frameworks of the simulation and recitation of the mythic imagination, chapter 2 sheds light on the defamiliarizing effects of popular culture and how they re-enchant the possibilities of believing.

Chapter 3 then analyzed the problem of re-enchantment through an analysis of the Marvel Cinematic Universe (MCU). By questioning what we mean when we use the terms enchantment, disenchantment, re-enchantment, and post-disenchantment, chapter 3 offered an exegesis of re-enchantment in the MCU, primarily of the metaphysical, religious, and decolonial contributions of Phase Four, to articulate that the myth of re-enchantment should more properly be understood as post-disenchantment which understands enchantment in light of the modern problem of disenchantment. Then chapter 4 offered an analysis of *The Lion King* through a post-Christian deconstruction of how Christians can read *The Lion King* inter-religiously and what moral problems that creates for them as it resources religion. It not only reflects on the practice of resourcement, but raises moral issues for Christians to take into account when something in popular culture isn't entirely, nor can solely be interpreted as, Christian. Chapter 5 offered an analysis of the show *Lucifer* to theologically articulate elements of a post-Christian theology and *applied* the method of rescription through a theological exegesis of the show. In doing so, it gave a practical example of how to interpret both Christian latencies and departures from Christian theology in popular culture. Arguably, rescription becomes the most used constructive method in the exegeses that follow in parts III and IV.

Part III began this application of methods in complex ways through analyses of how *Cloud Atlas*, *Black Panther*, and *Wakanda Forever* prophesy the wake and futurity of the dehumanizing effects of modernity. Chapter 6 illustrates how *Cloud Atlas* prophesies the futurity of modernity in ways that demonstrate how the book and film resource and rescripts themes from multiple religious and philosophical traditions for post-Christian purposes—like Indian ideas of karma and anekantavada, Christian eschatology and apocalypse, and postmodern critiques of modernity. Each of these resourcements and rescriptions argues for an implicit re-enchantment of the possibilities of believing—of how love humanizes us and how belief and hope are rescripted and resourced in *Cloud Atlas* to reveal post-Christian sensibilities that sustain hope in the face of hopelessness—and the ability to believe our world differently through love as a counter-tradition that shapes how we ought to live.

Furthermore, chapter 7 illustrates how *Black Panther* and *Wakanda Forever* prophesy an imaginary of Black humanity that wrestles with the afterlives of slavery and the modern colonial structures that negate the integrity and humanity of Black being. This is done as an example of an Afro-pessimism that must be held in tension with the Afro-futurism imagined in my original analysis of *Black Panther*. Chapter 7 illustrates the challenging effects of the modern systemic dehumanization of Black humanity and how *Black Panther* and *Wakanda Forever* envision the futurity of Black humanity as it grieves in the wake of modernity. Chapter 7 speaks a silence in my original work on the topic by resourcing Black philosophy to make sense of *Black Panther* and *Wakanda Forever* in ways that generate the reality of the need for wake work, of processing and grieving in the wake of modernity—even for Shuri in *Wakanda Forever*.

It is in the continuities of grief between part III and part IV that we begin to see glimpses of how the approaches of this book begin to make sense of brokenness in part IV. Part IV emphasizes primarily the method of rescription—the post-Christian rescription of sin as brokenness. Chapter 8 wrestles with the feelings and sensibilities of the millennial experience through an analysis of whether sin is the appropriate term to use when we discuss brokenness as it is found throughout the post-Christian doxologies of Machine Gun Kelly, Halsey, and Linkin Park. I chose these three musical artists because they reflect a level of popular consumption across the early twenty-first century, especially in its second decade for all three artists. I also chose these three because, as a millennial who is both a Christian and feels deeply the brokenness of their music in his own life, I think these artists reflect something of the cries, resignation, and heart of what it means to be a millennial—to wrestle with, but often without answers to, the brokenness that comes from suffering, heartbreak, drugs, abuse, and suicide.

Chapter 9 continues the question found within chapter 8 of whether sin is an adequate term when we take into account the systemic effects of modern, urban poverty as it is presented in *Shameless*. Like chapter 8, chapter 9 offers a rescription of sin as brokenness—but with an emphasis on the systemic nature of it through a sociological analysis of the "poverty of sin" and how it reflects a Christian latency when it comes to echo, like chapter 8, latent cries or intimations of and for redemption. Here we see not only that the cries or intimations for redemption in post-Christian popular culture reflect a Christian latency. We also see that these cries or intimations for redemption are rescripted in light of a new problem—brokenness—and are answered by a new theological trend—absence theology—where organized religion is either irrelevant to everyday life or irreverently distorted to reflect the basest truths of religion. Each of these reflects a new setting in which post-Christian religion must be contextualized and articulated.

Without contextualizing the conditions in which post-Christian religion may be understood, interpreting post-Christian religion in popular culture would not be able to be constructively articulated. This book has sought to articulate a set of constructive theological exegeses of post-Christian religion in contemporary Western twenty-first-century popular culture. It has done so by developing and applying three methodological approaches—re-enchantment, resourcement, and rescription—to both the dehumanizing effects found in the wake and futurity of modernity and in the doxological and systemic rescriptions of sin as brokenness that cries out for justice in the face of suffering and injustice that echoes and reverberates against something—even in the absence of God. At the heart of post-Christian religion, however, are a set of virtues—the longing for love and the insistence on endurance—that may help to shape and make sense of what it means to believe in a post-Christian context. But this post-Christian context is both shaped by certain theological messages and the effects of modernity on the possibilities of believing—which the next two sections each address.

POST-CHRISTIAN THEOLOGICAL MESSAGES IN POPULAR CULTURE

Before we turn to examine the problems of post-Christian religion, it is worthwhile, in light of the prior section, to reflect on the contents of this book and articulate the post-Christian theological messages found throughout this book. To do so, we will examine the theological messages of ambiguity, presence, and absence to articulate what post-Christian theology in popular culture presents to us. When it comes to the messages of ambiguity, there are three types: Theological, Moral, and Demonic. When it comes to presence, this is presented as advocating for learning to *live and dwell in the tensions of the present*—of "presencing the present." In turn, absence can be understood as the idea of the absence of God as it is compared to the fleeting or episodic presence of God.

The theological ambiguities are marked by both the theological rescriptions of who God is, away from traditional views of Christian belief. Not only do we see this in *Lucifer's* depiction of an *imperfect* God, but we also see this in Machine Gun Kelly, Halsey, and Linkin Park with their doubts about the belief in the presence of a God who loves sinners and who can change the contextual conditions of their lives. We also see this in the MCU in Thor's reflections on the unworthiness of the gods for human worship. These messages present a theological ambiguity that doubts the belief in a God when traditional beliefs in God as good, loving, perfect, and worthy of worship are denied. Each of these theological ambiguities arises in the postmodern sentiment of doubt—particularly of traditional Christian characteristics of God because of the failure of God to meet humans in the contextual conditions of their lives.

Another instance of theological ambiguity comes within both *Wakanda Forever* and *Cloud Atlas*. In the print version of *Cloud Atlas* and the presentation of religious beliefs, particularly of Buddhism in Sonmi-451's timeline and in the timeline of Zachry Bailey with the beliefs of Meronym, there are intimations of both disbelief as well as something powerful and true in those beliefs. The disbelief in the Buddha as having attained spiritual enlightenment is held in tension with the belief that his message presents a symbolic message of peace and flourishing for humanity. Meronym's disbelief in the afterlife is held in tension with the reality that the Valleysmen's beliefs are messages that humanize us against the violence of the will to power.

In *Wakanda Forever*, Shuri's solution to grief is not originally found in the religious rituals of her people, but in the technological hope to recreate the heart-shaped herb as the source of Wakanda's strength. The tension between technology and religion for Shuri is reconciled through her character formation, through the remembrance of the death of her mother, her visit to Talokan, and the choices she has to make between seeking vengeance and showing mercy to her enemies. Within each of these is a theological ambiguity as to whether the technology or the rituals of her people can help her grieve the loss of her brother and mother. Rather than one or the other, for Shuri, both played a role in helping her process her grief when no concrete answers were offered other than trusting in the memories that shaped her identity.

We also see a distinct theological ambiguity in *Shameless* when we come face to face with soft, yet stinging portrayals of theological beliefs across the show. This can be found in two instances: when Frank turns to religion to cope with the death of his lovers and when Ian challenges traditional Protestant Christianity with the creation of the Church of Gay Jesus and searches for the voice of "Shim" in multiple religious traditions when he stops hallucinating the voice of God. What we see in these analyses is the marked *absence* of the *power* of God to shape and speak to the contextual conditions of life for those in *Cloud Atlas*, *Wakanda Forever*, and *Shameless*.

The moral ambiguities of a post-Christian theology are found throughout this book, especially again, with Thor and Gorr's articulation of the unworthiness of the gods, but also again with *Lucifer's* depiction of the Devil as having the moral integrity to keep his word and not being able to lie. But we also see in *Lucifer*, as well as *Shameless*, the inversion of sexual morals that problematizes the tensions between traditional and contemporary sexual morals, and the presence of the goodness of agapeic love even in contemporary sexual norms. We also see the moral ambiguities in how *The Lion King* presents a moral problem as to whether Christians ought to consume objects in popular culture that both do and do not present Christian themes. These present problems of moral theology that may cause Christians to pause in their objections against popular culture just because something may go against what we deem is against our religious beliefs. The resolution I would pose to Christians is not to merely avoid or condemn things in popular culture that are non-Christian. Rather, the challenges and resolutions I would pose to Christians are to: live in the tensions popular culture poses between Christian faith and formation and the malformation it may cause; enjoy and nuance the common graces in popular culture; and redemptively reorient our hearts in light of the brokenness and sin even in things that are non-Christian in popular culture.

This is an important test case when it comes to the demonic ambiguities, especially as presented in the irreverent humor of *Lucifer*. There is something to truly enjoy in *Lucifer's* redemption of the Devil through the power of love. That God would gift Chloe life to be the redemption of love for the Devil implies uncomfortable inversions of how we perceive the demonic. Even with Mazekeen desiring a soulmate and a soul, we see the cries for a soul and love even while for demons a soul and love are not promised. At the heart of both of these is an unspoken promise: the answer is left open and ambiguous without a final resolution. The demonic ambiguity not only leaves open, but unresolved, the possibility of redemption. Moreover, it also represents the Devil not as pure evil, but rather as a complex combination of goodness, pride, sexual licentiousness, and imperfection. Tied to this is the idea that demons are reflected as imperfect and as prone to faults and fallenness—that is, the demonic ambiguity reduces the demonic to reflect what it means to be not just created, but human. This demonic ambiguity holds in tension the presentations of God, the Devil, demons, and angels as *human—as good but imperfect*. A demonic ambiguity does not, however, imply a mere rescription of evil as good or good as evil. Rather it implies a subversion of traditional theological understandings of the divine through the traditional theological lens that says humans are inherently good though fallen. Here the demonic ambiguity lies in the humanization of the divine while still retaining supernatural powers.

Throughout the previous paragraphs, we have seen the sense of presencing that is so central to what popular culture presents as a theological message: *by living in tension between ambiguities, one learns to be present to the complexities of what is good and what is broken in what it means to be human.* Here, presencing comes to mean being present to brokenness—to weep and rejoice in all that comes between them in the lived realities of human existence. This sense of presencing implies messages against injustice, oppression, and violence—it signals the cries of the oppressed as something that must be addressed. Whether this signals liberation theology or the philosophy of Martin Heidegger, to practice presencing means to be present to those whom we know, love, and engage with through the spheres of our lives.

We see this presencing in Lucifer toward Chloe, Meronym toward Zachry, and Mufasa toward Simba, among many other places across the scriptures of popular culture analyzed throughout this book. To be present and practice presence means to take the time to dwell, understand, and share in the life of those we intentionally commit our lives to—and this requires a level of vulnerability that poses the risk of being hurt—both those we are vulnerable with and to those we expose our hearts, struggles, and fears to. Learning to practice presence implies the reality of being hurt, but this is also lived in tension with the hope of a shared life marked by wholeness and healing with others.

Finally, the third theological message is one of absence. Where is God throughout all of the analyses offered in this book? Is this book a theological reflection on the nature of God? In both cases, we must affirm the absence of traditional Christian views of and reflections on God. How orthodox Christian theology presents the nature of God is clearly at odds with the theological presentations of God found throughout this book. What is striking throughout these analyses is remarkably the sense of the absence of God, not just as a perfect, loving, and good God, but also of the loving concern of God for the goodness and flourishing of humanity and creation.

Where is God in the post-apocalyptic fall of Hawaii or the catechisms of the consumer capitalist corporations of Neo-Seoul? Where is God before Amenadiel is elevated to the status of God? Where is God throughout the poverty of *Shameless*, other than as a hallucination, crutch for grief, or excuse for shady acts? Where is God throughout the MCU? Surely Captain America's reference to the One God is not adequate evidence of the presence of the Christian God in the MCU.[1] While *The Lion King* does present more clearly Christian theological themes, where is a doctrine of God? Where is God when the cries of Machine Gun Kelly, Halsey, and Linkin Park for love and healing lead to broken relationships in the presence of an absent God? Surely each of these presents a salient theological theme of the absence of God throughout contemporary popular culture as a hallmark of post-Christian religion.

Here we see that the theological messages of contemporary popular culture are presenting to us not just the fragmentation of belief, but also the tensions between theological, moral, and demonic ambiguities, between doubt and disbelief, and between the call to presence and/in the absence of God. Where is the power of God when the contextual problems of our world must be addressed by human action? And yet, even human action in the absence of God can be shaped by Christian theological ideas, contents, and practices that may be contextually applied to the conditions of human life. Before we continue these reflections on what I will call below "post-Christian theological virtues," let us begin to address the problems of post-Christian religion.

THE PROBLEMS OF POST-CHRISTIAN RELIGION

Throughout parts III and IV of this book, common themes have focused on the problems of modernity and the cries of the broken. The brokenness of modernity cries out to an absent God against the dehumanizing effects of systemic sin found within the structures of modernity. And yet, what these illustrate of post-Christian religion are not only the systemic patterns of brokenness and dehumanization. They also illustrate a sense of post-Christian religion—the *cries* of the broken. But another theme this book has illustrated about post-Christian religion is not only the latency of Christianity but moreover the loss of theological orthodoxy through its rescription and resourcement in the development of a post-Christian theology and religion. This rescription of theology and religion throughout this book illustrates the turn away from cliché answers while at the same time reflecting on the indebtedness to traditional theology in ways that chart new pathways for understanding what may be deemed the elements of a post-Christian theology. It is to these issues that we now address the problems of post-Christian religion: the loss and transformation of theological orthodoxy and the broken, dehumanizing effects of modern structures.

The Loss and Transformation of Theological Orthodoxy

An implicit concern of this book has been to interpret certain popular cultural sources as inscriptions of post-Christian theological belief. But what these have revealed is not so much a theological doctrine of God. Rather, by interpreting popular culture as containing a set of theological and religious messages revealed through consumptive practices, this book shows not so much a single overarching theological system or doctrine of God when it comes to post-Christian belief. Rather, this book pays attention to and exegetes the fragments and sensibilities of post-Christian belief that are reflected in the practiced consumption of contents of belief found within twenty-first-century popular culture to demonstrate how post-Christian religion opens us to the grief that shines through modern systemic structures of dehumanization and cries of brokenness in the absence of God.

What happens when we pay attention to the implicit messages found within the recited messages of the practiced consumption of popular cultural contents of belief? It is not just that we hold firm beliefs that then can intentionally shape our practices, but also, as Pierre Bourdieu noted decades ago, that when we examine the practices, these practices themselves reveal the assumed beliefs of how we live out our lives in and through the practices. Here we see a glimpse not only of how beliefs can intentionally shape and influence the messages of popular culture but also how the practice of consuming popular culture itself reveals and speaks a variety of implicit beliefs that manipulate and help us imagine anew the possibilities of belief. This book reveals interpretations of various instances of twenty-first-century popular culture that pay attention to the religious and theological messages implicit within popular culture. And what results from this—when we interpret and let the messages of popular culture speak for themselves—is a distinct element of post-Christian religion: *the loss and transformation of theological orthodoxy*.

The plethora of religious options in the contemporary West reveals the reality that religion is transforming in a new pluralistic cultural context. Within our pluralistic milieu, religion—and Christianity—is *transforming* in new ways as it begins to address problems of racism, classism, ecology, and so on, and the dehumanizing effects of modern structures that range from injustice, poverty, oppression, power, wealth, and domination. Within this context, Christian theological orthodoxy must learn to constructively address complex issues in the world in ways that are conducive to redemption, reconciliation, flourishing, and wholeness.

And yet, what post-Christian religion also entails is the *loss* of theological orthodoxy. When we begin to pay attention to, listen to, and come to believe the pluralized plethora of messages that move through the skies overhead, on the pages before us, through our ears, and on the screen, what these entail—when we pay attention to the content and meaning of those recitations—is that there is certainly a loss of theological orthodoxy. This loss comes not only when we are exposed to a plurality of sources that can (re-)shape and recite what we believe, but also when we are unable to discern how to evaluate the complex messages from the (in)adequacies of our exposure to religious traditions and theological convictions.

What several chapters illustrate is not only the indebtedness of a post-Christian interpretation of popular culture to traditional Christian theology. Certainly, the discussions of sin as brokenness in chapters 8 and 9—and of traditional theological understandings of the Devil in chapter 5—reveal a set of Christian theological latencies that shape how we may discuss elements of a post-Christian theology. But they also reveal how post-Christian theology questions the relevance and (in)adequacies of Christian theological perspectives in ways that take us beyond traditional Christian and/or theological perspectives. Chapter 4 offers a case in point. When examining *The Lion King*, the analysis reveals a plethora of religious resources that are implicit within the film.

Chapter 4 also articulated a moral problem of how Christians ought to read *The Lion King*—if it does indeed draw on a multiplicity of religious and theological traditions. This *differance*, as Jacques Derrida would call it, *defers* the question of religious truth when we read the religious messages within *The Lion King* and offers *differing* messages of truth through which we can read those religious messages by demonstrating the centrality of inter-religious resourcement. In turn, this opens us to the ability to read texts and popular culture in a multiplicity of differing ways without emphasizing absolute truths while allowing us to defer the moral questions of whether we ought to engage in popular culture if it does not explicitly present a message that is distinctly Christian or of a particular religious tradition. This means popular culture can present not only pluralistic messages but also that how we interpret popular culture reveals a level of complexity that denies the exclusive vision of creating Christian versions and visions of popular culture. Often, the Christian response to this is to limit what Christians and Christian families may watch or listen to in pop culture because they are "sinful," "tempting," or lead people astray from the truth of God through Christ.

This implies not only a post-Christian interpretation that *denies* the "purity" and "impurity" of the church/world dichotomy that opposes Christians to the world (and one that fosters the false dichotomy that produces the potential of an unnuanced hatred or opposition to the world because of the claim that the world is against God and Christians because of the world's hatred of Christ). It also implies a post-Christian interpretation that calls Christians to a more nuanced analysis of the complexity and discernment of what they ought to consume in popular culture. This requires a critical engagement towards the formative effects the world has upon Christians and the church.[2] The awareness of these worldly effects upon the church must be listened to, engaged with, and discerned if the Christian church is to better witness to a post-Christian society and culture.

It is only through self-awareness of the church's indebtedness to the structures and affections of the world that the church can come into fellowship with the brokenness of the world. This witness must be conducive to the world's redemption in and through Christ by the Spirit's empowering of the church to be agents of reconciliation in the world to Christ through the Spirit of God, drawing all things to the glory of God the Father through the reconciling work of the Spirit of God through Christ. It is by listening to the ache, and pressing and presencing into it, that the church and the Spirit of Christ can come into the broken-heartedness of the world to redeem it. The question of effective witness to a post-Christian culture lies not merely in apologetics or correct theology, though the latter especially is still necessary. It rather lies in *how* Christians enact and embody their *presence in and to this brokenness*. *How* Christians live and engage with the world becomes the key to witnessing to post-Christian culture and society. And yet, we must pay attention to the cries of the broken in ways that pay attention to the systemic nature of sin and the structural, dehumanizing effects of modernity. It is to these effects of modern structures that we now turn.

The Effects of Modern Structures

Throughout this book, a focus has been on how popular culture illustrates the dehumanizing effects of modern structures that lead to the brokenness of the human condition. Chapters 6 and 7 illustrated in two instances (*Cloud Atlas* and *Black Panther/Wakanda Forever*) how visions of modernity not only *may* lead to a nuclear holocaust and the collapse of human societies and the human ability to love but also how visions of modernity *have led* to the dehumanizing effects of slavery and its afterlives for Black humanity across modern history. Furthermore, chapters 8 and 9 explored a post-Christian interpretation of the human condition as broken(ness) through the doxologies of Machine Gun Kelly, Halsey, and Linkin Park and the television show *Shameless*. Through each of these, we see glimpses of the effects of modern structures.

First, through *Cloud Atlas*, we see the potential ends of modernity, tracing across a fictional narrative a karmic teleology of history that recites strategies of domination and the tactics of love. Chapter 6 painted the former as dehumanizing and the latter as subversions that humanize us against the totalizing modern visions of control, power, and domination and their ability to take away what it means to be human: to hope in an ideal that helps us affect changes in the world by how we imagine, desire, and believe (in) the world in renewing ways. Adam Ewing at the end of the book displays a striking clarity in this. *The trajectory of humanity lies in how we act in the world through what we believe and desire humanity to be.*[3] When we believe in the will to power, this leads to both the potential destruction of the earth and the extinction of humanity. But if we can believe in the human ability to transcend the human will to power and desire towards a world marked by faith, hope, and love, then we can become the agents to work towards that end. *Cloud Atlas* serves as an important catalyst that can help us to imagine not only the dehumanizing potential and trajectory of modern structures but in those also lies both the tragedy of modernity and its ability to make way for what it means to be human—to love.

Second, through the powerful imaginaries of *Black Panther*, *What if...?*, and *Wakanda Forever*, we see glimpses of the afterlives of slavery in modernity's dehumanizing effects against Black humanity. The dehumanizing effects of modern slavery, colonialism, and the treatment of Black humanity reduced Blackness to animality, non-being, and a perpetuated reproductive labor force. In the afterlives of slavery, Black humanity has faced systemic injustice in the United States in ways that have reduced their freedoms in systemic and subtly strategic ways. The question of how we imagine Black humanity is so intertwined with the effects of the afterlives of slavery induced by modern structures that they are inescapable.

But what *Black Panther* envisions is an alternate, if fictional, possibility of imagining Black humanity in ways that are conducive to the empowerment and self-determination of what it means to be Black through the power of remembrance, endurance, and insisting on existence in the wake of suffering.

Third, chapter 8 analyzed what I call doxologies of brokenness through interpretations and analyses of twenty-first-century popular music via Machine Gun Kelly, Halsey, and Linkin Park. Each of these subtly illustrates a theological repercussion of modernity: when God is no longer trusted or relevant to the everyday contours of our lives, God becomes unbelievable, undesirable, and discredited. What results is the felt ennui and absence of God that echoes throughout the reverberations of the cries of our hearts. Absence theology is a contemporary theological by-product of the interaction between continental philosophy stemming from the thought of Martin Heidegger and modern theology. Part of this movement in theology pays attention to the reality that presence *implies the potential* for the absence of God *and* that absence implies the *need and space* for the presence of God. We can only know and value God when we recognize what it means to lose God. That is, once we recognize the absence of God, *there* are potential connection points that cry out *for* the presence of God. In the echoes of longing throughout secular doxologies, we hear cries not only for justice but for love—and yet it is a love that we defer because we neither believe we can be loved nor can receive that love in functional, healthy ways. The modern effects of brokenness are hearkened to throughout chapter 8 as the cries of unbelief and dysfunction for love and a God that we long for, yet deem absent.

Fourth, chapter 9 analyzes, through the show *Shameless,* the systemic effects of modernity, illustrating how sin and brokenness appear in the systemic structures of modern poverty. Not only does it adopt a Bourdieusian analysis that illustrates the systemic structures of urban poverty, but it also adopts a theological analysis that illustrates how structural and systemic sin cries out for justice for the poor and oppressed. Yet chapter 9 also highlights the dysfunctional dynamics of sin in the Gallagher family and how their conditions as urban white trash inhibit them from rising out of the structures of their condition of poverty. The logic and strategies of sin and poverty reveal the systemic and structural conditions of modernity that bind the Gallaghers not only to further patterns of sin but also to the structural conditions that bind them to further poverty. But underlying each of these effects of modern structures are also the promises of modernity found in the enduring cries for love. To articulate this, it is worth developing what may be deemed the affections of post-Christian theological virtues: love, longing, endurance, and insistence.

RESCRIPTING (POST-)CHRISTIAN THEOLOGICAL VIRTUES

This section addresses a post-Christian rescription of Christian theological virtues—not as faith, hope, and love, but as love, longing, endurance, and insistence. First, it analyzes how the Christian theological virtues of faith, hope, and love are grounded in key elements of Christian theology. Then it offers an inversion of Christian hope—one that wrestles with despair—as a transition to help set the mood for developing a set of post-Christian theological virtues. It ends by offering a theological rescription of post-Christian theological virtues as the longing, endurance, and insistence upon love in the absence of God amidst the contextual experience of brokenness, dehumanization, and suffering in late modernity. These points not only reflect a Christian theological reflection on the integration of the theological virtues but also a post-Christian theological reflection on the contextual conditions of late modern, post-Christian experience.

Integrating Christian Theological Virtues

In the Christian tradition, the theological virtues of faith, hope, and love are hallmarks of what it means to believe and how to live as a Christian. Faith in the Christian tradition is understood not merely as obedience, but rather as a trust-forming relational dependency upon the faithfulness of God through Christ. If faith is trust-forming, it implies that through dependence upon the *faithfulness* of God through Christ, *there* is the reality of a spiritual formation that shapes the character of the Christian believer. Furthermore, hope in the Christian tradition is often understood as expectation, but more properly as anticipation. But this hope as anticipation is not ungrounded—its ground lies in the promises of God demonstrated through the resurrection of Christ and the anticipation of his return after his ascension to Heaven. Finally, love in the Christian tradition is the practice of intentionally sacrificing our desires for the good of others for the righteousness of God through Christ as someone more worthy than ourselves. The practice of love then, is a form of self-renunciation for the greater good found ultimately in the grace of God demonstrated in the promises of God through the atoning death, burial, and resurrection of Christ—as well as the human participation in this grace towards others in the anticipation of the Parousia of Christ. To love is to intentionally serve, suffer, and work with others towards God's glory in the tension *between* practicing presence and love in the here and now in a broken world, *with* the anticipation that all things will be made right when Jesus comes again.

And yet, underlying these definitions of faith, hope, and love is a latent teleology that finds expression in the thought of Saint Thomas Aquinas, who links the theological virtues to human nature as ordered toward its end in the beatific vision that finds its completion in God. Aquinas' teleological account of the theological virtues as ordered towards their end in God illustrates how theological they actually are. That is, faith, hope, and love are theological insofar as they are ordered and gifted by God for humans towards their completion in God. Aquinas locates the reality of faith, hope, and love as incomplete if they are without their theological end. However, when faith, hope, and love find their completion and orientation in and toward God, they are completed by God as the end of human existence.[4] However, this way of thinking about the theological virtues is not the only way to think about them. Arguably, one way to rescript this classical Christian theological account of the Christian theological virtues is to locate them in their relationship to theological doctrines inherent to the Christian faith. These doctrines include the resurrection, realized eschatology, and the Parousia as loci to make sense of faith, hope, and love.

The resurrection remains a central theological doctrine in the Christian tradition that grounds the reason why a Christian has faith in God through Christ. Not only is the resurrection the best proof of the divinity of Jesus of Nazareth, but if it did not happen, Paul argues that Christian faith is futile and Christians are the most to be pitied.[5] And yet, if the resurrection did happen, it serves as the most fundamental reason why Christians have faith in God through Christ and *hope for redemption in anticipation of Christ's return.* Is it enough to merely believe in God as transcendent, loving, just, and merciful? There is implicit in the atoning work of the incarnation and resurrection of Jesus Christ a reason *why* humans should have faith in God through Christ. This is the picture of a God who condescends to be with us, to become human, suffer with us, and become like us in our human fleshly experience—but in infinitely redemptive ways. But the resurrection and incarnation of God through Christ serve as the ground for faith in ways that cannot be understood apart from the hope, anticipation, and expectation of the second coming of Christ.

Hope in the Christian tradition and the New Testament evokes the central theme of anticipation and expectation for the return of Christ. But it is also tied to the central New Testament theological theme of a realized eschatology. Christians believe that the Kingdom of God is already here since the first advent of God in and through Christ and that the kingdom is sustained in creation and throughout history through the Holy Spirit indwelling the faithful and redeemed dwelling in the church. These "Christians" are sojourners in and as agents of the Kingdom of God in the world in the here and now between the first and second advents of Christ. And yet, the Kingdom is *not fully* here *until* the Spirit draws all creation to its completion in and through the second coming of Christ when righteousness, peace, and wholeness are restored and wickedness is justly judged. Just as faith in God through Christ serves as the foundation of the theological virtues, hope in the second coming of Christ serves as the horizon toward which Christians believe they are moving and what they are intentionally aimed at. But in the time between the first and second advent of Christ, how Christians are to live is to intentionally and sacrificially live by the way of love.

There is a reason why Paul locates love as the central identifying characteristic of the Christian faith. It is not only that I have faith in God and hope in and anticipate God's return in and through Christ, but how I live in the midst of this story must demonstrably reflect not just the ability to feel (the) love (of God), but also to *practice* love intentionally and sacrificially for those whom God has put into my life. The praxis of love becomes the tangible means not only of Christian practice and the identifier of who reflects Christ-likeness in the world—it also becomes how we come to reflect Christ through the sustained practice of faith, hope, and love in ways that move us beyond ourselves while yet perfecting who we are in God through Christ.

The Inverted Hope of Post-Christian Theology

But if the Christian theological virtues consist of the integration of faith, hope, and love in the way a Christian is to live toward their completion in and through their dependence upon God, then the theological virtues also give voice to their opposites. While it is beyond the purposes of this section to fully illustrate how doubt, despair, and hate invert faith, hope, and love, it is worthwhile to reflect on the relationship between hope and despair in the theological and philosophical works of Jürgen Moltmann and the Heideggerian tradition. By offering an inverted perspective of hope and despair, it can help shape and give transitions to the post-Christian theological virtues of love, longing, insistence, and endurance.

Jürgen Moltmann's *Theology of Hope*[6] remains of central significance here, locating the reality of Christian hope within not the eschaton—the end of time when Christ returns and sets things right—but rather in the presence of God in the time and space between and beyond the first and second advent of God through Christ. This *duration* between the first and second coming is marked by a realized eschatology where the not yet is imbued and permeated within the presence of the already: *God remains present through his Spirit in the time and space between the first and second coming* of Christ in ways that signify God's presence to and in God's creation and people as a reality already here to be realized, while not yet fully actualized. By locating hope in the already and not yet dimension of a realized eschatology, Moltmann offers important insights that imply not only reformations of how we think about hope but also how to hope in God through the presence of God's Spirit in and to us here and now in the already.

Central to Moltmann's rebuttal of the reality of hopelessness and despair lies the paradoxical reality of God's overcoming of death through the resurrection of Christ as the first fruits of salvation. Not only does this imply that "salvation" will be eschatologically embodied in spiritually resurrected, transformed, and transfigured physical bodies that reflect the glory of God, but also that when death is overcome through Christ and the resurrection, this becomes the promise *from* which the Christian witnesses and proclaims in love a tactical countermove to the resignation to, and obsession with, the death and brokenness we find so much in post-Christian culture. The overcoming of death in and through Christ allows Christians not only to paradoxically hope and trust that God will overcome death, but that God has already done so through Christ *even while we still experience death here and now*. Here the realized eschatology of death makes the Christian not despair over death, but paradoxically hope in death's overcoming as both already here in and through the presence of the Spirit of Christ and not yet fully here until the second advent of Christ. Moltmann emphasizes that this time between is where hope is located—not only in the *telos* of creation in and through the Parousia but also in the here and now as a tactical counter-movement to the power of death that may lead us to despair.[7]

And yet the nature of despair in post-Christian religion also lacks the realized eschatological flavor of the Christian tradition. Moltmann states that "the despairing surrender of hope does not even need to have a desperate appearance. It can also be the mere tacit absence of meaning, prospects, future, and purpose."[8] It is marked by a "smiling resignation" and "faded hope . . . where hope does not find its way to the course of new, unknown possibilities" that ironically "play with the existing possibilities" that end "in boredom, or . . . outbreaks of absurdity."[9] He goes further to state that this despair is marked by the absence of "any prospect of fulfillment" where "there is no hope and no God anymore."[10] Because of this, we can say with Moltmann that

> Hope alone is to be called "realistic" because it alone takes seriously the possibilities with which all reality is fraught. It does not take things as they happen to stand or to lie, but as progressing, moving things with possibilities of change. Only as long as the world and the people in it are in a fragmented and experimental state which is not yet resolved, is there any sense in earthly hopes. The latter anticipate what is possible to reality, historic and moving as it is, and use their influence to decide the processes of history. Thus, hopes and anticipations of the future are not a transfiguring glow superimposed upon a darkened existence, but are realistic ways of perceiving the scope of our real possibilities, and as such they set everything in motion and keep it in a state of change.[11]

In contrast to positivistic utopian hopes that hope for an unactualizable future, Moltmann argues that the eschatological visions of the Christian tradition hope in the promise of an end that calls from the end of history the promise to make all things new.[12] It is with this sense of realism that Moltmann argues that the Christian views of a realized eschatology hope in a future that is actualizable—but one that can only be actualized by the one who calls creation and humanity to its completion in Him.

As such, "Christian hope" summons and empowers human beings to and for the "creative transformation of reality, for it has hope for the whole of reality."[13] The power of this hope is linked, for Moltmann to the "inventive imagination of love" in ways that "constantly provokes and produces thinking of an anticipatory kind" of love in and "to man and the world, in order to give shape to the newly dawning possibilities in light of the promised future."[14] This is done so in ways that always allow the possibility of imagining the future and our conditions anew. As Andrew Chignell states,

> Moltmann's main contribution was to develop the Augustinian idea that a proper understanding of the eschaton views it as *coeval* with the present vale of tears, rather than as some far-off idealized future. The eschaton is "adventus": still coming and yet *already here*.[15]

And yet, another way in which we can wrestle with the tension between hope and despair is offered by Ryan Coyne and Andrew Chignell in their reflections on radical hope and hopeful pessimism in the philosophical contributions of Immanuel Kant, Friedrich Nietzsche, and the tradition stemming from Martin Heidegger. Troy DuJardin states that Coyne argues "that any truly radical hope must involve an unflinching engagement with abysmal despair" in ways that potentially converge with it.[16] Furthermore, working with Kant, Chignell distinguishes "between hope, expectation, and optimism in order to argue for a kind of 'hopeful pessimism' that may avoid the naïve self-deception of excessive, unwarranted certainty or expectation" while still allowing us to press on "in trying times."[17]

Coyne makes use of Nietzsche and Heidegger to make sense of the despair that comes in light of nihilism. He states that for Nietzsche, there is a distinction between passive and active nihilism. The former is marked by paralysis and collapse, while the latter is marked by "the will to self-destruction that takes hold among those who cannot fully accept the goallessness of existence."[18] And yet, active nihilism is also marked by a hopeless despair that is only overcome "through the conversion of hopeless despair into the highest hope."[19] And yet, while we face the reality of our negation in the affirmation of hopeless despair, what this also entails for Heidegger is the transcending of hope for the presence of God in the present hope of awaiting the presence of

God in the aftermath of the death (or absence) of God.[20] But in this absence for Emmanuel Levinas, there is also the space for presence in ways that rescript the potential for hope for the present with a despairing eschatology that aims for a time beyond time.[21]

Furthermore, Jacques Derrida locates a sense of messianicity in the eschatology of an absence theology—one which is characterized by both a radical hope that commits to justice while leaving it exposed to the possibility of its transgression, contestation, and the violence left behind on the obverse side of its messianic deferral.[22] Coyne offers an important point throughout his analysis: to speak of hope is not so much to articulate it as a virtue but rather as a way of discerning between the possibilities and fragilities of "projects sustained by hope" that are threatened by violence and injustice.[23] A post-Christian theology of hope, as such, must discern the potential of modern structures and ways of living and loving in such a way as to prophesy about the dehumanizing trajectories of modernity while at the same time wrestling with the reality of brokenness and despair in the absence of God. It is by wrestling with these themes that we can now turn to what may be deemed the "post-Christian theological virtues" of love, longing, endurance, and insistence.

Post-Christian Theological Virtues

Throughout this book, there has been an enduring insistence that the central markers of post-Christian religion have been the realities of brokenness, suffering, despair, and dehumanization. And yet these central markers of post-Christian religion also reveal throughout the analyses above certain post-Christian virtues: insistence, endurance, love, and longing. It is to these that this section turns to explicitly address in light of the analyses throughout the book.

Underlying the realities of suffering, dehumanization, brokenness, and despair are tacit inversions of these themes that defer the hope for redemption through the reality of continuing to live, love, and hope even in the resignation to their deferral. The heart of this is the reality not only of enduring brokenness, dehumanization, and suffering but also of insisting on love and life through the struggles of everyday life when there seems to be no hope in the absence of God. Here we see both an insistence and an endurance: post-Christian religion insists that even without a realizable or actualizable hope for a future that leads to flourishing, we must still learn to endure through the struggles of life against the seemingly hopeless contours of a world that we cannot fix, but one that we suffer under. This is a world marked by meaninglessness, but yet also the endurance of life through the insistence on and a longing for love in ways that move us to continue on even under unbearable weights and atrocities. The spirit of insistence insists not only that the weight is unbearable, but also insists that we endure under it in ways that cry out for justice and long for love even when it seems unimaginable. It is in this *holding*, this *suspension*, that we learn to endure, to insist on endurance through an enduring insistence to carry our hurts, burdens, and weights between both an uncertain but discernible future marked by the shadows and wake of grief found in the systemic sins of modern structures.

Arguably, the key to this holding and this suspension is not only love but more particularly the longing for love. The human longing for love is something noted throughout the Christian tradition, especially since Augustine's famous statement that our heart longs for a rest it can only find in God through Christ.[24] For Augustine, the very longing for love and rest is evidence that there is a God who loves us and gives us rest. Longing is a fundamental human phenomenon that, for Augustine, displays something theological: our longings point to God as the final end and *telos* of existence. And yet, our longings are distinctly disordered. Desire, for Augustine, is something disordered and fallen. The evidence of our fallenness can be found in our own self-centeredness and unlove for others. For Augustine, our longings and loves must be re-ordered by the redeeming grace of a God who loves us first. It is in the grace of God's love demonstrated through Christ that our longings are fulfilled. It is through the grace of God's love in Christ that our longings motivate us to love others. And yet, what does the longing for love leave us with in the absence of God?

Throughout much of this book, there has been a certain ennui that has reverberated throughout the book: God may be absent in the doxologies of brokenness and *Cloud Atlas*, and reference to Christ may remain silent in *Lucifer*. Still, theology may remain polysemic in *The Lion King*. Moreover, systemic sin and brokenness may reveal the irrelevance of the answers of organized religion in *Shameless*, and though technology may find its end through its resourcement of religion and the renewed (synthetic) return to the sacred in *Wakanda Forever—there* remains a Christian latency that has been continually recited, rescripted, and simulated across the chapters. This reverberation echoes off an emptiness, a feeling left behind when recitations of Christianity are distorted and broken in the hearts of those who feel the pangs at the loss and brokenness of Christian religious plausibility structures. What are we left with in this brokenness? We are to long for love. This longing for love is not passive, however. It is grounded in the active, tactical practices of love that speak to a level of (vulnerable) hope and faith that things can be otherwise. This belief that things can be otherwise carries with it the scars and abuses of modernity, the faults of Christianity, as well as the graces of faith, hope, and love that cry out into the silence of an absent God for justice, wholeness, and flourishing when what has or had grounded our identities has been disenchanted or ripped away from us. Post-Christian theological virtues long for love in ways that insist on the enduring power of love to rescript, resource, and re-enchant what was left behind of Christianity—and yet in ways that point to its enduring presence displayed throughout post-Christian religion.

POST-CHRISTIAN THEOLOGY AS POST-DISENCHANTMENT THEOLOGY

Throughout this chapter, and indeed this book, I have been exploring what it means to believe in late modernity through theological exegeses of post-Christian religion in popular culture. It has sought to construct a post-Christian theology through popular cultural exegesis of various texts that predominantly date to the twenty-first century, or straddle the new millennium. But underlying this book, and this chapter especially, has been to articulate how post-Christian theology is a post-disenchantment theology. It does so in several ways. First, post-Christian theology defamiliarizes traditional views of God and religion in ways that cast doubt on traditional plausibility structures while also rescripting them with various theological inversions and deferrals. Second, the theological content of late modern believing is constituted by the imagined and simulated beliefs that we consume in popular culture—which subtly shape what is imaginable, credible, and desirable for us to believe. Third, the struggle to believe in late modernity must wrestle with the reality of a world where enchantment is both present as well as absent. It is in this condition where the possibility of believing in late modernity is held up as a contested possibility against (imagined) structures of everyday meaning and believing that functionally exist apart from or against traditional religious structures—even while belief may be a strange option in a broken world that holds out hope for a different world. Finally, a post-disenchantment theology emphasizes that the possibilities *of* belief, *to* believe, and *for* belief in late modernity must hold out for an enduring insistence on presence in a broken world. This presence is held up against, and cries out for, an absent God, and yet calls humans to be agents of justice, wholeness, and flourishing in a broken world whose future is contingent upon how we imagine the possibilities of love and longing for a better world.

NOTES

1. Rhiannon Grant and Jo Henderson-Merrygold, "Old Gods in New Films: History, Culture, and Religion in *Black Panther*, *Doctor Strange*, and *Thor: Ragnarök*," in *Marveling Religion: Critical Discourses, Religion, and the Marvel Cinematic*

Universe, ed. Jennifer Baldwin and Daniel White Hodge (Lanham, MD: Lexington Books, 2022), 67–85, 70.

2. C.f. James K. A. Smith, *Desiring the Kingdom: Worship, Worldview, and Cultural Formation*, vol. 1, 3 vols., Cultural Liturgies (Grand Rapids, MI: Baker Academic, 2009); James K. A. Smith, *You Are What You Love: The Spiritual Power of Habit* (Grand Rapids, MI: Brazos Press, 2016).

3. C.f. David Mitchell, *Cloud Atlas* (New York: Random House, 2004), 508.

4. Frederick Christian Bauerschmidt, *The Essential Summa Theologiae: A Reader and Commentary*, Second Edition (Grand Rapids, MI: Baker Academic, 2021), 145–147.

5. Stanley Grenz, *Theology for the Community of God* (Grand Rapids: William B. Eerdmans Publishing Company, 1994), 251–260; 1 Cor. 15:14-19.

6. Jürgen Moltmann, *Theology of Hope: On the Ground and the Implications of a Christian Eschatology* (New York and Evanston: Harper and Row, 1967).

7. Moltmann, *Theology of Hope*, 21–22.

8. Moltmann, *Theology of Hope*, 24.

9. Moltmann, *Theology of Hope*, 24.

10. Moltmann, *Theology of Hope*, 24.

11. Moltmann, *Theology of Hope*, 25.

12. Moltmann, *Theology of Hope*, 25–26.

13. Moltmann, *Theology of Hope*, 34.

14. Moltmann, *Theology of Hope*, 34–35.

15. Andrew Chignell, "Hopeful Pessimism: The Kantian Mind at the End of All Things," in *Faith, Hope, and Love: The Theological Virtues and their Opposites*, ed. Troy DuJardin and David Eckel (Cham: Springer, 2022), 125–144, 139.

16. Troy DuJardin, "Introduction: Virtue and Vice," in *Faith, Hope, and Love: The Theological Virtues and Their Opposites*, ed. Troy DuJardin and David Eckel (Cham: Springer, 2022), 1–7, 4.

17. DuJardin, "Introduction," 4.

18. Ryan Coyne, "Radical Hope, Despair, and Time: Responses to Nietzsche," in *Faith, Hope, and Love: The Theological Virtues and their Opposites*, ed. Troy DuJardin and David Eckel (Cham: Springer, 2022), 109–123, 113.

19. Coyne, "Radical Hope, Despair, and Time," 113.

20. Coyne, "Radical Hope, Despair, and Time," 115–119.

21. Coyne, "Radical Hope, Despair, and Time," 120.

22. Coyne, "Radical Hope, Despair, and Time," 121.

23. Coyne, "Radical Hope, Despair, and Time," 122.

24. Augustine, *Confessions* I.1, trans. R. S. Pine-Coffin (New York: Penguin, 1961).

Bibliography

"A Chance at a Happy Ending." Streaming. *Lucifer*. Burbank, CA: Netflix, May 28, 2021.
Abbey, Ruth. *Philosophy Now: Charles Taylor*. Princeton, NJ: Princeton University Press, 2000.
———. "Theorizing Secularity 3: Authenticity, Ontology, and Fragilization." In *Aspiring to Fullness in a Secular Age: Essays on Religion and Theology in the Work of Charles Taylor*, edited by Carlos Colorado and Justin Klassen, 98–124. Notre-Dame, IN: University of Notre-Dame Press, 2014.
Abraham, Roshan, and Gabriel McKee, eds. *Theology and the DC Universe*. Lanham, MD: Rowman and Littlefield, 2023.
Adorno, Theodor W., and Max Horkheimer. *The Culture Industry*. London: Routledge, 1991.
Asad, Talal. *Formations of the Secular: Christianity, Islam, and Modernity*. Stanford, CA: Stanford University Press, 2003.
Astley, Jeff. *Ordinary Theology: Looking, Listening, and Learning in Theology*. Burlington, VT: Ashgate, 2002.
Astley, Jeff, and Leslie J. Francis, eds. *Exploring Ordinary Theology*. Burlington, VT: Ashgate, 2013.
Augustine. *Confessions*. Translated by R.S. Pine-Coffin. New York: Penguin, 1961.
Baldwin, Jennifer. "'Open Your Eye': Psychedelics, Spirituality, and Trauma Resolution." In *Marveling Religion: Critical Discourses, Religion, and the Marvel Cinematic Universe*, edited by Jennifer Baldwin and Daniel White Hodge, 179–94. Lanham, MD: Lexington Books, 2022.
Baldwin, Jennifer, and Daniel White Hodge, eds. *Marveling Religion: Critical Discourses, Religion, and the Marvel Cinematic Universe*. Lanham, MD: Lexington Books, 2022.
Barker, Eileen. "Preface." In *Handbook of Hyper-Real Religions*, edited by Adam Possamai, ix–xii. Leiden and Boston: Brill, 2012.

Barkman, Adam, and Bennet Soenen. "The Worthiness of Thor." In *Marveling Religion: Critical Discourses, Religion, and the Marvel Cinematic Universe*, edited by Jennifer Baldwin and Daniel White Hodge, 87–100. Lanham, MD: Lexington Books, 2022.

Baudrillard, Jean. *Simulations*. Translated by Paul Foss, Paul Patton, and Philip Beitchman. Fourteenth Edition. USA: Semiotext[e], 1983.

———. *Simulations and Simulacra*. Translated by Sheila Faria Glaser. Ann Arbor, MI: The University of Michigan Press, 1994.

———. *The Consumer Society: Myths and Structures*. Revised Edition. London: SAGE, 2017.

Bauerschmidt, Frederick Christian. *The Essential Summa Theologiae: A Reader and Commentary*. Second Edition. Grand Rapids, MI: Baker Academic, 2021.

Bauman, Whitney, and Imran Khan. "Religion, Science, and the Marvel Universe: Reimagining Human-Earth Relations." In *Marveling Religion: Critical Discourses, Religion, and the Marvel Cinematic Universe*, edited by Jennifer Baldwin and Daniel White Hodge, 159–77. Lanham, MD: Lexington Books, 2022.

Bauman, Zygmunt. *Freedom*. Milton Keynes: Open University Press, 1988.

———. *Globalization: The Human Consequences*. New York: Columbia University Press, 1998.

———. *Intimations of Postmodernity*. London and New York: Routledge, 1992.

———. *Legislators and Interpreters: On Modernity, Postmodernity and Intellectuals*. Malden, MA: Polity Press, 1987.

———. *Liquid Modernity*. Cambridge, MA: Polity Press, 2000.

———. *Postmodernity and Its Discontents*. Washington Square, NY: New York University Press, 1997.

———. *Thinking Sociologically*. Malden, MA: Blackwell, 1990.

———. *Work, Consumerism, and the New Poor*. Second Edition. Maidenhead: Open University Press, 2004.

Behr, John. *Irenaeus of Lyons: Identifying Christianity*. Oxford: Oxford University Press, 2013.

Berger, Peter, ed. *The Desecularization of the World: Resurgent Religion and World Politics*. Grand Rapids, MI: William B. Eerdmans, 1999.

———. *The Sacred Canopy: Elements of a Sociological Theory of Religion*. New York: Anchor Books, 1967.

Bilgrami, Akeel. "Might There Be Secular Enchantment?" In *The Philosophy of Reenchantment*, edited by Michiel Meijer and Herbert De Vriese, 54–77. London and New York: Routledge, 2021.

———. "Secularism: Its Content and Context." In *Secularism, Identity, and Enchantment*, edited by Akeel Bilgrami, 3–57. Cambridge, MA: Harvard University Press, 2014.

Boersma, Hans. *"Nouvelle Theologie" and Sacramental Theology: A Return to Mystery*. Oxford: Oxford University Press, 2009.

Bourdieu, Pierre. *Outline of a Theory of Practice*. Cambridge: Cambridge University Press, 1977.

———. *The Logic of Practice*. Stanford, CA: Stanford University Press, 1990.

Božovič, Miran. *Jeremy Bentham: The Panopticon Writings*. London: Verso, 1995.
Brake, Matthew William, Kimberly Hampton, and Travis Harris, eds. *Theology and Black Panther*. Lanham, MD: Rowman and Littlefield, Forthcoming.
"Buckets of Baggage." Streaming. *Lucifer*. Burbank, CA: Netflix, September 10, 2021.
Calhoun, Craig, Eduardo Mendieta, and Jonathan VanAntwerpen. "Editor's Introduction." In *Habermas and Religion*, edited by Craig Calhoun, Eduardo Mendieta, and Jonathan VanAntwerpen, 1–23. Malden, MA: Polity Press, 2013.
Calvin, John. *Institutes of the Christian Religion*. Massachusetts: Hendricks, 2008.
Carson, D.A. *Christ and Culture Revisited*. Grand Rapids, MI: William B. Eerdmans, 2012.
Cartledge, Mark. "Ordinary Theology and the British Assemblies of God Doctrinal Tradition: A Qualitative Study." In *Explorations in Ordinary Theology*, edited by Jeff Astley and Leslie J. Francis, 107–16. Burlington, VT: Ashgate, 2013.
———. *Testimony in the Spirit*. Burlington, VT: Ashgate, 2010.
Casanova, José. "A Secular Age: Dawn or Twilight?" In *Varieties of Secularism in a Secular Age*, edited by Michael Warner, Jonathan VanAntwerpen, and Craig Calhoun, 265–81. Cambridge, MA: Harvard University Press, 2010.
———. "Exploring the Post-Secular: Three Meanings of 'the Secular' and Their Possible Transcendence." In *Habermas and Religion*, edited by Craig Calhoun, Eduardo Mendieta, and Jonathan VanAntwerpen, 27–48. Malden, MA: Polity Press, 2013.
———. *Public Religions in the Modern World*. Chicago, IL: The University of Chicago Press, 1994.
Chignell, Andrew. "Hopeful Pessimism: The Kantian Mind at the End of All Things." In *Faith, Hope, and Love: The Theological Virtues and Their Opposites*, edited by Troy DuJardin and David Eckel, 125–44. Cham: Springer, 2022.
Cloke, Paul, Christopher Baker, Callum Sutherland, and Andrew Williams. *Geographies of Post-Secularity: Re-Envisioning Politics, Subjectivity, and Ethics*. London and New York: Routledge, 2019.
Cloud Atlas. DVD. Warner Bros. Pictures, 2012.
Cobb, Kelton. *The Blackwell Guide to Theology and Popular Culture*. Malden, MA: Blackwell, 2005.
Cole, Graham A. *Against the Darkness: The Doctrine of Angels, Satan, and Demons*. Wheaton, IL: Crossway Publishing, 2019.
Colebrook, Claire. "Certeau and Foucault: Tactics and Strategic Essentialism." *South Atlantic Quarterly* 100, no. 2 (2001): 543–74.
———. *Gilles Deleuze*. London and New York: Routledge, 2002.
Connolly, William E. *Pluralism*. Durham, NC and London: Duke University Press, 2005.
Coyne, Ryan. "Radical Hope, Despair, and Time: Responses to Nietzsche." In *Faith, Hope, and Love: The Theological Virtues and Their Opposites*, edited by Troy DuJardin and David Eckel, 109–23. Cham: Springer, 2022.
Cusack, Carole M. *Invented Religions: Imagination, Fiction and Faith*. Burlington, VT: Ashgate, 2010.

Cusack, Carole M., and Venetia Laura Delano Robertson. "Introduction: The Study of Fandom and Religion." In *The Sacred in Fantastic Fandom: Essays on the Intersection of Religion and Pop Culture*, edited by Carole M. Cusack, John W. Morehead, and Venetia Laura Delano Robertson, 1–13. Jefferson, NC: McFarland, 2019.

D'Sa, Francis X. "Time, History, and Christophany." In *Raimon Panikkar: A Companion to His Life and Thought*, edited by Peter Phan and Young-Chan Ro, 171–93. Cambridge: James Clarke and Co., 2018.

"Daniel Espinoza: Naked and Afraid." Streaming. *Lucifer*. Burbank, CA: Netflix, May 28, 2021.

De Certeau, Michel. *Culture in the Plural*. Edited by Luce Giard. Translated by Tom Conley. Minneapolis, MN: University of Minnesota Press, 1997.

———. *The Practice of Everyday Life*. Translated by Steven Randall. Vol. 1. 2 vols. Berkeley, CA: University of California Press, 1984.

De Vries, Hent, and Lawrence E. Sullivan, eds. *Political Theologies: Public Religions in a Post-Secular World*. New York: Fordham University Press, 2006.

Deleuze, Gilles. "The Actual and the Virtual." In *Dialogues II*, edited by Claire Parnet and Gilles Deleuze, 148–59. Indianapolis, IN: Bloomsbury Academic, 2006.

Doberenz, Jake. "Reading Religious Texts as a 'Cinematic Universe.'" *Popular Culture and Theology* (Blog). June 22, 2020. https://popularcultureandtheology.com/2020/06/22/reading-religious-texts-as-a-cinematic-universe/

DuJardin, Troy. "Introduction: Virtue and Vice." In *Faith, Hope, and Love: The Theological Virtues and Their Opposites*, edited by Troy DuJardin and David Eckel, 1–7. Cham: Springer, 2022.

Dunn, George A., and Jason T. Eberl. "'I See a Suit of Armor Around the World': Tony Stark's Techno-Idolatry and Self-Sacrificial Love." In *Marveling Religion: Critical Discourses, Religion, and the Marvel Cinematic Universe*, edited by Jennifer Baldwin and Daniel White Hodge, 3–18. Lanham, MD: Lexington Books, 2022.

Ellul, Jacques. *The Technological Society*. Translated by John Wilkinson. New York: Vintage Books, 1964.

Estes, Douglas, ed. *Theology and Tolkien*. 2 vols. Lanham, MD: Rowman and Littlefield, Forthcoming.

"Family Dinner." Streaming. *Lucifer*. Burbank, CA: Netflix, May 28, 2021.

Fanon, Franz. *Black Skin, White Masks*. Translated by R. Philcox. London: Grove Press, 2008.

Flynn, Gabriel, and Paul D. Murray, eds. *Ressourcement: A Movement for Renewal in Twentieth-Century Catholic Theology*. Oxford: Oxford University Press, 2012.

Forbes, Bruce David. "Introduction: Finding Religion in Unexpected Places." In *Religion and Popular Culture in America*, edited by Bruce David Forbes and Jeffrey H. Mahan, Third, 1–24. Berkeley, CA: University of California Press, 2017.

Foucault, Michel. *Discipline and Punish: The Birth of the Prison*. New York: Vintage, 1995.

Freeman, Austin M. "Gods Upon Gods: Hierarchies of Divinity in the Marvel Universe." In *Theology and the Marvel Universe*, edited by Gregory Stevenson, 157–72. Lanham, MD: Rowman and Littlefield, 2020.

———. "Sins of the Imagination." In *Theology, Fantasy, and the Imagination*, edited by Andrew D. Thrasher and Austin M. Freeman, 19–34. Lanham, MD: Rowman and Littlefield, 2023.

Gardiner, Michael E. *Critiques of Everyday Life*. London and New York: Routledge, 2000.

Geoffroy, Martin. "Hyper-Real Religion Performing in Baudrillard's Integral Reality." In *Handbook of Hyper-Real Religions*, edited by Adam Possamai, 23–35. Leiden and Boston: Brill, 2012.

Giard, Luce. "Introduction: Opening the Possible." In *Culture in the Plural*, edited by Luce Giard, translated by Tom Conley, ix–xv. Minneapolis, MN: University of Minnesota Press, 1997.

Graham, Elaine. "'What We Make of the World': The Turn to 'Culture' in Theology and the Study of Religion." In *Between Sacred and Profane: Researching Religion and Popular Culture*, edited by Gordon Lynch, 63–81. London and New York: I. B. Tauris, 2007.

Grant, Rhiannon, and Jo Henderson-Merrygold. "Old Gods in New Films: History, Culture, and Religion in *Black Panther*, *Doctor Strange*, and *Thor: Ragnarök*." In *Marveling Religion: Critical Discourses, Religion, and the Marvel Cinematic Universe*, edited by Jennifer Baldwin and Daniel White Hodge, 67–85. Lanham, MD: Lexington Books, 2022.

Grenz, Stanley. *Theology for the Community of God*. Grand Rapids, MI: William B. Eerdmans, 1994.

Habermas, Jürgen. *An Awareness of What Is Missing: Faith and Reason in a Post-Secular Age*. Translated by Ciaran Cronin. Malden, MA: Polity Press, 2010.

———. *Religion and Rationality: Essays on Reason, God, and Modernity*. Edited by Eduardo Mendieta. Translated by Eric Crump and Peter Kenny. Cambridge, MA: The MIT Press, 2002.

———. *The Structural Transformation of the Public Sphere: An Inquiry into a Category of Bourgeois Society*. Translated by Thomas Burger and Frederick Lawrence. Cambridge, MA: The MIT Press, 1989.

Hall, Gerard. "Anthropology: Being Human." In *Raimon Panikkar: A Companion to His Life and Thought*, edited by Peter Phan and Young-Chan Ro, 194–216. Cambridge: James Clarke and Co., 2018.

Halsey. *More*. Manic 14. Los Angeles, CA: Capitol Records, 2020.

———. *So Good*. Single. Los Angeles, CA: Capitol Records, 2022.

———. *Without Me*. Manic 9. Los Angeles, CA: Capitol Records, 2020.

———. *You Should Be Sad*. Manic 4. Los Angeles, CA: Capitol Records, 2020.

Hart, David Bentley. *The Beauty of the Infinite*. Grand Rapids, MI: William B. Eerdmans, 2003.

Hartman, Saidiya. *Lose Your Mother: A Journey Along the Atlantic Slave Route*. New York: Farrar Straus Giroux, 2007.

Heelas, Paul. *Spiritualities of Life: New Age Romanticism and Consumptive Capitalism*. Malden, MA: Blackwell, 2008.

———. *The New Age Movement: The Celebration of the Self and the Sacralization of Modernity*. Malden, MA: Blackwell, 1996.

Heidegger, Martin. "The Question Concerning Technology." In *Basic Writings*, edited by David Farrell Krell, 307–42. New York: HarperCollins, 2008.

Herring, Josh. "The Hero as God: An Exploration of Mormon Soteriology in the Fantasy Novels of Orson Scott Card and Brandon Sanderson." In *Theology, Fantasy, and the Imagination*, edited by Andrew D. Thrasher and Austin M. Freeman, 155–75. Lanham, MD: Rowman and Littlefield, 2023.

Hodge, Daniel White, and Jennifer Baldwin. "Preface: Marveling Religion: Visual Culture as a Common Tongue." In *Marveling Religion: Critical Discourses, Religion, and the Marvel Cinematic Universe*, edited by Jennifer Baldwin and Daniel White Hodge, vii–xviii. Lanham, MD: Lexington Books, 2022.

Holdrege, Barbara. "Dharma." In *The Hindu World*, edited by Sushil Mittal and Gene Thursby, 213–48. New York: Routledge, 2004.

Horkheimer, Max, and Theodor W. Adorno. *Dialectic of Enlightenment: Philosophical Fragments*. Edited by Gunzelin Schmid Noerr. Translated by Edmund Jephcott. Stanford, CA: Stanford University Press, 2002.

Illenium and Call Me Karizma. *God Damnit*. Single. Santa Monica, CA: UMG Recordings, Inc., 2018.

Jackson, Zakiyyah Iman. *Becoming Human: Matter and Meaning in an Antiblack World*. New York: New York University Press, 2020.

Jasper, David. "*The Pilgrim's Regress* and *Surprised by Joy*." In *The Cambridge Companion to C. S. Lewis*, edited by Robert MacSwain and Michael Ward, 223–36. Cambridge: Cambridge University Press, 2010.

Jennings, Willie James. *After Whiteness: An Education in Belonging*. Grand Rapids, MI: William B. Eerdmans, 2020.

———. *The Christian Imagination: Theology and the Origins of Race*. New Haven and London: Yale University Press, 2010.

Jindra, Michael. "It's About Faith in Our Future: Star Trek Fandom as Cultural Religion." In *Religion and Popular Culture in America*, edited by Bruce David Forbes and Jeffrey H. Mahan, Third, 223–41. Berkeley, CA: University of California Press, 2017.

Joas, Hans. *Faith as an Option: Possible Futures of Christianity*. Translated by Alex Skinner. Stanford, CA: Stanford University Press, 2014.

———. *The Power of the Sacred: An Alternative to the Narrative of Disenchantment*. Translated by Alex Skinner. Oxford: Oxford University Press, 2021.

Josephson-Storm, Jason A. *The Myth of Disenchantment: Magic, Modernity, and the Birth of the Human Sciences*. Chicago, IL: The University of Chicago Press, 2017.

Kantorowicz, Ernst. *The King's Two Bodies*. Princeton, NJ: Princeton University Press, 1957.

Keat, Russell, Nigel Whiteley, and Nicholas Abercrombie. "Introduction." In *The Authority of the Consumer*, edited by Russell Keat, Nigel Whiteley, and Nicholas Abercrombie, 1–19. London and New York: Routledge, 1994.

Kellner, Douglas. *Jean Baudrillard: From Marxism to Postmodernism and Beyond*. Stanford, CA: Stanford University Press, 1989.

Kelsey, David H. *Eccentric Existence: A Theological Anthropology*. Louisville, KY: Westminster John Knox Press, 2009.

Bibliography 221

Kohn, Livia. *Cosmos and Community*. Cambridge: Three Pines Press, 2004.

Kraemer, Christine Hoff, and A. David Lewis. "Comics/Graphic Novels." In *The Routledge Companion to Religion and Popular Culture*, edited by John C. Lyden and Eric Michael Mazur, 210–27. London and New York: Routledge, 2015.

Levinas, Emmanuel. *Totality and Infinity: An Essay on Exteriority*. Translated by Alphonso Lingis. Pittsburgh, PA: Duquesne University Press, 1969, n.d.

Lewis, C. S. *Out of the Silent Planet*. New York: Scribner, 2003.

———. *Perelandra*. New York: Scribner, 2003.

———. *The Screwtape Letters*. New York: HarperOne, 2015.

———. *The Space Trilogy*. New York: Simon and Schuster, 2011.

Linkin Park. *Crawling*. Hybrid Theory 5. Los Angeles, CA: Warner Bros., 2000.

———. *In the End*. Hybrid Theory 8. Los Angeles, CA: Warner Bros., 2000.

———. *Lost*. Single. Los Angeles, CA: Warner, 2023.

———. *Numb*. Meteora 13. Los Angeles, CA: Warner Bros., 2003.

———. *One More Light*. One More Light 9. Los Angeles, CA: Warner Bros., 2017.

———. *Somewhere I Belong*. Meteora 3. Los Angeles, CA: Warner Bros., 2003.

———. *What I've Done*. Minutes to Midnight 6. Los Angeles, CA: Warner Bros., 2007.

Lovejoy, Arthur. *The Great Chain of Being: A Study in the History of an Idea*. Cambridge, MA: Harvard University Press, 1961.

Low, U-Wen. "Cosmology as Agnostic Self-Actualization in Terry Pratchett's *Discworld*." In *Theology, Fantasy, and the Imagination*, edited by Andrew D. Thrasher and Austin M. Freeman, 115–31. Lanham, MD: Rowman and Littlefield, 2023.

Lyden, John C., and Eric Michael Mazur, eds. *The Routledge Companion to Religion and Popular Culture*. London and New York: Routledge, 2015.

Lynch, Gordon. *Understanding Theology and Popular Culture*. Malden, MA: Blackwell, 2005.

Machine Gun Kelly. *27*. Bloom 13. Santa Monica, CA: Bad Boy/Interscope Records, 2017.

———. *Bloody Valentine*. Tickets to My Downfall 4. Santa Monica, CA: Bad Boy/Interscope Records, 2020.

———. *God Save Me*. Mainstream Sellout 2. Santa Monica, CA: Bad Boy/Interscope Records, 2022.

Machine Gun Kelly and Bring Me the Horizon. *Maybe*. Mainstream Sellout 3. Santa Monica, CA: Bad Boy/Interscope Records, 2022.

Machine Gun Kelly and Glaive. *More Than Life*. Single. Santa Monica, CA: Bad Boy/Interscope Records, 2022.

Machine Gun Kelly and Halsey. *Forget Me Too*. Tickets to My Downfall 5. Santa Monica, CA: Bad Boy/Interscope Records, 2020.

Mahan, Jeffrey H. "Reflections on the Past and Future of the Study of Religion and Popular Culture." In *Between Sacred and Profane: Researching Religion and Popular Culture*, edited by Gordon Lynch, 47–62. London and New York: I. B. Tauris, 2007.

Mannheim, Karl. *Ideology and Utopia*. London: Routledge, 1960.

Mbembe, Achille. *Critique of Black Reason*. Translated by Laurent Dubois. Durham, NC and London: Duke University Press, 2017.

Mbiti, John S. *African Religions and Philosophy*. Garden City, NY: Anchor Books, 1970.

McAvan, Emily. *The Postmodern Sacred: Popular Culture Spirituality in the Science Fiction, Fantasy, and Urban Fantasy Genres*. Jefferson, NC: McFarland, 2012.

McCall, Thomas H. *Against God and Nature: The Doctrine of Sin*. Wheaton, IL: Crossway Publishing, 2019.

McDougall, Joy Ann. "A Trinitarian Grammar of Sin." In *The Theological Anthropology of David Kelsey: Responses to Eccentric Existence*, edited by Gene Outka, 107–26. Grand Rapids, MI: William B. Eerdmans, 2016.

McDowell, John C. "Marveling at Captain Danvers, Or, What Is so Super About Our Heroes?: Contesting the Identity Politics of Self-Other." In *Marveling Religion: Critical Discourses, Religion, and the Marvel Cinematic Universe*, edited by Jennifer Baldwin and Daniel White Hodge, 197–215. Lanham, MD: Lexington Books, 2022.

Meijer, Michiel, and Herbert De Vriese. "Introduction." In *The Philosophy of Reenchantment*, edited by Michiel Meijer and Herbert De Vriese, 1–14. London and New York: Routledge, 2021.

Mendieta, Eduardo, and Jonathan VanAntwerpen, eds. *The Power of Religion in the Public Sphere*. New York: Columbia University Press, 2011.

Mettepenningen, Jürgen. *Nouvelle Theologie—New Theology: Inheritor of Modernism, Precursor of Vatican II*. London and New York: T&T Clark, 2010.

Milbank, John. *The Suspended Middle: Henri de Lubac and the Renewed Split in Modern Catholic Theology*. Second Edition. Grand Rapids, MI: William B. Eerdmans, 2005.

Milbank, John, Catherine Pickstock, and Graham Ward, eds. *Radical Orthodoxy: A New Theology*. London and New York: Routledge, 1999.

Mitchell, David. *Cloud Atlas*. New York: Random House, 2004.

Moltmann, Jürgen. *Theology of Hope: On the Ground and the Implications of a Christian Eschatology*. New York and Evanston: Harper and Row, 1967.

Moore, Rob. "Capital." In *Pierre Bourdieu: Key Concepts*, edited by Michael Grenfell, Second Edition, 98–113. London and New York: Routledge, 2012.

Newbigin, Lesslie. "Religion for the Marketplace." In *Christian Uniqueness Reconsidered: The Myth of a Pluralistic Theology of Religions*, edited by Gavin D'Costa, 135–48. Maryknoll, NY: Orbis Books, 1992.

Nichols, Michael D. *Religion and Myth in the Marvel Cinematic Universe*. Jefferson, NC: McFarland, 2021.

Niebuhr, H. Richard. *Christ and Culture*. New York: Harper and Row, 2001.

Niebuhr, Reinhold. *The Nature and Destiny of Man: A Christian Interpretation*. Vol. 1: Human Nature. 2 vols. Louisville, KY: Westminster John Knox Press, 2021.

"Nothing Lasts Forever." Streaming. *Lucifer*. Burbank, CA: Netflix, May 28, 2021.

"O, Ye of Little Faith, Father." Streaming. *Lucifer*. Burbank, CA: Netflix, May 8, 2019.

Oropeza, B. J., ed. *The Gospel According to Superheroes: Religion and Popular Culture*. New York: Peter Lang, 2005.
Ott, Taylor J., and Shaun Brown, eds. *The Theological World of Harry Potter*. Lanham, MD: Rowman and Littlefield, Forthcoming.
Packer, J. I. *Knowing God*. Downers Grove, IL: IVP Books, 1973.
Panikkar, Raimon. *Mysticism and Spirituality: Mysticism, The Fullness of Life*. Edited by Milena Carrara Pavan. Vol. I.1. XII vols. Opera Omnia. Maryknoll, NY: Orbis Books, 2014.
———. *The Cosmotheandric Experience: Emerging Religious Consciousness*. Edited by Scott Eastham. Maryknoll, NY: Orbis Books, 1993.
———. "Trisangam: The Jordan, The Tiber, and the Ganges—The Three Kairological Moments of Christic Self-Consciousness." In *Christianity: A Christophany*, edited by Milena Carrara Pavan, III.2:3–25. Opera Omnia. Maryknoll, NY: Orbis Books, 2016.
"Partners Til the End." Streaming. *Lucifer*. Burbank, CA: Netflix, September 10, 2021.
Partridge, Christopher. "Religion and Popular Culture." In *Religions in the Modern World: Traditions and Transformations*, edited by Linda Woodhead, Hiroko Kawanami, and Christopher Partridge, Second Edition, 490–521. London and New York: Routledge, 2009.
Patterson, Orlando. *Slavery and Social Death*. Cambridge, MA: Harvard University Press, 1982.
Pennington, Jonathan. *The Sermon on the Mount and Human Flourishing: A Theological Commentary*. Grand Rapids, MI: Baker Academic, 2018.
Posada, Tim. "The Gospel According to Thanos: Violence, Utopia, and the Case for a Material Theology." In *Theology and the Marvel Universe*, edited by Gregory Stevenson, 71–83. Lanham, MD: Rowman and Littlefield, 2020.
Possamai, Adam. *Religion and Popular Culture: A Hyper-Real Testament*. Brussels: Peter Lang, 2005.
———. "Yoda Goes to Glastonbury: An Introduction to Hyper-Real Religions." In *Handbook of Hyper-Real Religions*, edited by Adam Possamai, 1–21. Leiden and Boston: Brill, 2012.
Prabhu, Joseph. "Dharma as an Alternative to Human Rights." In *Studies in Orientology: Essays in Memory of Prof. AL Basham*, edited by S. K. Maity, Upendra Thakur, and A. K. Narain, 174–79. Agra: YL Publishers, 1988.
"Previously On." Streaming. *WandaVision*. Burbank, CA: Disney+, February 26, 2021.
"Really Sad Devil Guy." Streaming. *Lucifer*. Burbank, CA: Netflix, May 28, 2021.
Reisinger, Ernest. *The Law and the Gospel*. Reprint Edition. Cape Coral, FL: Founders Press, 2019.
Riis, Ole, and Linda Woodhead. *A Sociology of Religious Emotion*. Oxford: Oxford University Press, 2010.
Roeland, Johan, SteF Aupers, and Dick Houtman. "Fantasy, Conspiracy and the Romantic Legacy: Max Weber and the Spirit of Contemporary Popular Culture." In *Handbook of Hyper-Real Religions*, edited by Adam Possamai, 401–22. Leiden and Boston: Brill, 2012.

Rose, Marika. "Machines of Loving Grace: Angels Cyborgs, and Postsecular Labor." *Journal for Cultural and Religious Theory* 16, no. 2 (2017): 240–59.
Saunders, Ben. *Do the Gods Wear Capes? Spirituality, Fantasy, and Superheroes.* London and New York: Continuum, 2011.
"Save Lucifer." Streaming. *Lucifer.* Burbank, CA: Netflix, May 8, 2019.
Shai Linne. *Were You There?* The Atonement 6. Philadelphia, PA: Lamp Mode Recordings, 2008.
Shakespeare, Steven. *Radical Orthodoxy: A Critical Introduction.* London: SPCK, 2007.
Sharma, Arvind. *Classical Hindu Thought: An Introduction.* New York: Oxford University Press, 2000.
Sharpe, Christina. *In the Wake: On Blackness and Being.* Durham, NC and London: Duke University Press, 2016.
Smith, Dennis. *Zygmunt Bauman: Prophet of Postmodernity.* Malden, MA: Polity Press, 1999.
Smith, James K. A. *Desiring the Kingdom: Worship, Worldview, and Cultural Formation.* Vol. 1. 3 vols. Cultural Liturgies. Grand Rapids, MI: Baker Academic, 2009.
———. *Imagining the Kingdom: How Worship Works.* Vol. 2. 3 vols. Cultural Liturgies. Grand Rapids, MI: Baker Academic, 2013.
———. "Secular Liturgies and the Prospects for a 'Post-Secular' Sociology of Religion." In *The Post-Secular in Question: Religion in Contemporary Society*, edited by Philip S. Gorski, David Kyumankim, John Torpey, and Jonathan VanAntwerpen, 159–84. London and New York: New York University Press and Social Science Research Council, 2012.
———. *Thinking in Tongues.* Pentecostal Manifestos 1. Grand Rapids, MI: William B. Eerdmans, 2010.
———. *You Are What You Love: The Spiritual Power of Habit.* Grand Rapids, MI: Brazos Press, 2016.
Smith, Nicholas H. *Charles Taylor: Meaning, Morals and Modernity.* Malden, MA: Polity Press, 2002.
Stenmark, Lisa. "Science and the Marvel Cinematic Universe: Deconstructing the Boundary Between Science, Technology, and Religion." In *Marveling Religion: Critical Discourses, Religion, and the Marvel Cinematic Universe*, edited by Jennifer Baldwin and Daniel White Hodge, 143–58. Lanham, MD: Lexington Books, 2022.
Stevenson, Gregory, ed. *Theology and the Marvel Universe.* Lanham, MD: Rowman and Littlefield, 2020.
Suurmond, Jean-Jacques. "The Church at Play: The Pentecostal/Charismatic Renewal of the Liturgy as the Renewal of the World." In *Pentecost, Mission, and Ecumenism: Essays on Intercultural Theolog*, edited by Jan A. B. Jongeneel, 247–59. Frankfurt: Peter Lang, 1992.
Svetelj, Tone. "Rereading Modernity—Charles Taylor on Its Genesis and Prospects." Boston, MA: Boston College, 2012.
Taylor, Charles. "A Catholic Modernity?" In *A Catholic Modernity?*, edited by James L. Heft, 13–38. Oxford: Oxford University Press, 1999.

———. *A Secular Age*. Cambridge, MA: The Belknap Press of Harvard University Press, 2007.

———. *Dilemmas and Connections*. Cambridge, MA: Harvard University Press, 2011.

———. *Human Agency and Language*. Philosophical Papers 1. Cambridge: Cambridge University Press, 1985.

———. *Modern Social Imaginaries*. Durham, NC: Duke University Press, 2004.

———. "Modes of Secularism." In *Secularism and Its Critics*, edited by Rajeev Bhargava, 31–53. Delhi: Oxford University Press, 1998.

The Lion King. DVD. Walt Disney Pictures, 1994.

Thistleton, Anthony C. *The Living Paul*. Downers Grove, IL: IVP Academic, 2009.

Thompson, Peter. "Marxism." In *The Oxford Handbook of Atheism*, edited by Stephen Bullivant and Michael Ruse, 293–306. Oxford: Oxford University Press, 2013.

Thomson, Patricia. "Field." In *Pierre Bourdieu: Key Concepts*, edited by Michael Grenfell, Second Edition, 65–80. London and New York: Routledge, 2012.

Thrasher, Andrew D. *An Advaitic Modernity? Raimon Panikkar and Philosophical Theology*. Lanham, MY: Fortress Press, 2024.

———. "Fantastic Inter-religious Resourcement in Robert Jordan and David Eddings." In *Theology, Fantasy, and the Imagination*, edited by Andrew D. Thrasher and Austin M. Freeman, 133–53. Lanham, MD: Rowman and Littlefield, 2023.

———. "Modern Re-Enchantment and Dr. Strange: Pentecostal Analogies, the Spirit of the Multiverse, and the Play on Time and Eternity." In *Theology and the Marvel Universe*, edited by Gregory Stevenson, 221–33. Lanham, MD: Rowman and Littlefield, 2020.

———. "Wakandan Imaginaries of Black Identity: Wakandan Politics of Identity." In *Theology and Black Panther*, edited by Travis Harris, Matthew William Brake, and Kimberly Hampton. Forthcoming.

Tillich, Paul. *Theology of Culture*. New York: Oxford University Press, 1964.

Tobolowsky, Andrew. "The Thor Movies and the 'Available' Myth: Mythic Reinvention in Marvel Movies." In *Theology and the Marvel Universe*, edited by Gregory Stevenson, 173–86. Lanham, MD: Rowman and Littlefield, 2020.

Tolkien, J. R. R. "On Fairy Stories." In *The Tolkien Reader*, 33–99. New York: Ballentine Books, 1966.

———. *The Silmarillion*. Edited by Christopher Tolkien. Second Edition. New York: Del Rey, 2020.

Vanhoozer, Kevin J. *The Drama of Doctrine: A Canonical-Linguistic Approach to Christian Theology*. Louisville, KY: Westminster John Knox Press, 2005.

Wakanda Forever. Streaming. Walt Disney Pictures, 2022.

Ward, Graham. *Cities of God*. London and New York: Routledge, 2000.

———. "Introduction." In *The Certeau Reader*, edited by Graham Ward, 1–14. Malden, MA: Blackwell, 2000.

———. "Introduction: Where We Stand." In *The Blackwell Companion to Postmodern Theology*, edited by Graham Ward, xii–xxvii. Malden, MA: Blackwell, 2001.

———. "Michel de Certeau's 'Spiritual Spaces'." *The South Atlantic Quarterly* 100, no. 2 (2001): 501–17.

———. *The Politics of Discipleship*. Grand Rapids, MI: Baker Academic, 2009.

Ward, Michael. *Planet Narnia: The Seven Heavens in the Imagination of C. S. Lewis*. Oxford: Oxford University Press, 2008.

Warde, Alan. "Consumers, Identity and Belonging: Reflections on Some Theses of Zygmunt Bauman." In *The Authority of the Consumer*, edited by Russell Keat, Nigel Whiteley, and Nicholas Abercrombie, 58–74. London and New York: Routledge, 1994.

Warren, Calvin. *Ontological Terror: Blackness, Nihilism, and Emancipation*. Durham, NC and London: Duke University Press, 2018.

Westphal, Merold. *Whose Community? Which Interpretation?: Philosophical Hermeneutics for the Church*. Grand Rapids, MI: Baker Academic, 2009.

"What If... Killmonger Rescued Tony Stark?" Streaming. *What If...?* Burbank, CA: Disney+, August 11, 2021.

Wright, N.T. *Paul and the Faithfulness of God*. Vol. 1. 2 vols. Minneapolis, MN: Fortress Press, 2013.

Wynter, Sylvia, and David Scott. "The Re-Enchantment of Humanism: An Interview with Sylvia Wynter." *Small Axe* 8 (2000): 119–207.

"Yabba Dabba Do Me." Streaming. *Lucifer*. Burbank, CA: Netflix, September 10, 2021.

Index

African religiosity, 26, 59, 92, 94–96, 101, 141–42, 144, 149–51, 198, 204–5

Bauman, Zygmunt, 8, 45–46, 131
Berger, Peter, 9–11, 30, 212–13
Blackness, xiii, 3, 5, 8, 26, 80–81, 137–51, 157, 195–96, 204–5
Bourdieu, Pierre, 27, 175–84, 189, 201, 205
brokenness, xiii, 3–5, 27, 29, 157–61, 164–72, 175, 183–84, 189, 193, 196–97, 199, 201–6, 211, 213

character arc, 26–27, 29, 94–99, 110–11, 113–16, 130, 136, 158–59, 180–85
Christology, 12, 112–13, 115, 163, 203, 206–8
consumption, xii, 1, 3–5, 8–9, 13, 21–22, 27, 30–35, 38–39, 43–47, 50–51, 54, 56, 67, 86, 101–2, 124–25, 194–95

Daoism, 59, 94–97, 101, 200–1, 213
De Certeau, Michel, 1, 4–5, 8, 13–14, 26–27, 33–39, 44, 48, 52–53, 58, 121–23, 126–28, 131–34, 176, 179–80, 182–83, 204, 212

deconstruction, 5, 67–68, 79, 91–92, 99–102, 105, 117, 172, 194–95
defamiliarization, 43, 46, 48–52, 57–60, 193–95, 213
dehumanization, x, xiii, 4–5, 26, 117, 121, 123, 125, 131–32, 137, 142–43, 147, 157, 193, 195–97, 201–4, 206, 211
Derrida, Jacques, 10, 159–60, 202, 204, 211
disenchantment, 5, 11, 28, 30–31, 54–55, 68–71, 84, 193, 195

enchantment, x–xii, 1, 5, 11, 24, 45, 48, 53, 56, 60, 68–79, 82–84, 86, 129–30, 193, 195
eschatology, 5, 123, 128–29, 133–34, 137, 195, 200, 204, 206–10
evangelism, xii, 13, 106–7, 116, 132–34, 161–65, 172, 176, 184–86, 188–89, 194, 200, 203, 206–8, 212–13

fall, the/fallen, 26, 55, 107–9, 112, 114–15, 125, 129, 133–34, 158, 163, 167, 184–85, 199
Frankfurt School, 33–35, 38–39, 45–46, 51, 125

grief, xi–xiii, 26, 75, 77–78, 110, 121, 149, 160–61, 165–70, 196, 198, 200

Heidegger, Martin, 12, 81, 145–46, 199, 205, 210
Hinduism, 26, 59, 94–95, 97, 99, 101, 122, 128–31, 195, 204
humanism, x, 112, 114–16, 121–22, 130–34, 141, 151, 195, 198–200, 204
hyper-real religion, 30–33, 49–50, 52, 54–55

imagined realism, x, 1–2, 13, 23–24, 29–30, 32–38, 43–45, 47–60, 67, 71–79, 85–86, 93–94, 101–2, 105–6, 172, 194–95, 201–2, 204–5, 213

Judaism, 13, 94, 98–99, 101, 109

Levinas, Emmanuel, 123, 126–27, 132, 204, 211
Lewis, C. S., 55, 158–59
literary genres: apocalyptic, 3, 5, 121, 125, 133, 137; comics, x, xii, 13, 24–26, 53–55, 72–73, 80–82, 109; fiction, x, 13, 24, 26, 53–56, 124, 151, 158–59, 205; prophetic, xiii, 3, 5, 26, 28–29, 121, 137–38; wisdom, 27, 29, 175
longing, xii, 2, 4, 26–27, 157, 159–61, 165–71, 184–86, 194, 197, 211–13
love, xii–xiii, 4–5, 14, 26–27, 29, 74–76, 78, 106, 108–11, 114–16, 121, 123, 128–29, 131–34, 157, 159–61, 165–70, 172, 175, 180–81, 183–89, 194–95, 197, 199, 204, 206–8, 211–12

magic, 11, 24, 56–57, 59, 68–80, 84, 86, 150
modernity, xii–xiii, 3, 5, 7–9, 11–13, 21–22, 26, 28–29, 46, 51, 68–71, 80–86, 117, 121–28, 131–33, 137–51, 157–58, 193–97, 201, 203–5
Moltmann, Jürgen, 208–10
music, 3–5, 7, 13, 26, 29, 129–30, 157, 159–61, 164–72, 196–97, 200, 204–5

mythic/myth, x, 5, 21, 24, 32, 37, 43–45, 52–53, 55–56, 58–60, 68, 71, 80, 82–86, 149, 195

Panikkar, Raimon, 12, 101, 130, 132
plot, 25, 26, 94–99, 125–26, 128–31, 200
pluralism, x, xii, 7–8, 11–12, 28, 59, 70, 91–102, 105, 195, 202–3
post-disenchantment, 5, 28, 67–68, 70–72, 79–86, 193–96, 198–99, 201–4, 211–13
postmodern, xii, 8–9, 22, 28, 31, 39, 46, 49, 51, 57, 67, 71, 101, 122–27, 137, 194–95
postsecular, 9, 12, 32, 48, 50, 58–60, 70–71, 85, 102, 127, 194
poverty, 4–5, 27, 29, 126, 157, 175–76, 180–86, 188–89, 196, 205

race, xiii, 81–84, 125–26, 128, 137–51, 202, 204–5
re-enchantment, x, xii, 1, 3, 5, 11, 13, 24, 28, 30–32, 39, 43, 45, 47–48, 52–60, 67–79, 84–86, 101, 105, 172, 193, 195, 197, 213
reincarnation, 59, 122, 128–32, 204
rescription, xii, 1, 3–5, 7, 11–13, 24–25, 28–29, 35, 39, 45, 53–56, 58, 60, 67–68, 71, 82, 85, 102, 105–17, 160–61, 164, 171–72, 193–97, 201, 207, 213
resonance, xi–xiii, 2–7, 14, 25–27, 35, 38, 157, 160, 164–72, 196, 212
resourcement, xii, 1, 3–5, 11–13, 24, 39, 45, 53, 55, 56, 60, 67–68, 71, 91–99, 101–2, 105, 117, 122–31, 133–34, 193–95, 197, 201, 203, 213
rhythm, 26, 130–31, 165–70, 176–77
ritual, x, 85, 149–51, 198

scripture, xii–xiii, 3–4, 12, 21–30, 39, 85, 194, 199
secular, x, xii, 5, 9, 30, 32, 44, 48, 69–71, 121, 160, 163–70

Index

simulation/simulacra, 1–2, 4, 13, 24, 30–32, 34–35, 37–39, 43, 45–46, 48–53, 58–60, 75, 91–94, 100–1, 105, 166, 176, 195, 213
sin, 3, 5, 111–12, 114–16, 157–65, 170–71, 175–76, 180, 184–89, 196–97, 199, 202–3, 205
slavery, xiii, 26, 125, 128, 134, 138–48, 162–63, 195–96, 204
sociology of religion, xii, 6, 9–12, 30, 32–33, 35–38, 45, 122–23, 176–80, 196
spirit, 12–13, 68, 148, 149
subversion, xii–xiii, 8, 26, 36–39, 43–46, 50–52, 59–60, 86, 106–16, 121–23, 128, 132–33, 204
suffering, 4–5, 7, 125, 149, 157, 197, 205–6, 211

Taylor, Charles, 9–11, 69–70, 101, 124, 127
technology, 7, 24, 46, 51, 68, 71–72, 80–81, 86, 123, 125–27, 131, 133–34, 139, 150, 198, 212
theology: absence, xiii, 5, 22, 27, 29, 35, 37–38, 157, 159–60, 164–67, 169–72, 175–76, 188–89, 196–98, 200–1, 205, 211–13; decolonial, 7, 26, 67, 72–73, 79–84, 86, 140–41, 195–96, 204; demonic, 8, 25, 29, 106–16, 158–60, 197, 199; inverted, 24, 45, 59, 106–16, 133–34, 158, 171–72, 197–98, 200, 202, 205–6, 208, 210–12; liberation, 186–88, 197, 199, 201–2, 205, 213; moral, xiii, 5, 7, 22, 24, 27, 73, 83–84, 92, 100–102, 140, 158, 195, 197–98, 203; ordinary, 12, 25, 35–38, 47–48, 70, 105, 161, 164, 166, 196, 205, 213; of religions, xii, 5, 7, 24–25, 28, 91–102; traditional, xii–xiii, 5, 12–13, 22, 25, 29, 38, 45, 67, 85, 105–9, 161–62, 164, 193, 197, 201–2, 206–10, 212
time, 25–26, 74–79, 95–96, 117
Tolkien, J. R. R., x, 23, 44, 47, 53–59

wake, 3, 5, 26, 137–40, 146–51, 195–97, 205
Weber, Max, 11, 30, 68–69
will to power, xiii, 11, 25–26, 29, 71, 121–22, 124–26, 128–29, 131, 134, 137, 140, 143, 145, 148, 157, 159, 198, 202, 204

About the Author

Andrew D. Thrasher is a part-time professor and instructor of Religions Studies at George Mason University and in the Virginia Community College System. He is a contributor to *Theology and the Marvel Universe*, *Theology and Game of Thrones* and is a co-editor of *Theology, Fantasy, and the Imagination*. He currently resides in Virginia outside of Washington, DC.